LITERARY REFLECTIONS

LITERARY

R.W.B. LEWIS

Northeastern University Press

Boston

REFLECTIONS

A Shoring of Images

1960–1993

Northeastern University Press

Copyright 1993 by R. W. B. Lewis

Library of Congress Cataloging-in-Publication Data

Lewis, R. W. B. (Richard Warrington Baldwin)
   Literary Reflections : a shoring of images, 1960–1993 /
R. W. B. Lewis.
      p.   cm.
   Includes bibliographical references and index.
   ISBN 1-55553-160-1
   1. Literature—History and criticism.   I. Title.
PN511.L375   1993
809—dc20   92-46687

Designed by Virginia Evans

Composed in Galliard by Coghill Composition, Richmond,
Virginia. Printed and bound by Princeton University Press,
Lawrenceville, New Jersey. The paper is Glatfelter Writers Offset,
an acid-free sheet.

MANUFACTURED IN THE UNITED STATES OF AMERICA
98 97 96 95 94 93 5 4 3 2 1

For Daniel Aaron
After all these years

CONTENTS

IV. A View from the Source

PREFACE

This collection is, in an irregular kind of way, a retracing of cultural steps. I was familiar with classical and Renaissance literature, for example, long before I knew that anything called "American literature" even existed; so the sequence of the first two sections from "Classical and Transatlantic" to "Americans" makes a certain sense. Indeed, I responded so quickly and vocally to the *Aeneid* in my senior year at school, outside Philadelphia, that the school yearbook spoke of me (not without an amiable derision) as having some sort of private understanding with its author. A decade and a half later, I wrote essays on the *Odyssey* and the *Aeneid* for the Ph.D. comprehensive examination at the University of Chicago, part of the point of which (not original with me) was that the *Aeneid* was the Homeric epics written backward. These essays were among my first appearances in print when they were published in *Furioso*, thanks to its co-editor Howard Nemerov, my Bennington College colleague at the time. The Virgilian piece included here, as it happens, dates from a considerably later period.

At Exeter and in my first two years at Harvard, I moved into Greek literary study: Homer, the *Antigone* of Sophocles, the Greek lyric poets (I remember Sappho, Archilochus, and Anacreon today better than I do Pindar, whose rhetoric seemed to me excessively public in tone). My unforgettable mentor at Harvard was John Huston Finley, Jr., ineffably charming, cultivated, and witty; he described Greek as "the champagne of studies." In my third year, I took a course in Shakespeare conducted by F. O. Matthiessen. This was the spring of 1938 and the New Criticism was just coming into flower (the enabling text, *Understanding Poetry,* edited by Cleanth Brooks and Robert Penn Warren, came out in that same year). Matthiessen was a quietly inspiring New Critical pathfinder through the thematic structures and linguistic textures of the six Shakespearian plays we read with such care. Nothing like it had ever come our students' way before; and I still recall how, on the final exam, I dilated in lordly fashion upon the unity of *Henry IV, Part I,* thematic and verbal unity, beneath a surface of discordance.

But Matthiessen, it must be added, was always alert to the social and political implications of the work under view, and he drew our attention to them insistently. We came to the moment in act IV of *King Lear* when Albany turns on his wife, Goneril, to excoriate her for her inhuman treatment of her father. "No more," says Goneril; "the text is foolish." And Albany:

> Wisdom and goodness to the vile seem vile;
> Filths savor but themselves. What have you done?
> Tigers, not daughters, what have you performed?

And then, a few lines later:

> If that the heavens do not their visible spirits
> Send down to tame these vile offenses,
> It will come,

Humanity must perforce prey on itself
Like monsters of the deep.

Matthiessen read the passage in his low, intense voice; and after some moments of absolute silence, he said: "Some of you may have occasion to think about those lines in a concentration camp." This was, as I said, the spring of 1938.*

The present essay on Shakespeare's *Pericles* derives from that seminar with Matthiessen, though at a goodly remove; at critical base, it is pretty plainly in the New Critical mode, dealing as it does with imaginative designs and echoing allusions and invocations. But the essay was written in 1962, almost a quarter of a century after my tutelage with Matthiessen; and two other strains, for what it is worth, may be observed in it. The first I would call an early sign of the Yale influence. I joined the Yale faculty, with an appointment in English and American Studies, in 1960; and it was not long before my congenital "classical," or formal-structure, approach to literature was being impinged upon by the "Romantic" approach deployed by the younger Yale English instructors. An instance of this is the remark, in the essay's second paragraph, that *Pericles* had to do not only with chastity and lust and with birth and death, but also, "more obscurely," with the relation of these matters "to the poetic and creative act." The Yale literary commentators would soon be propagating the notion, and with extraordinary flair, that every important work of literature is mainly or even exclusively concerned with the poetic and creative act out of which it emerged. It was a notion I would both resist and at times draw upon.

*A different but not much less expressive reaction to that *King Lear* passage was provided for me once by Howard Nemerov. We had fallen into the habit of reading aloud to each other, of an evening at Bennington, some of our favorite moments in Shakespeare. One evening, with the Matthiessen episode in mind, I read aloud Albany's speech to Goneril. After a longish pause, the phrases still hanging in the air between us, Nemerov said thoughtfully: "He sure could . . . couldn't he?"

The *Pericles* essay, though, is controlled conceptually by a cultural posture of an altogether different nature, and an imposing influence from college and graduate days. The posture owed much to Jacques Maritain, the French philosopher (*Creative Intuition in Art and Poetry*, 1953, is his most capaciously literary book*) and longtime resident of this country, whose writings gave so persuasive an impetus to the intellectual movement known as Neo-Thomism. I came to the edges of this movement (for reasons of temperament, I was never a convert nor could have been) in the natural course of things educational. At Harvard, disaffected by what I took to be the methods and emphases of the English department, I majored in the History and Literature of the Renaissance (hence the seminar on Shakespeare). One item on my program, offered by that genial giant Theodore Spencer, was called "Transitions from Medieval to Modern Culture," and it involved a reading of the *Divine Comedy*. I absented myself from all classes for several days and read the poem in its entirety. It was one of the two or three most powerful literary experiences of my life—I was carried straight up to *paradiso* before I was through. At the same time, I was trying to read in the work of Dante's intellectual master, St. Thomas Aquinas; and someone put me on to Jacques Maritain's *True Humanism*, as a guide for the Thomistically perplexed. The book seized and captivated me; its account of the relation between human nature and divinity touched some deepest chord. The book's central thesis, for me, was the one summed up in the final paragraph of the *Pericles* essay, where I refer to "the tradition Shakespeare is reviving in *Pericles* (some [supply Jacques Maritain] have called it the tradition of 'theocentric humanism')." According to this view, in the great work of redemption, "grace does not need to destroy human nature; it rather lifts it up; it enlarges, fulfills, and perfects it." I would not say that I have "believed" in any such doctrine for many years, and have not in fact had cause to

*See the full-scale analysis of this volume by Robert Fitzgerald in *Enlarging the Change* (1985).

think or write about doctrinal issues for quite some time. But that image of the relation between God and humanity, or grace and nature, as reformulated out of St. Thomas by Maritain, still strikes me as enormously appealing. I find it an invaluable corrective or balance to its ancient opposite, the Neo-Augustinian outlook, which has the worst possible opinion of human nature and finds that God (like the American general in Vietnam) very properly has to destroy human nature in order to save it.

I knew something of Maritain at the time I read *True Humanism*. He had been exerting a powerful and benign influence on that segment of the University of Chicago that was espousing Neo-Aristotelianism in literary criticism (Aristotle's *Poetics,* with its strict formalism, that is, was the Gospel-text) and Neo-Thomism in philosophy; and I had a family connection of sorts with the university. The thoroughgoing Great Books curriculum of St. John's College in Annapolis was an offspring of Chicago, and my uncle Stringfellow Barr was the president of St. John's in its new incarnation. I went out to the University of Chicago to begin graduate study in 1939 as though by avuncular propulsion. I fell at once under the intellectual spell of Richard P. McKeon, the great scholar of Aristotle and medieval philosophy; and I became somewhat differently entranced by Mortimer Adler, he of the whiplike mind and cascading dialectics. Adler—his position in the university was never quite clear, but it was formidable—had a tremendously springy personality, all mental energy and joyful combativeness. He was very kind to me personally, and I liked and admired him; but I was aware from an early stage that he had almost no interest in history (one of my own favorite branches of study) or even any sense of history, and very little appreciation of the pleasures of literature. He soon gave up on me as a potential philosophy student. "You have a literary mind," he once told me accusingly, a remark I have repeated to myself at intervals ever since, especially when confronted by some new flight of intellectualized and abstract theorizing *about* literature.

The last three items in the first part of this collection come in various ways out of a book about contemporary fiction, mostly European— *The Picaresque Saint,* published in 1958. This began as a study of the career of Ignazio Silone, the Abruzzese-born author of *Bread and Wine* and other chronicles. I sought out his work after getting to know his native Abruzzi fairly intimately during the fall of 1943 (part of the time being actually spent behind the lines with a courageous and hospitable peasant family). Later, I managed to get in touch with Silone, and in 1951 I enjoyed the first of several visits, in Rome, with Silone and his exceedingly *simpatica* wife, the Irish-born Darina Delacey. My study of Silone, however, turned out not to be sizable enough for a book (though it was in fact published as a small paperback book, in Italian translation *Introduzione all'Opera di Ignazio Silone,* in 1961); and to enlarge the enterprise to bookworthy proportions, I added sections on Alberto Moravia, Camus, Faulkner, Graham Greene, and Malraux.

During the last phases of the larger work-in-progress, I made a point of calling upon Albert Camus in Paris, and found him caught up in rehearsals (*répétitions*) of his play *Caligula.* What remains most vivid from the meeting (apart from the pleasure of introducing Camus to Francis Fergusson, an incident described in the Fergusson article below) was Camus's directorial emphasis upon the *comic* dimension of his play. Harrowing and moving as it might be by turns, it was also and always exhilarating. Or so Camus intended: I can still see him, taking the role of Caligula and gliding about the stage in surreptitious manner, looming up behind this or that Roman senator to frighten the fellow half to death, his face wreathed in a smile that made him look like no one so much as Fernandel. In the piece I wrote on *Caligula* for Yale French Studies a couple of years later, I tried to suggest something of this spirited comicality.

That same year, 1957–1958, much of it spent in Munich, where I was a Fulbright Lecturer in American Literature, my wife, Nancy Lewis, and I passed an afternoon in Milan with Elio Vittorini, the author of that luminous and haunting fictional meditation *Conversations in Sicily.*

We had encountered him several times before. The Silone undertaking had led me not only to Alberto Moravia (in person and in his writings), but to those other Italian fiction writers who were then being referred to as "the second generation": that is, the generation after that of Proust and Mann, and preceding the generation of young Italians of different literary persuasion who dubbed themselves *la terza generazione* (a magazine was founded with this name). Elio Vittorini was a conspicuous figure in this middle group, along with Cesare Pavese, Vitalio Brancati, Carlo Levi, Mario Soldati, Elsa Morante, Vasco Pratolini, and Emilio Gadda. I felt a commitment to these writers in some sort, a commitment at least to learn more about them and in particular about their postwar interplaying of the political and the poetic. Vittorini was himself a master of such interplay; he had indeed the greatest sensitivity to the impact of politics upon the creative imagination of anyone I have ever known; and he was a peculiarly apt guide to those contemporaries of his.

As to Paul Fussell's diverting and handsomely informed book *Abroad,* about English travel writing between the two wars, I was drawn to it at once and welcomed an opportunity to review it (the review being here submitted), and not only because Fussell was an old and cherished friend, a Rutgers colleague, and a Princeton neighbor who stood in a godfatherly relation to our older daughter. I was also attracted to the literary materials being examined, having explored Graham Greene's colorful travel books *Journey Without Maps,* about Liberia, and *The Lawless Roads,* about Mexico, for my section on Greene in *The Picaresque Saint.* In a sense and very partially, I had hit in advance upon Fussell's central thesis: that both English travel and English travel writing in the 1920s and 1930s were a response to a felt boredom and dinginess in the native country, a search for what Greene envisaged in his religiously slanted way as the terror and the evil in alien places that might bring an individual fully to life.

My immersion in American literature began in the spring of 1945, during the last months of the war, in an apartment in Florence commandeered for my small mobile intelligence unit. It was there that I happened upon a copy of *Moby-Dick* in an Armed Forces edition and read it right through. The experience was overwhelming, akin to that of reading the *Divine Comedy* over those three timeless days at Harvard, and culturally speaking it turned me completely around. The impact of that quintessentially American book in that Tuscan-European environment led me to wonder for the first time about the phenomenon of being an American, about American habits of speech and behavior as contrasted with the European varieties, about American literature and its own characteristics and traditions. F. O. Matthiessen would begin his book *From the Heart of Europe* (1948) with the remark that he came to Europe to discover what it meant to be an American, and I realized later that I could say almost the same thing. Or to put it more spaciously: that all my previous study of classical, medieval, and Renaissance culture had brought me to the point where I could start to think sensibly about what it meant to be an American.

When I returned to the University of Chicago in 1946 to continue graduate study, consequently, I shifted over into American cultural history, in an interdepartmental program called The Committee on Social Thought. (Its founder and chairman was John U. Nef, a French historian of remarkable educational vision and verve; Daniel Boorstin was a key figure in it; and much later Saul Bellow would conduct its affairs.) I began from almost absolute scratch, my ignorance of American literature being close to total. I read such overviews of the subject as Vernon Parrington's *Main Currents in American Thought*, making careful notes on the unfamiliar names of Jonathan Edwards, Oliver Wendell Holmes, Sr., and the like. Coming to this study, as I did, from three war years in Europe, I found myself focusing inevitably on the question: what was so especially *American* about American literature? I was struck to begin with by the tendency of New World residents to Americanize their places—naming a region *New* England,

and towns *New* London and *New* York—and by the way writers positioned themselves in so many important respects vis-à-vis the European. Then I began to make out a more profound impulse, toward a more radical newness, until the representative American began to be defined as a new kind of man: a being in fundamental and epochal contrast with the archetypal European; a creature coming from nowhere, newborn, lacking any history but poised on the brink of a history to come. Out of such observations came the image that gave rise to my doctoral dissertation, to which I gave the title *The American Adam.*

From that time forward, I have been engaged, to a greater or lesser degree, in American literature and its history. But I have continued to go back to Europe, in something like a commuting fashion: literally, by boat (when that was still possible) or plane, and most often to Florence—since 1950, Nancy Lewis and I have lived in Florence, for anything from two months to a year, more than a dozen times—but also imaginatively and literarily. The book mentioned earlier, *The Picaresque Saint,* was the successor volume to *The American Adam;* and having seen to the publication of a biography of the James family a year ago, I am now caught up in two simultaneous enterprises, a book about Florence in (as the subtitle says) "a personal and historical perspective," and a life of Robert Penn Warren (with a stress on his poetry).

The gathering here of articles on American writers reflects aspects of the critical temper in the 1970s and 1980s. The case arises of Edgar Allen Poe, for example: a writer generally neglected during the concerted effort four and five decades ago to identify American literature and its main components and stages; downplayed by Matthiessen in *American Renaissance;* and scarcely mentioned in Leo Marx's *The Machine in the Garden* (or *The American Adam*). But Poe has persisted in exerting an appeal, as critic, as poet, as storyteller; my little article of 1980 looks at some of the sources of that appeal, and at other observers (Richard Wilbur and Daniel Hoffman in particular) who have recognized it. Yet at a time when the American canon is being dis-assembled and re-organized nearly by the month, the status of Poe appears to be a challenge the canon makers have a singular difficulty coping with. Here is a rich subject—Poe's literary standing—for an inquirer with sufficient savvy, tenacity, and sense of humor.

The review of Henry Nash Smith's *Democracy and the Novel* dates itself when it refers to that volume as old-fashioned, first of all in its beguilingly good intellectual manners, the habit of bad-mouthing as a form of self-promotion was already (in the late 1970s) becoming evident in meetings of the Modern Language and the American Studies Associations—the recurring attempt by this or that academic to gain more professional or departmental power by a denigration of predecessors. And it was old-fashioned, also, in Smith's manifest humanism and his concern with cultural environment. "Cultural environment counts for nothing in the newest critical talk," it is then declared; "texts are purified of association with external reality to a degree that would have left the *old* New Criticism dizzy; and novels and poems are seen as concerned largely with the internal convulsions attendant upon their own begetting." This was, obviously, the heyday of deconstruction; fourteen years later, when—in the critical quarters we hear most about—cultural environment counts for practically everything, the sentence has an odd historical flavor: and all the odder, since Professor Smith's stress, as an instance, on Mark Twain's pursuit of the book-buying public sounds so timely.

In a not entirely different manner, the essay on Melville's *Pierre* argues that that befuddling romance was "most markedly modernist" in the "contempt for the cultural environment" that it displays at every turn. Modernism was a thing of the past by 1981, the time of the essay; but the contempt referred to lingered on as a valid posture, and not least in that new phase of things called postmodernism, about which there were the first sounds of confused and confusing talk. The discussion of Edwin Arlington Robinson, meanwhile, describes the more unhappy situation of a gifted writer whose cultural surroundings simply gave him too little to resist or oppose or exploit. The piece on Ralph Ellison and Toni Morrison, finally, likewise places itself when it confesses to a certain aversion or turning away from current styles in criticism, and toward the realm of the mythopoetic subtly entered by *Invisible Man* and *Song of Solomon*.

The title of the next-to-last section, "Critics of Literature," signals a group of literary critics who really are literary, who devote themselves in their writings to literature itself, and not, as one of them (V. S. Pritchett) says, "to its surrogates." These are critics whose natural tendency is to deal with poems and work of fiction and dramas and literary essays, and with the lives and personalities of their authors— and not with social warfare or sexual psychology and secret practices or doctrinaire theories of history. Some of those latter studies can undeniably add to literary understanding, and gratitude is in order; but they can have a bad effect on those who go in for them. One of the least attractive aspects of the contemporary academic literary scene (and the reference in this context is restricted to the academic area) is the pretentiousness displayed: the claim that the critic is more important than the writer, and the theory being elaborated more interesting than the literary text being used. That Shakespeare or Dickens is more interesting and important by any reckoning, larger-spirited, more intelligent and quick-minded, and writes better than any critic in the land is something the critics here considered would hardly pause to argue.

Almost as a footnote, and as a sign of my own predilections, I may say that in preparing this volume I glanced at and discarded articles going back to the 1950s on a number of other literary critics: Lionel Trilling, R. P. Blackmur (several pieces on Blackmur, with whom I had a long association that I am happy to remember), Kenneth Burke (I made a start on a book about Kenneth Burke, but that great intellectual junkball pitcher, probably the greatest critical mind of our time, always defeated me), Alfred Kazin, Mark Van Doren, and Richard Chase.

Had those articles been included, or some of them, they would have added further testimony to the general thesis about the critical obligation to literature; but enough, I decided, was enough.

These essays and reviews, too, take notice of the passing critical fancies of the last twenty years or so, and especially the 1980s. But although the same note was sounded in preceding pieces, even this reviewer had to blink when he came upon the statement, in the article on Francis Fergusson, that Fergusson's absorbing concern with the *historical* level of major literary texts was "downright un-American." "The American critical mind," I deposed in that year of 1969, was immune to history, indifferent to anything a text might have to say about historical development.

The pervasive theme of these pieces, in fact, is the extent to which these critics—Fergusson, Wilson, Cowley, Pritchett, Ellmann, and Howe—have so variously emphasized the historical dimension. The New Historicists have pushed to the academic forefront in recent years: as a now-all important external reality takes its revenge for the obliteration of external reality by the deconstructionists. But what is valuable about the New Historicism, its restoration of historical considerations to literary discussion in academia, is of course not new at all in literary criticism at large. The critics here examined have taken for granted the importance of history for literary analysis. What *is* new, unfortunately so in one perspective, is the principle of "historicism." This used to be a pejorative term, signifying a *reduction* of everything to the *merely* historical, in a superficial disregard of general ideas. Now that reductive methodology is apparently honored, and capital letters are installed to indicate the same.

In any event, the phrase "critics of literature" should be understood to include history as inseparable from literature. For Fergusson, Wilson, and the others, the combination went without saying, as it has done for this writer ever since he majored, at college, in the department of History and Literature. A superb test case of this whole matter is the episode of the Bollingen Prize and its award in 1948 to Ezra Pound for *The Pisan Cantos*. Howe tells of the affair in his autobiographical *A Margin of Hope*, and he writes so well about it that I would invite the reader to consult his book, or at least the passages quoted in my article on Howe toward the end of this collection. At the time Howe was composing his memoir, the opposition to any historicomoral judgment on Pound's poetry was the view that literature had no relation to "the world of familiar experience"—the New Criticism extended or narrowed into deconstruction. One would like to hear Howe's comments today, when the opposition to any sort of value judgment on literature would come instead from a neo-Marxist form of history.

As to that, we may get a hint via Howe's allusion to Louis Kampf, an M.I.T. professor who managed to get himself elected head of the MLA in the 1960s, and argued at a public forum that all of Greek tragedy, along with the likes of Jonathan Swift and Marcel Proust, should be dismissed from the academic curriculum on the grounds of being counterrevolutionary. To this preposterous and self-ridiculing contention, Howe turns a tolerant smile: "I know Louie, he isn't really a commissar, he wouldn't hurt a fly, he has simply been driven out of his wits by the *zeitgeist*." Today, with Kampf being joined by other seemingly demented Marxifying academics, Howe might well be less amused.

The final entry, on Robert Penn Warren and his personal canon of forerunners, is at once a contribution to the ongoing critical dialogue and a preparatory if partial look at Warren's literary career. The essay will find its place eventually, intact or dispersed, in the biography of Warren touched on earlier.

My own view about literary canon making in our American culture, or any other, is set forth as unequivocally as may be in the early pages: namely, that in the real life of literature, where it really counts, it is not the theorists, academic or otherwise, who determine the canon, but the writers themselves. Warren is an exceptionally valuable figure in this regard: a literary critic and historian of highest distinction, enormously well read in Western literature of nearly all ages and, in his later years, especially, in American writing of all levels and from all sources. The manner in which Warren makes a creative ally out of Dante, Coleridge, Hawthorne, Whittier, the authors of the black spirituals, Chief Joseph of the Nez Percé: this, for me, is a story worth rehearsing. I am intrigued no less by Warren's exploitation (in a poem like "Dragon Country") of the philosophic ideas of William James. This is not only canon making of the truest kind; it is how literary history actually happens in our country.

Bethany, Connecticut   R.W.B. LEWIS
August 1992

PART ONE

Classical and Transatlantic

1 YIF THAT I CAN

> *But as I romed up and doun,*
> *I fond that on a wal ther was*
> *Thus writen, on a table of bras:*
> *"I wol now singe, yif that I can,*
> *The armes, and al-so the man. . . ."*

The House of Fame, *I, 140–144*

T he lines descried by Chaucer's visionary dreamer on the walls of the Temple of Venus are not only an English rendering in a fourteen-word couplet of the opening three words of Virgil's *Aeneid: Arma virumque cano*. They also manage to say, or imply, a good deal about the difficulty of translating the whole or any part of that extraordinary poem. The words Chaucer has added are wonderfully suggestive. They comprise a sort of built-in awareness by the first of the great English poet-translators of the utter precariousness of the task he now proposes to attempt, and one of the major reasons therefore, all with the equally untranslatable Chaucerian air of serenest and most knowing amusement. The cautionary phrase "yif that I can" (or "gif" in another variant, or elsewhere, more modernly, "if") is addressed by Chaucer to himself. The translator, while Englishing the first three words, adds his own comment in his own voice: yif that he can—not sing, but translate: recreate in another language the complex beauty of the Latin song. And the grounds for caution are hinted at in the well-placed vocables of the next line: "And al-so." Those words are likewise commentary, or built-in footnote. For this poem challenges any translator by dealing not only with warfare, but also with other vast reaches of human experience, including a heroic human character. So massive a task has it always been to compose a translation of the *Aeneid*—or even to paraphrase Chaucer's compressed and witty little critical essay on the problem.

Chaucer, in point of fact, gave up after the third line of the poem; and the balance of the first book of *The House of Fame* offers, instead, the dreamer's account of a series of "curious portreytures" and "queynt maner of figures" he saw adorning the temple walls, illustrations of the Virgilian epic through to the final triumph of the hero—with Chaucer plucking only occasionally at the Latin for his English purposes, as in the lines admired by Ezra Pound describing the appearance of Venus to her son (I, 319):

> Goinge in a queynt array,
> As she had ben an hunteresse,
> With wind blowinge upon hir tresse.

Chaucer was wise; and I should like to borrow his self-admonition, and maybe even a small portion of his wisdom, and attach that admonition to an effort, not to translate myself (much less to sing), but to reflect upon the virtual impossibility of anything like a complete translation of the *Aeneid:* which is to reflect, of necessity, on some aspects of the poem's peculiar greatness and its beauty. Yif that I can. The caution will, I hope, be remembered: partly because I can refer only to a handful of translations into English, wilfully including Douglas's sixteenth-century Scottish under that head, and leaving aside other English versions and versions in any other language. Partly, also, because this observer is not in any way a classical scholar, but in every sense an amateur of Virgil, albeit of reasonably long standing. So it should be clear that I come not to scold translators of the *Aeneid,* nor to rank them invidiously, but mainly to sympathize.

Among the many kinds of difficulties that confront the translator of Virgil, I want to focus on that phase of his mastery of language that is revealed in an almost Shakespearian exploitation of imagery: exploitation, that is, to intensify, to illuminate (often by way of irony), and to carry forward the *action* of the poem. (A superior and indeed pioneering example [in English] of the study of this aspect of the *Aeneid*—and a work to the contents and author of which I am much indebted—is "The Serpent and the Flame" [on the imagery of *Aeneid* II] by Bernard M. W. Knox in *American Journal of Philology*, LXXI [October 1950].) Virgil's imagery has been sometimes, though by no means regularly, admired; and his action has been investigated within a variety of allegorical frames; but the relation between imagery and action has rarely been detected in criticism or caught in translation. John Dryden, in the lengthy dedication of his 1697 *Aeneid*, offered some of the most incisive comments ever made on Virgil's "similitudes"; Dryden was the first, and arguably the best, of the new critics; no one has noticed more accurately, for example, how Virgil's figures "are not placed, as our unobserving critics tell us, in the heat of any action; but commonly in its declining, when he has warmed us in his description, as much as possibly he can; then, lest that warmth should languish, he renews it by some apt similitude"—the one Dryden chooses being that of Neptune calming the storm (in Book I), as a venerable man calms an urban uprising with his eloquence. But for the most part, Dryden restricts his rhetorical analysis to the sweet harmony of Virgil's verses: "His words are not only chosen, but the places in which he ranks them for the sound; he who removes them from the station wherein their master sets them, spoils the harmony." Again, Dryden's feeling for, and in fact his intellectual comprehension of, verbal harmony was uncommonly keen. He has much to say, and always shrewdly, about the relative balance of vowels and consonants in Latin, Italian, French, and English. Yet he does not indicate in his preface or suggest in his translation the manner in which Virgil's figurative language participates vitally in the essential action that unfolds and consummates itself in the course of the poem. More recently, Rolfe Humphries, in the introduction to his 1951 version, has stressed the vigorous movement that characterizes the *Aeneid*. "This is a composition . . . that *moves* in more senses than one. . . . Hear how the themes vary and recur; how the tone lightens and darkens, the volume swells or dies, the tempo rushes or lingers." But in practice (as, later, I shall briefly illustrate), Mr. Humphries tends to limit all that activity to the narrative alone, reducing the element of metaphor to mere static, or inactive, quality. But the poem's activity has both its source and to a great extent its very meaning within the dimension of imagery, even though it is perhaps my main point that that is the dimension least accessible to satisfactory translation.

Here are two exemplary passages containing two key figures, which may be offered as representative both of the poem and of its special difficulty.* Taken individually and together, the passages comprise two interplaying synecdoches, so to say, of the entire epic. The first gives us the initial appearance of Queen Dido (following the picture of the Amazon Queen Penthesilea that Aeneas sees on the wall of the Temple of Juno)—I, 490–504:

> *Ducit Amazonidum lunatis agmina peltis*
> *Penthesilea furens, mediisque in milibus ardet,*
> *aurea subnectens exsertae cingula mammae,*
> *bellatrix, audetque viris concurrere virgo.*
>
> *Haec dum Dardanio Aeneae miranda videntur,*
> *dum stupet, obtutuque haeret defixus in uno,*
> *regina ad templum, forma pulcherrima Dido,*
> *incessit magna iuvenum stipante caterva.*
> *Qualis in Eurotae ripis aut per iuga Cynthi*
> *exercet Diana choros, quam mille secutae*

*A translation of these two passages by C. Day Lewis—his version chosen for reasons indicated—appears at the conclusion of this essay.

hinc atque hinc glomerantur Oreades; illa pharetram
fert umero, gradiensque deas supereminet omnis;
Latonae tacitum pertemptant gaudia pectus:
talis erat Dido, talem se laeta ferebat
per medios, instans operi regnisque futuris.

The second passage, lines 141 to 150 in Book IV, gives us the look of Prince Aeneas, as he rides forth on the fateful day to join in the hunt with Dido:

Ipse ante alios pulcherrimus omnis
Infert se socium Aeneas atque agmina iungit.
Qualis ubi hibernam Lyciam Xanthique fluenta
deserit ac Delum maternam invisit Apollo,
instauratque choros, mixtique altaria circum
Cretesque Dryopesque fremunt, picti Agathyrsi;
ipse iugis Cynthi graditur, mollique fluentem
fronde premit crinem fingens atque implicat auro;
tela sonant umeris; haud illo segnior ibat
Aeneas; tantum egregio decus enitet ore.

An ideal, or shall we say an angelic, translation of those passages would not only solve particular questions of phrasing and seek for some English equivalent of the intricate variety of rhythm and tempo. It would also reflect the highly animated paralleling, the insistent echo of language and of metaphoric structure: the similitude *between* these two similitudes. It would adopt the Jamesian principle of point-of-view and would suggest—possibly by pace and weight—that the first passage is not description so much as the impression made by a regally beautiful woman upon a very masculine man; and the second, the impression made by a princely man upon a very womanly woman. And it would so manage the language of translation as to make evident to the reader's imagination, ultimately and in retrospect, the synecdochic nature of each passage: the way each adumbrates a major part of the action, and the way the two together adumbrate the whole of the action. Which is, of course, altogether impossible.

Let me, anyhow, try to justify the conditions laid down. The echoes and parallels, for example, are at once striking and profound; nor are they mere formulaic repetitions or epic clichés (it was Dryden's mistake, or his unavoidable choice, so to read them). In the *Aeneid* there are almost no formula-lines in the Homeric manner; his song was primarily a written one, not dependent on a bardic memory. And as to the conventional phrase, he tended to recharge it in a way more reminiscent, for the modern, of T. S. Eliot, and frequently to the same ironic or paradoxical ends. Scrutinizing the two quoted similes, then, we observe that *pulcherrima* Dido is, in the first of them, presented in her likeness to the goddess Diana, leading the dances *(choros)* on the ridges *(iuga)* of Mount Cynthus, on the island of Delos; and in the second, *pulcherrimus* Aeneas is described in his likeness to the god Apollo, restoring the dances *(choros)* on the ridges *(iuga)* of Mount Cynthus, on the island of Delos. Further similarities gather about the two divinities themselves. Both carry weapons on their shoulders *(umero, umeris)*; both are depicted as they walk *(gradiens, graditur)*. And, more important for the kind of knowing reader on whom Virgil was able to depend, there is the shared allusion to the mother—to Latona, whose still maternal heart rejoices as Diana, her daughter, leads the ceremonies, and, implicitly, to Latona again, as Apollo abandons wintry Lycia and goes back to his mother's home, the *Delum maternam* where he was born.

Diana and Apollo are, of course, sister and brother, the twin children of Delian Latona. The close similarity in structure and language of the two passages serves to join the *human* figures, Dido and Aeneas, in a relationship comparable in closeness to that of the *divine* figures, according to an almost geometric premise of likeness. The union accomplished in the imagery is then consummated in the fact, when, fifteen lines later in Book IV beyond the Apollo simile, Dido and Aeneas—driven by a divinely contrived storm—bind themselves in the act of love: in the *coniugum* enacted in the mountainside cave of Carthage; "for with this name, *coniugum,*" Virgil remarks gravely, "did Dido cover up her fault."

It was perhaps Gawin Douglas, Bishop of Dunkeld, in his *XII Bukis of Eneados* (1553), who was most alert, among Virgilian translators, to the existence and the dramatic value of those multiple parallels. Ezra Pound may be right in his belief (in "Notes on Elizabethan Classicists," *Literary Essays of Ezra Pound,* 1954, p. 245) that Douglas "gets more poetry out of Virgil than any other translator," though Pound has rendered his opinion suspect in advance by contending tersely and somewhat inanely that "Douglas's *Eneados* [is] better than the original, as Douglas had heard the sea." Pound detested Virgil and resented having in part to go through him to get at Homer. One does, however, see what Pound means when he adds that Gawin Douglas gives "a clue to Dante's respect for the Mantuan," something that had plainly puzzled him. Douglas's version of the two passages is muscular and alive, and it abounds with meaningful echoes.

> The queyn Dido, excellent in bewte,
> To tempill cumis with a fair menye
> Of lusty yinkeris walkyng her about.
> Lyke to the goddes Dian with hir rowt
> Endlang the flude of Eurot on the bra
> Or undir the toppis of hir hill Cynthia
> Ledand ryng dansys. . . .
>> To Latone her moder this
> Gevis rejosyng and secrete hartis blyss.

And in Book IV:

>> hym self that kyng
> Enee gan entir in falloschip, but dout,

And unto thame adjonyt hys large rowt.
Lyke quhen Apollo list depart or ga
Furth of hys wyntring realm of Lysya,
To vissy Delos, his moderis land and ile
Renewand ryngis and dansys, mony a rowt. . . .
Als fresch, als lusty dyd Eneas ryde,
With als gret bewte in hys lordly face.

In addition to the more commonplace references in both passages
to *bewte, rowt, lusty,* and *flude,* Douglas has caught the binding action
of the two images of dancing—"ledand ryng dansys" and "renewand
ryngis and dansys"—and of the recurring awareness of the mother—
"to Latone her moder" (doubly admirable, since the phrase "her
moder" is in fact contributed by Douglas, knowledge of the relationship being, as he saw, essential) and "his moderis land and ile." By
contrast, one hundred and forty-odd years later, John Dryden gives
almost no suggestion of the extent to which the similes are actively
and creatively involved with one another. Dryden aimed first of all at
registering his sensibility of the sweet flow and harmony of Virgil's
verses (something he went far toward achieving in the melody of his
English), so that the harmony of Virgil's concrete subject remained
largely unnoticed. The verbal echoes are limited to such conventions
as "above the rest" and "lofty mien"; the divine and human persons
are transfixed by the bloodless and inactive adjective ("beauteous
Dido," "great Aeneas," "fair Apollo"); and the island of Delos suffers
a yet further reduction to mere "native." Dryden was a very remarkable
judge of certain aspects of Virgil; but his *Aeneid* seems well below his
translation of, say, the satires of Juvenal. His talent for vigorous, even
aggressive phrasemaking was thoroughly stimulated by Juvenal; but
his Englishing of Virgil is a demonstration of another of Ezra Pound's
notions—namely, that "The quality of translations declined in measure
as the translators ceased to be absorbed in the subject matter of the
original. They ended in the 'Miltonian cliché.' "

How valid that notion is becomes clearer when we return to the subject matter of the *Aeneid* as a whole, taking note, this time, of the participation in it of our two exemplary passages. Looking at them in reverse order, we can now observe that in the Aeneas-Apollo simile, the god is not only leading the dances on the slopes of Mount Cynthus. To do so, Apollo must first abandon his wintry Lycia *(hibernam Lyciam)*, go *back* to his mother country, to maternal Delos, and there *renew* the dances *(instaurat:* renew, celebrate again; Douglas, as usual, is exact: *"renewand* ryngis and dansys"). It is with this surprising and seemingly maladroit figure that Virgil characterizes the man Aeneas, who is actually dallying in Carthage with Dido, all negligent of duty. This is the sort of image for which Virgil has been accused of incompetence across many centuries; in fact, it is an instance of his greatest strength. The Apollonian image is more dynamic, so to speak, than pictorial; it is at once ironic and prophetic; it implies what Aeneas must himself eventually do, and measures his present erotic idling against that destiny. (This article must perforce—since it deals with Virgil—make use of the helplessly unavoidable term "irony"; and in the present case, assuming the Apollo image to exist in Dido's consciousness, we witness again a deeply Jamesian irony—that of one character recording more and other than she knows, and of a nature that would destroy her if she *did* know.) For Aeneas, too, must soon abandon his winter palace in Carthage; must return to the mother country of his Trojan race (that is, to Italy); and there must renew the ceremonies of his people—while around him will murmur *(fremunt)* the mingled voices, if not (as with Apollo) of Cretans and Dryopes and Agathyrsi, at least of Latins and Arcadians and Trojans.

The same Apollo who returns figuratively to his mother country in Book IV, 144, also explains in the actual narrative and on the actual Delos that they must undertake an exactly analogous journey. Landing at Delos, the Trojans worship at the shrine of Apollo and beseech his guidance; and the god answers: the land that first produced them will in good time take them back. *"Antiquam exquirite matrem,"* he enjoins

(III, 96); and though Anchises, already rather senile, supposes this to mean Crete, a later oracle specifies Italy as the place of tribal origin.

The astuteness of Gawin Douglas's translation, his attunement with the Virgilian epic, is peculiarly evident at this point. The references to "Latone her moder" and "Delos, his moderis land and ile" have their dramatic justification in the very nature and design of the Trojan mission—in the actual statement of Apollo, which Douglas renders as follows:

> The ilke grond, fra quham the first stok cam
> Of your lynnage, with blyth bosum the sam
> Sal you ressave thiddir returnyng agane:
> To seik your ald moder mak you bane.

(*Bane*, as Professor Helge Kökeritz has been kind enough to explain to me, is a variant of the word *bain*—and a derivative of the Old Norse word, *beinn*—meaning ready or prepared: "Make you ready to seek your old mother.") That last line deserves italicizing, since it amounts to a definition of the poem's central action. I am here accepting the concept of "action" as propounded in various essays by Francis Fergusson: as something best defined by an infinitive of purpose, as "to find the killer of the king," or "to revenge the murder of the father." It is in this sense of the term that the action of the *Aeneid* has been so sharply identified by Douglas; for it is, exactly, "to seik your ald moder." And the grounds, or better the sanction, for such an enterprise, the grandeur, the propriety, and indeed the holiness of it: all this is established by Virgil's reminder, in Book IV, that a comparable endeavor is characteristic—and according to legend, annually so—of the god Apollo. Nor is Apollo, for Virgil, any common sort of divinity. The god whose rhythmic and habitual movement provides the pattern for the heroic human mission is the god of poetry: a designation Virgil himself insists upon (especially in certain lines of *Aeneid* VI, and in the *Georgics*). In seeking out his race's ancient mother, Aeneas is thus acting in consonance with nature, with art, and with religion, and the significance of his adventure is thereby heightened out of all bounds, made truly epic: at the same time his momentary dereliction in Carthage is made to appear reprehensible to the edge of sacrilege.

It is just this microcosmic action in the Apollo simile that all but vanishes from the version of it offered by Rolfe Humphries. The potent charm of his translation does not compensate for its dramatic thinning out:

> Aeneas
> Comes to her side, more lordly than Apollo
> Bright along Delos's ridges in the springtime
> With laurel in his hair and golden weapons
> Shining across his shoulders. Equal radiance
> Is all around Aeneas, equal splendor.

The dramatic details have there been dropped in favor of an intense, and beguiling, lyric glitter. The original Latin image, however, participates in the poem's action by itself containing an action (as Virgil's similes almost always do): Apollo leaves, visits, renews, steps. With Humphries, the image is simply a quality, seen variously as bright, shining, radiant, and splendid. Humphries equates the appearance of Aeneas with the appearance of Apollo; but Virgil compares their conduct, what they do. And the reason, as I have suggested, is that Virgil throughout the *Aeneid* is not so much picturing something as pressing toward or enacting something: enacting with all the resources known to poetry and on many different "levels" the classic drama of a necessary and sanctified return—the return of the dead to life, the return of the race to its homeland, the restoration of peace and order out of violence and disorder, along with the renewal of the year, of the ceremonies, of the human spirit.

Or rather, to be precise, he is enacting all that in part: in part, the *Aeneid* steadily mirrors an action of an opposite kind, a self-propelled movement toward defeat and death. It is hard, in our tension-ridden age, not to apprehend the *Aeneid* in terms of an unresolved tension or duality: a duality that persists to the very end, where it is fixed forever in that closing glimpse, not only of the victorious Aeneas but simultaneously (and perhaps more memorably) of Turnus's *vita indignata* ("Unconsenting spirit"—C. Day Lewis) fleeing to the shades below. It is that dark underhalf of the poem that is secretly present in the other of our two passages, in the image of Dido-Diana, following immediately, as it does, the portraiture of Penthesilea on the temple wall. I do not myself see how translation could effectively manage to suggest this secret presence; but it may be pointed to, at least, in the language of criticism. The character and both the present high position and the tragic future destiny of Queen Dido are here indicated by means of not one but two similes: one of them (to Diana) explicit, and one (to Penthesilea) implicit and by juxtaposition.

As to Penthesilea, Virgil assumes one's knowledge of the legend about her in the epic cycle and in vase paintings: the valiant and beautiful young virgin warrior and queen who fought on the Trojan side in the old war and was slain by Greek Achilles, who, grieving over her corpse, was taunted by Thersites. Such is the memory, stimulated by the image, that Virgil asks us to carry into the first glimpse of Dido; for even as Aeneas stands wondering at the painted Amazon, the living queen steps into view. Over the description of Dido's beauty, authority, and grace, the image of Penthesilea casts a very dark shadow. For Dido, too, is a valiant young queen; herself possibly a virgin, and now altogether chaste in her widowhood; able, like the Amazon, to hold her own with the heroes, the dangerous neighboring princes. And Dido, too, will eventually be slain, or anyhow driven to madness and self-slaughter, by the man who in this poem takes on the victorious aspects of Achilles and who will likewise grieve over her speechless ghost (as he will, incidentally, imitate Achilles as well by slaying the literal counterpart of Penthesilea in the *Aeneid*, the swift-footed Camilla).

Later, in Book IV, Virgil will attach to Dido some of the language used here, in Book I, about Penthesilea. "*Aurea subnectens exsertae cingula mammae,*" he says here; and the line is echoed by "*aurea purpuream subnectit fibula vestem*" in IV, 139, just ten words before the start of the Apollo simile. (The image of Dido at this moment also includes the very phrase attached, in the Book I simile, to the goddess Diana: "*magna stipante caterva.*") Far more significant are the key words *furens* and *ardet* that characterize the militant conduct of Penthesilea and that then turn up, in Book IV, to characterize the behavior of Dido. But it is exactly at this point that the full force of the two similes in Book I—the implicit and the explicit—realizes itself. The nature of that force is, as poetically it should be, the opposite of the force of the Aeneas-Apollo simile. The latter is immediately ironic (considering Aeneas's actual occupation), but it is ultimately descriptive, or perhaps *pre*scriptive. The two similes involving Dido, on the contrary, are immediately descriptive, but ultimately ironic, and very tragically so. When *furens* and *ardet* are associated with Dido in Book IV, they represent not (as with Penthesilea) the flaming heroics of a virgin warrior, but the sexual fires of a woman raging with physical passion. "*Totaque vagatur urbe furens,*" Virgil reports in IV, 69; and "*Ardet amans Dido, traxitque per ossa furorem,*" exults Juno, in IV, 101 ("She wanders raging through the city. . . . 'Dido burns and her whole frame rages with love' "—C. Day Lewis). Dido, likened initially to the virgin warrior and the rites-observing goddess of chastity, has by line 300 of Book IV pulled so far away from both, has so far betrayed her political and religious duties, as to be comparable to "some Bacchante driven wild and drawn at night to the Bacchic orgies." And by line 470, she is akin to Pentheus (is there a slight twisty echo of Penthesilea in that familiar name?), raving on the Theban hills, destined to be torn in pieces by the Bacchae.

The Aeneas-Apollo simile, I have argued, participates in the action of the *Aeneid* by providing a divine archetype which it is the business of Aeneas and his followers to emulate—in their huge enactment of the personal, moral, racial, and national *return*. In a considerably more complex and even paradoxical manner, the Penthesilea-Dido simile combines with the Dido-Diana simile to participate in an action of an opposite kind: in the multiple movement toward personal and moral and national death that the poem embraces. Just as, for example, the allusions to the mother Latona are grounded in the divine injunction to "seik your ald moder," so the allusions to *furens* and *ardet* and so on reach their fulfillment when the individual death and funeral pyre of Dido, in IV, 669–671, are analogized to the fall and destruction of the entire city by fire:

> *Non aliter, quam si inmissis ruat hostibus omnis*
> *Karthago aut antiqua Tyros, flammaeque furentes*
> *Culmina perque hominum volvantur perque deorum*

Of contemporary translators, C. Day Lewis is probably the one who has best perceived the crucial continuity of the imagery at work here:

> It was as if Carthage or ancient Tyre should be falling,
> With enemy troops breaking into the town and a
>   conflagration
> Furiously sweeping over the abodes of men and of gods.

Lewis has grounded that version in his earlier renderings of Penthesilea "storming through the melee like a fire," and in his English account (quoted, for example, in an earlier paragraph) of the burning fury of Queen Dido. The *Aeneid* of C. Day Lewis is not always exhilarating, nor has it been able to capture very much of the sheer beauty of the original; it has a somewhat dogged quality. But it also has the merit of leaving nothing out, and of staying with the exact line count of the Latin. Beyond that, it is a translation that usually tries and often succeeds in carrying over into English the steady, almost relentless drama of the Virgilian poem—in discovering in English an echo of the active Virgilian echoes. It is, therefore, by way of a tribute to this version that I borrow from it a full translation of the passages with which we have been concerned.

[Aeneas] picked out Penthesilea leading the crescent shields of
The Amazons and storming through the melee like a fire,
Her bare breast thrusting out over the golden girdle,
A warrior queen, a girl who braved heroes in combat.
Now while Aeneas viewed with wonder all these scenes,
And stood at gaze, rooted in a deep trance of attention,
There came in royal state to the temple, a crowd of courtiers
Attending her, queen Dido, most beautiful to see.
As by the banks of Eurotas or over the Cynthian slopes
Diana foots the dance, a thousand Oreads following
Weave a constellation around that arrowy one,
Who in grace of movement excels all goddesses,
And happiness runs through the still heart of Latona—
So Dido was, even as she went her radiant way
Through the crowds, eager to forward the work and growth
    of her realm.

I, 490–504

              But by far the handsomest of them all
Was Aeneas, who came to her side now and joined forces
    with hers.
It was like when Apollo leaves Lycia, his winter palace,
And Xanthus river to visit Delos, his mother's home,
And renew the dances, while round his altar Cretans and
    Dryopes
And the tattooed Agathyrsi are raising a polyglot din:
The god himself steps out on the Cynthian range, a circlet
Of gold and a wreath of pliant bay on his flowing hair,

The jangling weapons slung from his shoulder. Nimble as he,
Aeneas moved, with the same fine glow on his handsome
face.

IV, 141–150

(1961)

Afterword: The Art of Robert Fitzgerald

Some twenty-two years after the essay above was published, Robert
Fitzgerald brought out his translation of the *Aeneid,* and it instantly
took its place as the great English rendering of the poem in the
modern epoch. The enterprise came into being, Fitzgerald said in a
later interview, one afternoon in 1978 when he was sitting in Boston's
South Station waiting for a train and going over in his mind some
lines of Virgil he had been glossing with his Harvard students that
day. The lines came from Book II of the *Aeneid,* where Aeneas is
beginning his long account, for Queen Dido, of the fall of Troy:

> *Et iam nox humida caelo*
> *Praecipitat suadentque cadentia sidera somnos.*

Mentally rejecting the rather toneless literal translation of the lines—
"The humid night is going down the sky, and the sleeping stars are
persuading slumber"—Fitzgerald found himself almost spontaneously
composing a more musical version.

> Now, too, the night is well along, with dewfall
> Out of heaven, and setting stars weigh down
> Our heads towards sleep.

He said to himself. "My God, I've got that! *Now, too: dewfall*—the end
of the line is symmetrical with the beginning of the line. *Out of heaven,*

and setting stars weigh down: Out at the beginning of the line; *down* at
the end . . . If I can do a few lines with this pleasure, why don't I do
the whole thing?" And so he did. For the reader who, like me, is at
most an amateur and occasional Latinist, it might be noticed that
Fitzgerald got more than a subtlety and balance of music in his
English. There is also a sort of freshened activity, something happening, in the English phrasing. This is the effect when the translator
derives "dewfall out of heaven" from the simple juxtaposition of the
adjective *humida* and the noun *caelo,* and when *suadent . . . somnos*
becomes "weigh down / Our heads towards sleep." Music and action:
better, and in Fitzgerald's own formula, music "carrying the story on":
this is the hallmark of Fitzgerald's supremely artful *Aeneid.*

Robert Fitzgerald was Boylston Professor of Rhetoric and Oratory at
Harvard in the year 1978; he had held that honorable post, of ancient
lineage, since 1965. He was sixty-eight years old; and although he had
been living in New England on and off for fifty years—as a student at
Choate School and Harvard College and then a resident of Ridgefield,
Connecticut, before the Harvard appointment—there clung to him
traces of the Springfield, Illinois, where he had grown up: something
neighborly and direct and humorous, along with an easy, intimate
knowledge of the things of the natural world; not to mention a felt
closeness to Springfield's Lincoln. The Springfield connection helps
explain Fitzgerald's unfashionable affection and admiration for Vachel
Lindsay, an 1879 product of the same town who, in one of his best
poems, imagined the ghost of Lincoln pacing up and down at midnight near the old Springfield courthouse. "Vachel was a really great
fellow," Fitzgerald once said, "*molto simpatico,* and very good to me."

Not less ineradicable was the experience of loss in those early years.
Fitzgerald's mother died when he was three, his younger brother when
he was eight, and his father (after being bedridden for nearly a decade)
when he was seventeen. He learned early on, as he was to put it, "that
the fate of the breathing person was to be hurt." The lesson expressed

itself in a certain enduring air of sadness: a Virgilian sadness at mortality, and a sadness that rather colored than deflected from the quiet zest and the laughter.

After Harvard, class of 1933, Fitzgerald labored at the New York *Herald Tribune* for a while, as assistant to the business editor. In the later thirties he was on the staff of *Time* magazine and wrote a book review a week, mainly to keep himself in pocket money. Irving Howe, a fellow reviewer on the magazine, has (in his autobiography) remembered Fitzgerald at the weekly conferences maintaining his poise "by assuming an air of unbroken gravity, as if he were a monk bound hostage to a gang of heretics." (The figure is a nice twist, conscious or not, on the elder Henry James's image of Hawthorne, glimpsed at a meeting of the Saturday Club in Boston, looking like "a rogue who suddenly finds himself in a company of detectives.")

All the while, Fitzgerald was exercising and sharpening his remarkable skills as a translator of classical literature. With Dudley Fitts, his teacher and mentor at Choate, he translated three Greek plays: the *Alcestis* of Euripides, and the *Antigone* and *Oedipus Rex* of Sophocles. In 1952, he launched himself valiantly upon a verse translation of the *Odyssey*, having heard from many sources that such a thing was much needed in the burgeoning humanities courses in American universities. He had been living since 1946 in Connecticut, "having a baby every year," as he recalled, and commuting down to a part-time job at Sarah Lawrence in Bronxville. Now, simultaneously, he received a Guggenheim Fellowship and a quite respectable advance from Doubleday, payable over five years, to get ahead with the Homeric epic. He took his wife and their children to Italy, where in the course of time they bought a house in Perugia—"a tall old house near a road along a grand hillside looking out over the Tiber valley," in Fitzgerald's report—and here they lived until Robert was made a lecturer at Harvard.

The *Odyssey* came out in 1961. It was a staggering accomplishment whose implications—for the art of translating from Greek and for dramatic poetry under the modern cultural circumstances—are still being worked out. It was recognized almost at once as a masterpiece; indeed, in the words of Moses Hadas, the distinguished Columbia classicist, it was "the best and truest *Odyssey* in the English language." The translation was cast in a highly flexible blank verse: "too much iambic can ruin any subject matter," Ezra Pound once told Fitzgerald; and Fitzgerald himself said later that his metrical ideal was "a living rhythm" that "corresponds to a living voice," rather than a metronomic five-stress beat. Most of all, he met the enormous challenge he set himself: that of "reimagining the action of the poem, so that it was alive from start to finish."

A very faint sense of the achievement may be gained from a sequence in Book XIII, a favorite of mine, especially since it is a phase of the story that has to do with the art of story telling. Odysseus awakes in his homeland of Ithaka (in Fitzgerald's spelling), having been conveyed there in a Phoinikian ship, but he does not at first recognize the place. The goddess Athena appears in the guise of a young man, and, accosting the lad, Odysseus asks him, "what is this land, and realm, who are the people?" Athena replies that it is the island of Ithaka, famed for its pastures and vineyards. Odysseus, ever on guard, thereupon spins out an astonishing tale of how he had slain Orsilokhos, the son of Idomeneus, in Krete, and had been outlawed and had fled to Pylos, but had arrived by mistake at Ithaka, where his companions robbed him and left him alone. This delights Athena, always a bit enamored of Odysseus, and she asks him whether, in his own country, he will not give his trickeries a rest.

Odysseus's yarn is packed with plausible detail devised on the spot. The (wholly fictitious) man Orsilokhos, he says,

> could beat the best country runners
> in Krete, but he desired to take away
> my Trojan plunder, all I had fought and bled for
> cutting through ranks in war and the cruel sea. . . .
> I acted: I

hit him with a spearcast from a roadside
as he came down from the open country. Murky
night shrouded all heaven and the stars.
I made that ambush with one man at arms.
We were unseen. I took his life in secret,
finished him off with my sharp sword.

Listening to these brilliant inventions.

         the gray-eyed goddess
Athena smiled, and gave him a caress.
Her looks being changed now, so she seemed a woman,
tall and beautiful and no doubt skilled
at weaving splendid things. She answered briskly,
"Whoever gets around you must be sharp
and guileful as a snake; even a god
might bow to you in ways of dissimulation.
You! You chameleon!
Bottomless bag of tricks! Here in your own country
would you not give your stratagems a rest
or stop spellbinding for an instant?"

Honors and awards of many kinds followed upon the translation, and they increased with the appearance of Fitzgerald's *Iliad* in 1973. He also translated from the French of St. John Perse. He had brought out three volumes of his own poetry, through *In the Rose of Time* in 1956; and he might have left a larger body of poetry, as he knew, if he had not spent the years on translation. Remarking on this, his widow, Penelope Laurans Fitzgerald, said at a memorial service in January 1985 that Robert might equally have written more literary essays and personal memoirs. And yet—

in his translations *all* of his gifts—the capacity to imagine character, to drive a narrative forward, to pick exactly the right word for the right context, to bring ancient verities into modern thought, and to infuse at once directness and lyric power—combined to provoke and fit his special genius.

A better appraisal could not be asked for.

Robert Fitzgerald died in Hamden, Connecticut, on January 16, 1985, and in the wake of the event, those of us who knew him—some, like William Maxwell and James Laughlin, for upwards of fifty years, others, myself included, for a relatively few years—tried to say to each other just what it was that so drew us to the man. "I think," Penelope Fitzgerald said, "that Robert was one of the rare people who truly touch others' lives"; the classic simplicity of the statement should not hide the genuine rarity of the phenomenon, and the justness of the saying was made evident in the outpouring of messages of love and gratitude to Robert during the eight months' losing bout with cancer. On his last birthday, in October 1984, he was presented with a book containing notes, cards, letters short and long, telegrams, photographs, cartoons, a painting, a drawing, a card that sang "Happy Birthday" by computer chip, and no fewer then twenty-two original poems.

There was an immediacy to him, perhaps that was part of it: a shaped and outlined presence there close to one and always aware of one, something psychically vital and spiritually staunch, but also gentle, *dolce,* amused and amusing. In his fiftieth anniversary report for his Harvard Class of 1933, Robert Fitzgerald wrote—the Homeric tone mingling with the Christian, the modern, and the personal—

> So hard at best is the lot of man and so great is the beauty he can apprehend, that only a religious conception of things can take in the extremes and meet the case. Our lifetimes have seen the opening of abysses before which the mind quails. But it seems to me there are a few things everyone can humbly try to

hold on to: love and mercy (and humor) in everyday living; the quest for exact truth in language and affairs of the intellect; self-recollection or prayer; and the peace, the composed energy of art.

He was a celebrationist of life, but in the quietest way, almost whispering, as though celebrating a religious rite. There was an evening in the late spring of 1984 when a dozen of us forgathered for dinner at a friend's house in New Haven. Nancy and I drove up in time to see Robert and Penny getting out of the car ahead of us. We all wore evening garb. Robert turned and saw us; lifting up a bottle of champagne in the semi-darkness, he waggled it at us celebrationally, with a gleaming beatific smile, and said in the softest possible voice: "*Whoopee!*" It was that day, we discovered afterward, that Robert learned he had cancer.

Speaking of the author of the *Odyssey,* Fitzgerald told an interviewer that whoever it was who "composed this poem had imagined people in action and people feeling and saying things out of what they felt." For the translator, "that work of imagining had to be redone." And the aim in the redoing was to devise a poetic line in English "as graceful, as sinewy and as interesting" as the Greek line, while seeking "to avoid any stunting, metrical or otherwise, that might distract the reader from the main thing, which was always the dramatic action and narrative." In talking retrospectively about the challenge faced in translating the *Aeneid,* he put a comparable stress on the envisioning of individuals in action. Someone quoted Robert Lowell to him: "Virgil is dark, narrow, morbid, mysterious, and artistic." What did Fitzgerald think of those adjectives? "Well," Fitzgerald answered, "too much has been made of texture. One of the things I tried to bring out more fully as I went along was the pure narrative interest of this thing as a story."

Fitzgerald captured that quality and rendered that story from literally his first line. Several of us can remember Robert trying out versions of the line, the famous *arma virumque cano*. It was the *que* that tantalized him: what Chaucer had cunningly expressed in the phrase "and al-so." "War is my burden and the man of war" was one version Robert offered for our judgment; but he ended with "I sing of warfare and a man at war." There then came the eleven-line overview of the basic adventure up to the founding of Rome, followed by the twenty-eight-line account of the assorted reasons for the goddess Juno's relentless hostility toward Aeneas and the Trojans. The prologue ends:

> so hard and huge
> A task it was to found the Roman people.

Tantae molis erat Romanam condere gentem. Fitzgerald is off to a momentous start when from *tantae molis*—"of so great a toil," or "difficulty"—he elicits "So hard and huge / a task . . ."

We may move on to Fitzgerald's translation of the two passages from Book I and Book IV examined in the preceding essay.

> Then, leading the battalion of Amazons
> With half-moon shields, he saw Penthesilea
> Fiery amid her host, buckling a golden
> Girdle beneath her bare and arrogant breast,
> A girl who dared fight men, a warrior queen.
> Now, while these wonders were being surveyed
> By Aeneas of Dardania, while he stood
> Enthralled, devouring all in one long gaze,
> The queen paced toward the temple in her beauty,
> Dido, with a throng of men behind.
>
> As on Eurotas bank or Cynthus ridge
> Diana trains her dancers, and behind her
> On every hand the mountain nymphs appear,

A myriad converging; with her quiver
Slung on her shoulders, in her stride she seems
The tallest, taller by a head than any,
And joy pervades Latona's quiet heart:
So Dido seemed, in such delight she moved
Amid her people, cheering on the toil
Of a kingdom in the making

I, 490–504

Resplendent
Above the rest, Aeneas walked to meet her,
To join his retinue with hers. He seemed—
Think of the lord Apollo in the spring
When he leaves wintering in Lycia
By Xanthus torrent, for his mother's isle
Of Delos, to renew the festival;
Around his altars Cretans, Dryopes,
And painted Agathyrsans raise a shout,
But the god walks the Cynthian ridge alone
And smooths his hair, binds it in fronded laurel,
Braids it in gold; and shafts ring on his shoulders.
So elated and swift, Aeneas walked
With sunlit grace upon him.

IV, 141–150

Fitzgerald was willing to forgo some of the arguably Virgilian
features of the C. Day Lewis translation: a measured stateliness of
movement, an air of solemnity, the sense of attending a tale told in a
long perspective of time. By contrast, Fitzgerald's drama unfolds
before our very eyes. Nothing could be more appropriate; for what we
have (as I tried to indicate earlier) are, exactly, dramas unfolding
variously before the eyes and the image-making imaginations of Aeneas

and Dido; that is the tactical point. The narrative is direct, vibrant, alive to the quick, a condition enabled by the flexibly iambic line. The narrative *voice* can adjust itself in mid-sentence: so, the uncharacteristically awkward

> It was like when Apollo leaves Lycia, his winter palace,
> And Xanthus river

in Lewis becomes

>   He seemed—
> Think of the lord Apollo in the spring
> When he leaves wintering in Lycia
> By Xanthus torrent

in Fitzgerald.

The intricate multifarious activity is beautifully set forth, with all its pacing, striding, walking, observing, dancing, converging, braiding, binding, and buckling. Each element has its own distinctness, but what comes into view at last is a single large composite action. It is the essential action, triumphant and tragic, of the *Aeneid* as a whole.

(1991)

Until fairly recently, *Pericles* has been one of the least popular of Shakespeare's plays. It has been among the least read and the least performed, and it has somehow seemed to be one of the least accessible. Part of the "problem" it presents is, of course, the problem of authorship. Almost everyone feels that the first two acts are poetically and dramatically quite inferior to the last three; and from this it has usually been inferred that while Shakespeare may have written most of III, IV, and V, he can have contributed only an occasional touch to I and II. Some commentators doubt that Shakespeare wrote any significant part of *Pericles,* in which case we are interestingly confronted—at moments like III.i and iii, IV.vi, and V.i—with a writer whose creative powers were scarcely less than Shakespeare's. Others are convinced that he wrote just about all of the play, but that either he hurried the composition of I and II to arrive at the first point that really engaged his imagination, the alleged death and the actual birth at sea that begin the third act, or that the spottiness of the earlier portions is due merely to faulty recording by the person, whoever he was, who first copied it down. One or two critics even argue that Shakespeare wrote the whole of *Pericles* and that it is all equally good.*

The assumption behind the remarks that follow is that Shakespeare probably did take over a fragment of someone else's play, and that he recast and touched up the borrowed fragment so that it might lead naturally into the major section of *Pericles,* the last three acts, which he did indeed write himself. If this is so, we can learn a good deal by observing what Shakespeare was willing to let stand in acts I and II. Assuming, for example, as most people do, that the play's first scene is mainly by somebody else, the really fascinating critical question is not which words and phrases Shakespeare may have pushed into it, but why he retained the scene, its characters and incidents and language, in what must be pretty much its original form. The answer, needless to say, is that the scene as written fitted into the imaginative design that Shakespeare had for the work as a whole, and for which he was willing to be artistically responsible. That design has to do, in part, with fathers and daughters, and with chastity and lust: items that are obviously central to I.i. But the design has also to do with death and birth, and, more obscurely, with the relation of those radical events to the poetic and creative act. As such awkward and murky scenes as I.i give way to the vital dramatic beauty that succeeds them (beginning with III.i), we have the distinct impression that the play itself is quickening into life—a creative process that parallels and reflects the human process whereby first Thaisa and then Pericles are miraculously restored to consciousness. The aesthetic miracle, like the human one, is attended by music.

Speaking not of the actual but of the verbal music in *Pericles,* T. S. Eliot has contended that Shakespeare is here "experimenting to see how elaborate, how complicated, the music could be made without

*An outline of the plot of *Pericles,* scene by scene, will be found at the end of this essay.

losing touch with colloquial speech altogether." That is one of the reasons that Eliot believes *Pericles* to be, as he has said, a "very great play," and it is why he based his exceedingly moving lyric "Marina" (1931) upon it. A related reason, according to Eliot, is that the speech of *Pericles*—he is referring specifically to the fifth act—is that of "creatures who are more than human, or rather, seen in a light more than that of day."* It is very aptly put, and I am in full agreement. There is a greatness in *Pericles,* and it does come from "a light more than that of day," though nothing is more difficult to define. Let me risk the following. The notable rise in the reputation of *Pericles* in recent decades has been due to its being at last properly located within the career of Shakespeare's imagination. It has been seen as belonging to the so-called last plays (*Cymbeline, The Winter's Tale, The Tempest*), sharing with them a certain atmosphere, a certain music and symbolism, a certain preoccupation with loss and recovery; and it shares with them a tendency to reverse the habitual tone or "vision" of the great tragedies. In those, human experience seems surrounded by a darkness more than that of night:

> As flies to wanton boys, are we to the gods;
> They kill us for their sport.

There is the penultimate verdict on the human situation by blinded Gloucester in *King Lear,* speaking out of his terrible physical and psychological darkness; and the events of the play go far to confirm him. But in *Pericles,* which ushers in Shakespeare's final phase, it is rather the very kindness of the gods that seems unbearable.

> This, this! No more, you gods, your present kindness
> Makes my past miseries sports.

*The first remark quoted in this paragraph is from "The Music of Poetry" (1942; included in *On Poetry and Poets,* 1957). The second and third comments are quoted by Elizabeth Drew (*T. S. Eliot: The Design of his Poetry,* 1950) from an unpublished address of 1937.

We have entered a world that radiates with a light more than that of day, and Pericles is nearly blinded by it.

In the peculiar illumination of *Pericles,* we discover something more than a shift in attitude toward the gods: say, a new cheerfulness about them, or a new sense of their benignity. Along with that there has evidently come a basically revised judgment on human experience generally, and a new sense of what it means to be a human being, a new view of mortality. To convey all that, Shakespeare devised—and in the final phases of *Pericles* he can be caught in the very act of devising—a new dramatic method, a new manner of reference and of symbolism. But nowhere, I venture, are these other novel aspects better illustrated than in the play's handling of its religious dimension. It is a dimension that gets articulated primarily in pagan terms, but it contains an attitude toward divinity and toward the relation of god and man that belongs essentially to the Christian tradition—or, as I shall suggest, to one major segment of it.

The pagan articulation begins at once. The King of Antioch, in I.i, introduces his debauched daughter as one who is "clothed like a bride, / For embracements even of Jove himself"; that is, as resembling the goddess Juno. The connection is further stressed by the reference to Lucina, who reigned at the child's birth, Lucina being a name usually associated with Juno, though sometimes with Diana. Later on, the Prince of Tyre, speaking wildly of the maiden who stands before him (V.i)—his own daughter Marina, whom he has not yet fully recognized—says that, in resembling his drowned queen, Thaisa, Marina too resembles Juno: "in pace another Juno." At Marina's birth also, Lucina has been invoked:

> Lucina, o
> Divinest patroness, and midwife gentle
> To those that cry by night, convey thy deity
> Aboard our dancing boat.
>
> (III.i)

The two royal daughters are thus seemingly linked by these shared allusions to the queen of the gods. But of course the expressed parallel between Antioch's daughter and Marina only serves to make the more shocking our awareness of the enormous distance that separates them, a distance reflected as much in the quality of the poetry about each of them as in their moral characters. It is something like the distance between hell and heaven, and the action of the play requires traveling across the whole of it. Antioch's child (who is also, as the riddle dreadfully declares, his "mother" and his "wife") represents the infernal profanation of the principle of daughterhood. Marina (who, as she assists at his rebirth, becomes her father's spiritual parent: "Thou that beget'st him that did thee beget") is its ideal or perfect instance. The incestuous one threatens Pericles (I.i) with a "sharp physic"; but Marina will restore him with her "sacred physic" (V.i). The daughter of Antioch is really dedicated, one feels, to some dark goddess whose name may not be spoken. Marina entrusts her fortunes and her virgin honor to Diana.

Diana presides over much of *Pericles,* and where she is not the ruling deity the god Neptune has his province. Diana is in particular the goddess of Pericles' family or, shall we say, of his domestic community, the regular object of its prayer. Each member of it does homage to her; she is the key element in the family religion—which is, among other things, a religion *of* family; and she represents, even as she later actually becomes, in her own person, both cause and warrant of the family's salvation. At Mytilene, surrounded by bawds and panders, Marina prays: "Diana aid my purpose"; to which the bawd replies sardonically, "What have we to do with Diana?" and adds in a malicious pun, "Pray you, will you go with us?" But Marina and her father and mother have everything to do with Diana. Even Pericles swears "by bright Diana, whom we honour" when he leaves his daughter in Tharsus to (so it develops) the murderous hands of Dionyza and Cleon.* The entire life of Thaisa, or so much as Shake-

*There is a scholarly debate, not unentertaining, about just what Pericles is

speare wants us to know of it, is shaped by her involvement with Diana. While still a princess at Pentapolis, and as a device to ward off all suitors except Pericles, she vows (her father says) to "wear Diana's livery" for another twelvemonth, invoking Diana also by her patronym Cynthia: "This by the eye of Cynthia hath she vowed, / And on her virgin honour, will not break it." Cast ashore in her coffin at Ephesus, she returns to consciousness with the words: "O dear Diana, / Where am I?" And learning that her lord Pericles is reported dead at sea, she declares, "A vestal livery will I take me to, / And never more have joy." Cerimon informs her at once that there is a temple to Diana not far distant; and she enlists herself in it as a priestess for what she supposes will be the rest of her days. To Pericles, when after fourteen years' separation he finds his wife again in that holy temple, Thaisa seems Diana incarnate—if, as I take it, he is addressing her when he exclaims, "Immortal Dian!"

Pericles can call her that since he has just seen Diana herself, the goddess having appeared to him in a dream to summon him to Ephesus. Much could be made to hang upon that visitation. But though it may be difficult to stage persuasively, the event is not implausible. Pericles is at the moment a man exalted, carried beyond himself. He is attuned to a reality beyond the human. Only an instant earlier, he had heard the music of the spheres, sounds usually inaudible to the ear of man; and if he can hear the heavenly music, there is no reason he cannot see the heavenly goddess. Or we can say, humanistically, that Pericles' exaltation has created in his own mind a beauty of

---

swearing to do at this point (III.iii). One reading has him vow that "All unsister'd shall this heir of mine remain, / Though I show will in it"; i.e., that he will not remarry and beget another daughter until his first daughter, Marina, is wedded. The alternate reading, which is the one approved by Professor Sisson, is: "Unscissored shall this hair of mine remain, / Though I show ill in it"—that he will not cut his hair till Marina marries. The former version does involve the oath of personal chastity customarily associated with the prayer to Diana. But the latter seems confirmed by the concluding moment in V.iii—about which all readings agree—when Pericles announces that, to celebrate Marina's marriage to Lysimachus, he will at long last shave his beard: "This ornament / [That] makes me look dismal will I clip to form: / And what this fourteen years no razor touched, / To grace thy marriage day I'll beautify."

sound and sight more than humanity can normally arrive at; or again, Romantically, that the dramatic intensity of the play at this point has forced into concrete being something (Diana) that had hitherto figured as symbol and metaphor, as a mode of moral and spiritual statement. All these accounts come, on different levels, to the same thing, which is that Diana, or what she represents, has momentarily achieved a palpable reality.

What *does* she represent in the play—"celestial Dian, goddess argentine," as Pericles names her? Here as always, Shakespeare was not restricted by his classical sources, but took from them what was alive to his purposes. In Ovid's *Metamorphoses,* which Shakespeare knew and loved, Diana is rather an alarming than an endearing figure.* Like her Greek counterpart and source, Artemis, she is the virgin huntress, the woodland goddess of women and especially of female chastity; but she has become aggressively hostile toward men and coldly unforgiving toward the frailty of women. We hear of her revenge upon Acteon, the grandson of Cadmus, who by mischance espied her bathing, naked, in a forest pool; whereupon, with an arrogant cry, she turned him into a stag and his own hounds destroyed him. We see her banish one of her nymphs who had been seduced by Jove—making his assault in the garb of Diana herself!—and who was with child by him. Whatever modern psychology might suggestively make of these legends, for *Pericles* Shakespeare took only the principle of chastity.

Chastity, in the play, is a virtue important for men and women alike. Pericles too can swear by bright Diana, and envision her in a dream of hope. Similarly, it is a virtue exercised not only in the uncontaminated forests and mountains, but equally in the centers of courtly and urban life. It pertains to much more than the sexual aspect of human

*Shakespeare's classical knowledge was primarily Roman. He had famously even "less Greeke" at his command than Latin; and where he did borrow from a Greek tradition, he tended to Romanize it. In historic fact, for example, the temple at Ephesus was built in honor of Artemis; in *Pericles,* it is given over to Artemis's Roman successor, Diana.

behavior, though that aspect is crucial enough and seems the more so as it is manifested in the extreme forms that everywhere characterize this play. Marina's chastity is more impressive than the somewhat frigid and even suspect virginity of Ovid's Diana, for we understand it in juxtaposition with the "monstrous lust" of Antioch and his daughter, and we see it glow against the squalor of Mytilene. It is a very spirited kind of chastity, as Marina's spirited words to the bawd indicate (IV.ii):

> If fires be hot, knives sharp, or waters deep,
> Untied I still my virgin knot will keep.
> Diana aid my purpose.

But, as Marina's later words to Boult, the pander's servant, also make clear, chastity is a way of life and a way of being; it designates not simply virginity but the kind of conduct that can distinguish the human from the subhuman. "For what thou professest"—that is, the pander's trade—"a baboon, could he speak, / Would own a name too dear." Still, chastity is only *a* way of life; it is not the highest kind of life to which human nature may aspire (for Thaisa, we recall, the chaste temple life was a joyless one). For that highest kind, which in the play is marital and parental, chastity is a preparation and a preservative. It *preserves* the possibility of domestic fulfillment; and it is because Pericles, Thaisa, and Marina have alike sworn to and lived by Diana for fourteen years that they are morally and spiritually ready for one another, are fit members of their recreated domestic community, when they are brought together at last. They have made themselves worthy of the grace bestowed.

And by the curious but compelling logic of myth, it is the same goddess of chastity who restores the family, who brings Thaisa and Pericles back to their marriage bed (and Thaisa's intense physical, not to say sexual, reaction to her husband's appearance is made perfectly and beautifully evident) and oversees the engagement of Marina and

Lysimachus. At this moment in act V, Diana is doing more than rewarding the chaste by, as it were, releasing them from their vows. She is also performing another of her ancient traditional functions—which was to promote or to restore the community life. There is a hint of this phase of Diana in the hymn to her by Catullus, which Shakespeare is said not to have known. There is a more elaborate hint in those early books of Virgil's *Aeneid*, which Shakespeare had plainly absorbed. It emerges there from an intricate pattern of imagery that links Diana to Queen Dido of Carthage and in particular to Dido's work of organizing and controlling an entire kingdom. The Virgilian pattern is indeed intricate, but Shakespeare was supremely equipped to grasp the essential motif at a glance; and his own Diana represents—beyond chastity and yet by means of it—the force that begets out of separate and separated individuals a genuine and enduring community. This is exactly what happens when, in the temple at Ephesus, Diana's priestess removes her veil to become again the wife of Pericles, mother of Marina and queen of Pentapolis, and as Marina, once more the daughter of her living parents, is about to become the wife of Lysimachus (whom Pericles already speaks of as "our son") and queen of Tyre. One even imagines that Tyre and Pentapolis will unite within a larger community, bound by family ties and a common devotion to the goddess of the silver bow.

But while Diana presides over so much of the action of *Pericles*, it is Neptune who incites most of the great language of the play. The old sea-god is not mentioned by name until the final act; and he is addressed directly only in Pericles' muscular words in III.i: "Thou god of this great vast, rebuke these surges, / Which wash both heaven and hell. . . ." But his presence and power are steadily felt; and as always the sea, especially a tempestuous sea, draws from Shakespeare some of his most remarkable poetic effects. The world of *Pericles* is a world of coasts and islands; Pericles, during the first four acts, is constantly at sea, journeying from port to port, and usually the passage is a dangerous one. On four separate occasions we see or hear of him "thwarting the wayward seas," as Gower says (IV.iv) in one of the handsomest puns even Shakespeare ever contrived. In act II, his ship is "wrack'd and split," and Pericles is deposited naked and alone on the coast of Pentapolis ("Enter Pericles wet," as the stage direction quaintly declares). In act III, Thaisa—as her husband and the nurse Lichorida believe—dies giving birth to Marina during a ferocious storm at sea. "A more blusterous birth had never babe," Pericles tells his newborn daughter in a speech that goes on to encompass the play's whole supple movement from storm to calm and from grief to joy, under the mysterious but ultimately benevolent governance of the gods:

> Quiet and gentle thy conditions; for
> Thou art the rudeliest welcome to this world
> That ever was prince's child. Happy what follows;
> Thou hast as chiding a nativity
> As fire, air, water, earth, and heaven can make,
> To herald thee from the womb. Even at the first,
> Thy loss is more than can thy portage quit,
> With all thou canst find here. Now the good gods
> Throw their best eyes upon't.

The very lines wash back and forth with a powerful sea motion. In act IV, finally, Pericles makes his difficult way to Tharsus, and then, according to Gower, "He puts on sackcloth, and to sea. He bears / A tempest, which his mortal vessel tears, / And yet he rides it out"—a literal statement that at the same time refers prophetically to Pericles' inward and spiritual endurance.

It is therefore exactly fitting that the great "recognition scene" in act V, that extraordinary reversal of fortune and of spirit, should take place on the day of "God Neptune's annual feast" (by tradition, July 23), and at a moment when Pericles' storm-tossed ship lies peacefully at anchor. Neptune, in fact, was a figure more honored in the literature of the seagoing Elizabethans (as was his mythological ancestor Poseidon among the Greeks) than in the writings of the relatively landlocked Romans, though he appeared conventionally enough in Virgil and Ovid as the lord of the waters. But in Shakespeare and especially in *Pericles*, Neptune is at once the lord of the waters and of what the waters represent—which is nothing other than life itself. It is the characteristic stuff of human experience, both the ebb and flow of human fortune and the very principle of vitality (stressing that last word's etymology, which is from the Latin word—*vita*—for life). It is almost redundant to say that Pericles has been beset by storms at sea or by Neptune; it is enough to say that, in his life, he has been sorely beset. And what happens in V.i is a reversal of fortune, a sudden flood of happiness, that is essentially the sheer triumph of *life:* the reassertion of life quite simply as against non-life. That triumph occurs and is celebrated while the Mytilenians on shore are "honouring of Neptune's triumphs," and it is conveyed by language in which the imagery of birth and living fuses with the imagery of the sea. In the climax the elements are inseparable:

> O Helicanus, strike me, honoured sir,
> Give me a gash, put me to present pain;
> Lest this great sea of joys rushing upon me
> O'erbear the shores of my mortality,
> And drown me with their sweetness. O come hither,
> Thou that beget'st him that did thee beget,
> Thou that was born at sea, buried at Tharsus
> And found at sea again.

The passage really needs to be spoken aloud, listened to, and meditated, rather than commented upon. But we can observe that, just as Marina's "wayward fortune" (as she calls it) is wonderfully reversed, so the once "wayward seas" have now yielded to a "great sea of joys." And when Pericles in the same speech urges Helicanus to kneel and "thank the holy gods as loud / As thunder threatens us," he and the play announce a new sense of divinity (a reversal of the tragic sense) that is simultaneously a new sense of the very nature of human life. The god that thundered earlier is now the source of ecstasy and the object of celebration; and life itself suffers a sea change and becomes for Pericles and Marina something rich and strange.

The new sense of life, though it is dramatically realized in pagan terms, can be fully defined only by drawing on the Christian vocabulary. For just as there are two or more versions of most other ingredients in the play (fathers and daughters, for example; murderers; healers; storms; journeys; songs and dances; kinds of retribution), so, shaping the play's meaning, there are two religious structures. In this regard, *Pericles* reflects its combination of "sources"—for it is an Elizabethan version of a fourteenth-century narrative poem by John Gower (a fragment of his *Confessio Amanti*) drawn from a once popular Latin tale of perhaps the sixth century A.D. based on a no longer existent Greek romance. It retains several familiar items from the romance tradition, especially as it flowered under medieval Christianity: the quest, the riddle, the blighted city, the contest at arms, and so on. Beyond that, the language of the play often gives a momentary Christian coloring to its pagan subject matter: for instance, the word "sin," which is much used about the incestuous pair at Antioch, or the bawd's petulant remark that Marina's stubborn chastity "would make a Puritan of the devil." But of course the Christian theme runs very much deeper and broader than this.

It begins even before the play proper begins, with the reminder by Gower, the chorus, that the "song" we are about to hear

> hath been sung at festivals,
> On ember-eves and holy-ales;
> And lords and ladies in their lives
> Have read it for restoratives.

That is one of the most telling of the passages Shakespeare chose to keep from the dramatic fragment he was reworking. "Holy-ales" means holiday celebrations; it holds on to the root meaning of holiday—holy day—that a secular culture like our own has pretty well forgotten. "Ember-eves" are the evenings before Ember days: the three days (Wednesday, Friday, and Saturday) set aside by the Church in each of the four seasons for a period of religious discipline and prayer. In the Christian calendar, Ember days occur during Advent, Lent, Whitsun-tide, and September; but there is no doubt that they are another example of the absorption into the Christian scheme (the baptism, we might almost say) of earlier pagan elements. Behind them we make out the seasonal rites and festivals of the pagan world, the ritual celebration of the rhythm of the year. Diana (Catullus emphasizes this aspect) also presided over the monthly and the annual cycle; she was the goddess honored at those periodic moments that were converted by the Christian Church into Ember days. But the intermeshing relation between pagan and Christian in *Pericles* is most precisely enacted when a song (the play itself) to be sung by Christians on Ember-eves reaches its climax on the "holy-ale" of the pagan god Neptune.

The entire story, Gower says, has been read by lords and ladies "for restoratives." Ember days are restoratives: properly practiced, they serve to restrengthen one's Christian faith and to purify and refresh the soul. The relevance of *Pericles* to this solemn enterprise is that it presents the Christian practitioner with the storied experience of restoration. When we encounter him in act V, Pericles has been, so to speak, on a sort of extended Ember day, having lain motionless in sackcloth and having virtually fasted for three months (he has taken nourishment, Helicanus reports sadly, only to "prorogue"—prolong—his grief, only to keep his grief alive). And when his daughter and then his wife are restored to him, when the family community is restored to itself and Pericles to supreme happiness, we can read in his whole adventure an allegory of the Christian life: of the soul's passage through adversity and suffering, and by severe self-denial, to a radiantly new spiritual condition.

But the Christian life in question has to be very importantly distinguished from other traditional versions of it. In a Christian perspective, what we witness in *Pericles* is a dramatic image, first, of finite human nature—of "frail mortality," in the prince's phrase—and second, of human nature not only restored to spiritual health, but heightened and illuminated by divine grace: in the theological meaning of the word, "perfected" by grace. But if the vision that informs the play's pagan materials is essentially Christian, it does *not* belong to the Christian vision we are most of us accustomed to today. Contemporary Christianity, where it shows the greatest potency, is an adaptation of the teachings of Saint Paul and Saint Augustine, with their somber insistence on original sin, on the dark vigor of evil and the soul's helplessness to do anything at all about its own salvation. Shakespeare's Christianity in *Pericles* and the other last plays is far more humanistic than that.

Standing among the Ephesians in the holy temple, Pericles is clearly a man reborn. He is not, however, reborn from the conditions described to the later Ephesians by Saint Paul, who said in his epistle to them that "You hath [God] quickened who were dead in trespasses and sins. . . . Even when we were dead in sins, hath [God] quickened us together with Christ." But Pericles had not been "dead in sins"; so far as we are told, he never committed any sin whatever, nor had Thaisa and Marina. None of them has trespassed; but each of them has had to experience the limits of unaided human nature, and if Pericles was for a while spiritually and psychologically dead, he was simply dead of mortality. All have been exposed to the shocks and stresses that measure finitude because finite nature is unable to control or avert them. Pericles and his wife and daughter bespeak for us what it means to be merely human, and the grief it entails. According to one strain in the Christian tradition—the Pauline strain that is so alive today—this human nature is *innately* sinful and prone to evil, and so it must be destroyed, or at least thoroughly chastised, before grace can enter the soul. But in the tradition Shakespeare is reviving in *Pericles* (some have called it the tradition of "theocentric humanism"), grace does not need to destroy human nature; it rather lifts it up; it enlarges, fulfills, and perfects it. This is the miracle that occurs in the fifth act of *Pericles*. This is what we recognize when Pericles hears the music of the heavenly spheres. We recognize it too when each member of the restored family seems to each of the others to be godlike, a human self and yet more than human. And we recognize it most of all in that more than natural light of which T. S. Eliot has spoken, a light that shines in the very atmosphere of the final scenes and that plays in their language:

> Look who kneels here. Flesh of thy flesh Thaisa;
> Thy burden at the sea, and called Marina
> For she was yielded there.
>
> Blessed, and mine own.

(1962)

The Plot of *Pericles*

Pericles solves the riddle put to him by the king of Antioch, and thereby discovers the secret of the king's incestuous relation with his own daughter; he flees for his safety (I.i, ii). Pericles arrives at Tharsus, and rescues that city from a famine (I.iv). Later he is shipwrecked off the coast of Pentapolis; and in Pentapolis he wins the hand of Thaisa, the daughter of King Simonides (II.i, ii, iii, v).

With his pregnant wife, Thaisa, Pericles is on his way back to Tyre when a storm breaks out. Thaisa gives birth to a child, Marina, but she herself appears to have died in childbirth; she is placed in a chest which is dropped overboard (III.i). Thaisa is not dead, however; the chest is cast ashore at Ephesus, and here Thaisa is restored to life. Believing her husband to have drowned, Thaisa becomes a priestess of Diana (III.iii, iv).

Pericles, meanwhile, takes the infant Marina to Tharsus, and leaves her in the hands of Governor Cleon and his wife, Dionyza (III.iii). As Marina grows to young womanhood, she arouses the hostility of Dionyza, jealous for the popularity of her own daughter. She sends a henchman to kill the girl, but pirates seize Marina and carry her off (IV.i). Marina is sold into a brothel in Mitylene (IV.ii); from this she is rescued by the governor, Lysimachus (IV.vi), who will become her husband.

In a dream vision, Pericles is shown the (false) tomb of Marina in Mitylene (IV.iv). He goes to Mitylene; and there follows the recognition scene between father and daughter (V.i). Pericles is now directed by Diana to her temple at Ephesus; and here there takes place a second recognition scene, between husband and wife.

3

Within days of Camus's death, it was being said (with an air of surprise) that, for all he seemed so characteristically a man of the theater, his dramatic achievement was not, as it turned out, very large or impressive: four plays of uncertain merit, and nothing original since *Les Justes* in 1949; adaptations of Calderón, Lope de Vega, Faulkner, and Dostoyevsky; toward the end, administrative activities. The enumeration is not inaccurate; and in appraising the apostle of *mésure*, one does not want to make immoderate claims for his work in the theater, nor for *Caligula* in particular. But such reckoning can be as misleading as it would be for Camus's fiction (only one novel, really, along with a couple of novellas and a handful of short stories), or for his essays and articles. The fact is, of course, that Camus—as he always insisted—was one of those writers "whose works form a whole in which each one is illuminated by the others." Each one, it might be added, is a necessary aspect of the others, and often contains those others, including writings yet to come, in nearly visible essence. Camus's dramatic work, in short, is not a fragment to be isolated, for inspection, from his performance in other genres. It is a constant dimension, constantly expanding, of his total artistic accomplishment. It was, for him, one more vocabulary, one more set of resources, with which to take hold of the shifting chaos reflected everywhere in his pages—just as the actor was one more prototype (along with Don Juan and Napoleon) of what Camus used to call "the absurd man." Camus's theatrical dimension was large and pervasive; and no work, in my opinion, more rousingly illustrates the scope and intent of it—and its dependence, for full understanding, upon his other writings—than the first of his plays, *Caligula*.

In its first version, completed in July 1939, *Caligula*, likes *Noces*, is a prewar creation; the more definitive second version, finished in early 1941, emerges in part from the atmosphere of war, and one can clearly see the spiritual condition of late prewar continental France in the sagging morality and jumpy opportunism of the Roman patricians, as they whine and cower before the lethal derision of Camus's protagonist. The date of composition is important in other ways as an aid to identification (though the said date is instructively difficult to pin down*). Albert Camus, in 1939, was more or less the age of the twenty-

*In an exemplary act of literary scholarship, A. James Arnold in 1984, working with hitherto inaccessible manuscripts, established the text of what he calls "the first *Caligula*": that is, the 1941 version with the many changes inserted into the 1939 version. He added a lengthy and illuminating biographical and analytic essay. The whole was published by Gallimard as *Cahiers Albert Camus #4: "Caligula:* version de 1941, suivi de La Poétique du Premier *Caligula*, par A. James Arnold."

The textual adventures are a cautionary tale about revisions and dating. Professor Arnold informs us that the 1941 *Caligula* contained an entirely new act III, written in early 1941 after the completion of *L'Etranger* and while he was finishing *Le Mythe de Sisyphe*. Camus revised the play again in the fall of 1943, preparatory to its first publication in book form the following year. It was in this 1943 rendering, notably, that Caligula for the first time utters what would become the drama's most famous line: "Men die and they are not happy."

Camus had not yet finished with the text. After the play was produced in September 1945, the author made further emendations, probably based on the stage script. Again in 1947 (I am still following Professor Arnold), in the wake of another production, Camus made several important changes. They are visible in the next printing, in particular the expanded role of Hélicon—who

five-year-old Roman lad who began his own career, his blood-curdling four-year rule as emperor of Rome and successor to Tiberius, in 37 A.D. *Caligula* is, first of all, an emphatically youthful play about an emphatically youthful hero ("All young people behave like that," says one of the patricians, hopefully); and through all its persistent horrors there rings an irrepressible exuberance that—in Camus's case—the swift maturing process of the war years would soon dispel.

This communicated zest is, among other things, the sheer joy of artistic creation. *Caligula* expresses the same self-conscious literary excitement that we sense (to take one of countless examples) in young Christopher Marlowe's apprentice drama about an imperial superman, *Tamburlaine.* It is the excitement of the discovery of vocation: an emotion so powerful that, with *Caligula* as with *Tamburlaine,* the insatiable aspirations of the hero appear as vital analogues to the creative aspirations of the author. The life-begetting impulse apparent in the writing vies and mingles with the death and destruction enacted on the stage; story and tonality engage in a strained but artistically happy marriage; and poets and poetry, actors and dramatic presentations become literal and significant elements in the action of the piece, investing it with a quality of being that no summary of the plot could hope to suggest.† The result, as Camus describes the dark, congested reign of one of history's most repulsive tyrants, is (not a tragedy but) an extravaganza which takes as its inner and actual subject the very idea

---

was not even a person in the piece in 1939. The 1958 book edition, following a revival of *Caligula* directed by Camus, shows some additional tinkerings.

For Camus, Professor Arnold says, there was not, perhaps could not be, any final or definitive version of the play. Like Caligula, and unlike the timorous Roman senators, Camus was a man who really did believe in the theater and its creative energizing. (This footnote added in 1990.)

†It may be useful here to insert Camus's brief account of the play and its meaning, from his 1958 preface to the American edition. "Caligula, a relatively attractive prince up to then, becomes aware, on the death of his sister and mistress, Drusilla, that the world is not satisfactory. Thenceforth, obsessed with the impossible and poisoned by scorn and horror, he tries, through murder and the systematic perversion of all values, to practice a liberty that he will eventually discover to be the wrong one."

of extravagance: that is, strictly, of "wandering outside." The great attraction of supreme power, Caligula remarks thoughtfully, is that it gives the impossible a chance; and this play is the only work of Camus that really does so.

In *The Myth of Sisyphus* Camus would commit himself "to exhausting the field of the possible," and to hanging doggedly inside it. The urge to transcend, to wander outside the limits of human possibility, would then be denounced as one of the characteristic modern modes of suicide. To be sure, Caligula's transcendent urge was also, in a manner of speaking, suicidal, as Camus underlined in his 1958 preface to the American edition of the play. "*Caligula*," Camus declared—but this is the older and more austere Camus talking— "is the story of the superior suicide," who "does what is necessary to arm against him those who will eventually kill him." That is a neat capsule of the play's plot; though, as Camus went on to say, it is not the fact but the terms of the emperor's rebellion that must be seen as unacceptable. At the outset, indeed, Caligula plainly bespeaks Camus's own refusal to accept the condition of things: the condition which the shock of his sister Drusilla's death leads Caligula to recognize and reject—a universe in which "men die and they are not happy." In that extraordinarily bare and eloquent phrase of the pre-Christian Caligula, we hear the unmuffled voice of the post-Christian Camus, uttering his absolute statement about the source of the tragic nature of contemporary experience. Camus's personal response was to dedicate both his art and his moral energy to what, following Malraux here as elsewhere, he called the "refabrication" or "rectification" of the universe.

But to rectify the universe, according to Camus, was precisely to *humanize* it. The way of Camus's Caligula, on the contrary, was to dehumanize it, literally to attempt to depopulate it; and this, or so it would seem in retrospect, was the young man's grandiose error. And yet, as dramatized, Caligula's deadly ambition—set, as it is, amidst a good deal of erotic high jinks and set against the whimpering bewilderment of most of the other persons in the play—takes on a curiously exhilarating character, even as Caligula the man becomes a curiously, contradictorily engaging personality. For by giving its head, for once, to an extravagance he would thereafter resist with all his force, Camus composed what, within the framework of all his later writings, comes to us as the major showpiece for his compelling anti-themes.

These are the great themes that animate the realm of the impossible. Among them is the familiar awareness of nothingness, of *rien*. But nothingness is not grimly confronted here, acknowledged and deplored, as it would be in *Cross-Purposes* and *The Myth of Sisyphus*. It is, rather, reached out for, it is leaped toward and celebrated: from its multiple iteration in the play's opening scenes (when it is sounded with the booming regularity of the gong the emperor strikes, rhythmically, to accompany the nihilistic oath he forces on his terrified mistress, Caesonia) onward to Caligula's wild admission, a second before his assassination, that his entire quest has concluded in *"Rien! rien encore!"* The cry is a shout of triumph as well as an ultimate confession; for "nothing" has become an end to be accomplished, a reality to which Caligula nearly reduces the world he rules over. And throughout the quest, Caligula proceeds with a kind of fierce and knowing joy directly against the notion that Camus would erect into a central theme and a principle of right conduct: the theme of *mésure*, of balance, of control and limitation. Dr. Rieux, in *The Plague*, stands for Camus's ideal of well-balanced rebellion; but about Caligula everything is excessive, out of control—beginning with his extravagant grief over the loss of Drusilla (*"Cela dépasse les bornes,"* grumbles one of the patricians). "I invite you," Caligula says magniloquently to Caesonia, "to a feast without limit . . . to the most beautiful of spectacles." *Caligula* itself, needless to say, is that feast and that spectacle.

And the limit Caligula seeks mainly to surpass, equally obviously, is the limit of humanity. In *The Rebel*, the determining theme and the note of its unswervable humanism was Camus's contention—echoing the reply of Homer's Odysseus to the goddess's offer of divinity and a permanent home on her magic island—that "We shall choose Ithaca.

. . . This world remains our first and last love." The anti-theme of *Caligula* is the defiant rejection of Ithaca and the ultimate strangulation of the aging, faithful Penelope of the piece; Caligula himself assumes the role of the goddess and appears before the gaping nobles in the guise of Venus. That second-act scene is as antic and histrionic as anything in the play; but Caligula is impersonating the only divinity that he (or Camus) could manage to discern: something deceitful, perverse, malicious, and utterly unpredictable, the dispenser of a loathsome or, betimes, maddeningly prankish grace.

Such is the image of divinity implicit in *The Plague* and represented by the incalculable epidemic that mysteriously destroyed one person and spared another; and such is the image made quite explicit in *The Rebel*. In *Caligula*, it is the tribune Cherea who makes Camus's more customary thematic point:

> I have the taste and the need for security. Most men are like me. They are not capable of living in a universe where, at any moment, the most bizarre thought can enter into reality; where, most of the time, it does enter, like a knife in the heart.

Cherea's words define not only a whimsical tyrant and an insupportable Rome; they define an unsolvable godhead and an appalling kingdom of grace—as seen from the side of human reason. But where, in *The Rebel* and *The Plague*, the perspective was largely on the tough-hearted and clear-minded effort to resist so intolerable a deity, in *Caligula* the focus is on the deity itself. The figure of Cherea (unless the part is performed with uncommon skill) tends to fade before that of the emperor; and as it does so and as Caligula looms and expands, the anti-theme gets its full chance of expression, gets itself articulated with something like genuine high spirits and genuine high comedy. Both elements are grounded in the creative excitement I have alluded to; but within the play, the playwright's excitement is merged with the hero's excited aspirations toward, and notions of, divinity. "I have taken on the stupid and incomprehensible visage of the gods," he tells Scipio. "And that is blasphemy, Caius." "No, Scipio it is the dramatic art! The error of these men is that they do not believe enough in the theater."

Camus, in 1938, believed so much in the theater that his histrionic enjoyment illuminated not only the imaging of a hateful theology, but also the exposure of what is perhaps the most significant of *Caligula*'s anti-themes: the theme of total isolation. This, again, is not something asserted and feared; it is something lusted after and, at the end, accomplished, after the departure of Scipio, the revolt of Cherea, the killing of Caesonia, and the (presumed) assassination of Hélicon. Isolation is the chief anti-theme in the sense that its opposite—human fellowship as the key resource for those who stick to the possible in a senseless cosmos—would become the bedrock of Camus's compassionate humanism. And in the construction of *Caligula* it is a periodic tension between the lust for isolation and the longing for an authentic human encounter that moves the action forward.

Such an "agon" emerges consistently in the climax of each act. For the play is composed of a series of analogous movements, beginning in each case with a relatively crowded stage and thickening into a public spectacle of some kind, and then shifting and concentrating into the effort and the revealed failure of some personal and private relationship. Those parallel rhythms are analogies to each other; but they are also synecdoches, enactments in small, of the entire and overall action—which is, exactly, a deliberate movement from the crowded center of a populous empire to a position of complete solitude. The pattern I am suggesting warrants, perhaps, a brief elaboration.

After introductory moments wherein various patricians prowl and conspire, muttering their hopes or resentments or fears, we are treated—in act I—to a display of startling political and financial imperial decisions; in II, to a banquet modeled, one guesses, on those techniques of sexual humiliation discoverable in the Marquis de Sade's *Juliette;* in III, to an obscene religious rite, a histrionic Black Mass, with the Lord's prayer meticulously inverted to serve the worship of an androgyne Venus ("Spread across our faces thy impartial cruelty, thy objective hatred; open before our eyes thy hands full of flowers and murders"); and, in IV, to a poets' contest, at which the assembled court listens to hurried improvisations on the theme of death. Few modern plays have even attempted so rich and various a presentation of the public contours of experience, in the classical and Elizabethan manner; far more characteristic of this dramatic era is Camus's *Cross-Purposes*, with its tight and inward little domestic parable and its cast of five persons. But it is to be noted that the public spectacles that occupy the middle of each act in *Caligula* do not merely dramatize; they rambunctiously subvert the governmental, the social and familial, the religious, and the artistic dimensions of the "Roman" life being depicted. And it is to be noted that these recurring ceremonies lead regularly to a moment when some purely private encounter is investigated and then, similarly, invaded and subverted.

Four successive times, after the pageantry has been dissipated and the patricians dismissed, Caligula confronts one or another of the very few persons with whom a relationship is imaginable. In act I, it is his mistress whom the emperor submits to the exquisite torture of a dreadful oath of allegiance ("You will be cruel." "Cruel." "Cold and implacable." "Implacable." "And you will smile." "Yes, Caligula, but I am going mad!"). The second act concludes with a surprising intimacy springing up between Caligula and the young poet Scipio, whose father the emperor has had executed—and with Caligula's abrupt denial of the incipient relationship, or of any other ("Is there nothing in your life that resembles some silent refuge, like the approach of tears?" "Yes, Scipio, there is." "What is it?" "Contempt!"). It is the turn, in act III, of the rational tribune Cherea, who is persuaded despite himself that it is after all possible for two individuals "whose pride and spirit are equals, to speak to each other, once in their lives, from the bottom of their lives, from the bottom of their hearts"—only to have that experience, too, torn to pieces as an illusion, even as

Caligula tears to pieces the conspiratorial document Cherea had written. And finally, in the play's denouement, Caligula (having dispatched his one remaining companion, Caesonia) confronts Caligula, his own staring image in the mirror; haranguing himself in a long, last effort at relationship—only to demolish that possibility as well, in the conclusive gesture of smashing the mirror and turning to throw himself on the swords of the inrushing assassins.

The absolute solitude arrived at in the closing instant is then, dramatically speaking, altogether appropriate; the end toward which the play and its hero have been determinedly moving from the outset. In pursuit of his negative ideal, Caligula must explore the varieties of possible personal relationship, if only to demonstrate the fragility or fraudulence of all of them: the heterosexual relation (with its portion of mother-son involvement, and a hint of further incest); the relation of masculine love (with its portion of father-son involvement, for Caligula curiously but understandably replaces for Scipio the father he has murdered); the intellectual companionship of equals; and the relation of the psyche to itself. All are experimented with, undermined, and rejected; and the action fulfills itself—with a burst of horrified enthusiasm—in the established fact of utter and permanent alienation.

The movement, or action, I have been describing is plain enough in the printed text, and it was made glowingly evident in the Paris production of 1958, directed by Camus. But it was largely smothered in the American presentation of 1960, and in a way worth mentioning for the inverse light it sheds on the play. The performance, for one thing, was heavily overproduced; characteristically, the reviewers praised the production and dismissed the play that lay buried beneath it. The set was mammoth and overwhelming; hordes of extras, many of them naked to the groin, pounded up and down huge flights of steps in total disorder; one had the impression of klieg lights and Cecil B. DeMille. But such lavish expenditures merely concealed the exuberance *within* the play by imposing a spurious and distracting boisterousness from without. The production did not trust the play; and the play in action no longer trusted itself. It no longer, for example, trusted the obscenity in the Venus scene to become apparent through language and grouping, but required the unfortunate actress playing the part of Caesonia to contribute a series of pantomime obscenities ("bumps and grinds") to punctuate—and in fact completely to divert the American audience from—the superbly blasphemous words of the prayer.

But the graver defect of all this was to blur fatally the characteristic rhythm of the action—its progression in act after act, and throughout the play as a whole, from the collapsing public spectacle to the failing private encounter. The latter element was made impossible from the beginning, and for another reason. It is not possible to enact the subtle motion toward and the painful failure of the human relationship if the personages of the stage have—as actors—no visible relation, have nothing to do with one another, to start with. Cherea and Caesonia, Hélicon and Scipio, the assorted patricians and their wives: all, in the American production, appeared to have wandered on to the same set by accident. There was no surprise and little impact in Caligula's inability to arrive at some common basis for understanding or for love. This scattered quality is not, it should be added, peculiar to the American presentation of *Caligula*: it is something inherent in the contemporary American theater, and under present circumstances it is probably incorrigible.

The American production has closed (for the wrong reasons), but the play remains—complex and extravagant, nihilistic and exhilarating, perverse and blasphemous and profoundly moral.

(1960)

4

The Restoration of Reality

I n 1956, when Elio Vittorini published *Erica e i suoi fratelli (Erica and Her Siblings)*, a fictional fragment begun twenty years earlier, he appended a note accounting for his habit of abandoning a work even when well under way. "Any large public event," he said, "can unfortunately distract me and provoke a shift of interests just as much as can a personal misadventure or adventure." Vittorini has always exhibited an almost helpless responsiveness to "large public events." He has, in particular, what Henry James called the imagination of disaster: a sensibility that, like a peculiarly delicate seismograph, can register the stirrings of some human earthquake at enormous distances. The result can be a temporary loss of creative energy; but Vittorini has discovered in his personal life and dramatized in his fiction the way to recovery.

In 1956 the way involved, characteristically, a journey back into his own past: a reconsideration of previous literary and political impulses, a return in memory to his unique sources. This was just the way of

Silvestro, the narrator of *Conversazione in Sicilia (In Sicily)*, who, impelled by a similar sense of paralyzing distraction (or, to adopt the famous idiom of the opening pages, of "furious abstraction"), journeyed back to his Sicilian birthplace to find in the figure of his mother the embodiment of a past that Silvestro too had abandoned twenty years earlier. In outcome the two journeys were suggestively parallel. In his actual life, Vittorini produced one of his most impressive books, *Diàrio in pubblico*, a volume that tellingly juxtaposes passages from nonfictional writings dating back to 1929 with long comments added during the year of compilation. The value of such a juxtaposition is announced in the Sicilian novel by its narrator, reporting on the first confrontation with his mother. "My mother was this: the memory of her, young and awe-inspiring . . . and, in addition, her present self created during the years of separation: thus she was endowed with a twofold reality." The mother, that is to say, incarnates the very secret and principle of reality; for reality itself, in Vittorini's view of it (a view not unlike that of Marcel Proust, whom Vittorini had been celebrating since his days with the Florentine review *Solaria*), is a twofold affair. And it is perceived in its totality only when the immediate and historical reality becomes transformed or enlarged—through its vital relinking with the past—into what Vittorini calls "the greater reality."

Reality, in any case, and ambiguous as the word must of necessity remain, is a key word for Vittorini and probably the crucial one for an approach to his fiction. It is by reality that his special sensitivity is so agitated; or, more accurately, it is the loss of reality that his psychic seismograph habitually registers—the loss of that higher reality as a result of erratic disturbances on the lower or historical level. To say so, obviously, is to modify rather sharply the usual characterization of his primary impulses in essentially political terms. It has been argued that the relative lapse of Vittorini's literary productivity after 1947 and the novel called in English *The Twilight of the Elephant* (since then, so far as one can tell, he has completed one long novel, *Le donne di Messina*, which he has virtually disclaimed, and one short novel, *La garibaldina)* was due entirely to political causes: that it was due to his withdrawal, announced in open "letters to Togliatti" in Vittorini's magazine *Il Politecnico,* from the Communist party, with which, though not technically affiliated, he had been deeply involved. Vittorini, so it was claimed, had nothing with which to replace the communist base— hence nothing on which, artistically, to build. There is of course some important truth in that account: about as much truth, perhaps, as there would be in a comparable account of Ignazio Silone, a writer of a very different order who also, however, passed through the communist experience (which Silone regularly described in his favorite disaster image as an earthquake) and who wrote his way out of it by converting his personal past into a series of large and representative anecdotes. But the fact is that, like Silone, Vittorini is jolted less by politico-economic upheavals than by their effect upon—by the lesion they produce in—the sense of the real. And to heal that lesion, Vittorini believes (it is a belief he shares with André Malraux and Albert Camus), is a defining function of art: in his case, of the art of the novel.

Vittorini had that function in mind when he remarked in *Il Politecnico:* "I have always denied that it is the task of literature to make visible . . . the political motives of a revolution. . . . But there are human motives in a revolution which only the writer, the poet, can make visible." He had it even more clearly in mind when he came later to discuss the exhaustively debated subject of *engagement*—in the usual meaning, the writer's duty to enlist his art in the service of a political commitment. Rejecting that notion, Vittorini preferred, as he said, to talk about a *natural engagement*—a congenital artistic instinct, peculiarly valuable in moments of revolutionary change, to penetrate the historical and political surfaces in order to detect and make apparent "reality in depth." To do that, he insisted, is "to contribute to the transformation of reality," and thus to fulfill the purpose of art.

But of all art forms, the form known in Italian as *romanzo* would seem the least equipped to accomplish that transforming act, and precisely because the *romanzo* has traditionally been the most closely bound to surfaces, to the immediate and the actual. What Vittorini felt the need of was what he detected, as early as 1941, in the short stories of the American writer Sherwood Anderson—Vittorini's resemblance to whom, incidentally, is a good deal greater than his overly insisted upon resemblance to Ernest Hemingway. Anderson, as Vittorini quite accurately pointed out, both communicated the sense of a lost reality and also succeeded to a small degree in restoring it; his stories "contain a metaphysical ardor composed of obscure interior gestures . . . lost fragments of an unknowable absolute." And by metaphysical, Vittorini went on, he meant that the stories "tend to absorb the reality to which they bear witness into their own ideal order." This was the achievement as well of Italian opera, the musical element in which "liberated" any particular work in question from "the realistic references of the events being described, to the point of making resonant significations" beyond those of the actual here-and-now.

What in the novel could supply what music supplied for opera— that is, the resonance of larger significations? Larger significations, Vittorini has always been sure, are not to be got at by philosophic speculations, by the intrusive voice of the author ruminating digressively on the universal destiny of man. His own view of the significating art and the restorative function of the novel became virtually complete when he saw (this was in 1948) that what he had admired in Sherwood Anderson was in fact the chief quality of American fiction generally, from Hawthorne and Melville to Hemingway and Faulkner. It was the quality, as he put it, of "playing it by ear—by the ear of life, and not by reflecting *on* life." It was the quality of making evident the higher reality by dramatizing, not ruminating, by the truly novelistic resource of *action* rather than the philosophic resource of speculation. "Action" is, I venture, the best English word for the classic critical concept rendered in Vittorini's Italian by the word *racconto;* and so important, for a variety of reasons, is the notion of *racconto,* or action, that Vittorini is eager not only to distinguish it from the element of plot, or *stòria*, but to say (most unclassically) that *stòria* may, on occasion, be left out altogether. "The *stòria* is only the pretext [for the *racconto*] and if there is no actual need for it, it may be omitted."

Vittorini's major statement about the art of the novel appeared in his preface to an edition of *Il garòfano rosso (The Red Carnation,* completed in 1935). The two most interesting of the novels that followed that work were *Conversazione in Sicilia* (1939) and *Il Sempione strizza l'occhio al Frejus* (1947; literally, *The Simplon Winks at the Frejus,* but in English, as we will see, it was given the strikingly apt title of *The Twilight of the Elephant**). Let me take these three texts to illustrate several of the generalizations thus far introduced and to suggest one or two main points in addition. These three novels, I propose, give us, increasingly and progressively, actions rather than plots. They give us, moreover, actions that aim at restoring a reality previously disturbed by certain surface upheavals. They arrive, by doing so, at something so much beyond the surface and the actual as to approximate the mythic and archetypal. And these three novels, finally, may be taken not only as three separate actions of that kind, but as three moments of a single action—three parts of a single work.

Of the three, *Il garòfano rosso* has the most abundant plot. Its erotic and sentimental intrigues, its fascist connivings and liberal intellectual resistance, its dope peddling and disasters provide so busy a plot that its action remains blurred. But the book is not bound to the *stòria* of sixteen-year-old Alessio Mainardi, a particular boy in a particular place and time, his adolescent enthusiasm for fascism, his university friendships, and his sexual awakening through the mysterious prostitute Zobeida. Those incidents are so shaped and pressured as to enlarge into a *racconto,* an action of initiation, the ritual passage from child-

---

*The translation, published by New Directions in 1951, was by Cinina Brescia (who at that time was married to Robert Penn Warren). The Brescia translation was reprinted in *A Vittorini Omnibus* (New Directions, 1973), along with Wilfrid Davis's rendering of *In Sicily* and Frances Keene's of *La garibaldine.*

hood to a first maturity, the achievement of membership in the human tribe. In its sexual element *Il garòfano rosso* draws upon a very deep-seated European tradition whereby the maturing process for the young male turns upon an erotic involvement with a considerably older woman, a sort of surrogate mother (so different from the American tradition, exemplified by the Nick Adams stories of Vittorini's friend Hemingway, where the initiation of the young male turns on masculine companionship in the great woods or on the high seas). But it is in the political element that Vittorini's transforming art is here most conspicuous. For fascism in *Il garòfano rosso* is less the grubby histrionics that it actually was than, as Vittorini has himself insisted, an instance and image of force and hence an instance and image of life. Alessio's entrance into fascism is dramatized as initiation into a youthful mode of life.

But fascism, needless to say, was a mode or version of life that could not but end by seeming a mode or version of death. *Conversazione in Sicilia* begins with that sense of death: the seismographically registered sense of the loss of reality, the radical disempowering of the self. And its action is precisely the great and painful motion back to vitality. In this novel, Vittorini's finest to date, there is a good deal less plot than there had been in *Il garòfano rosso;* and what there is appears hazy and enigmatic, partly because Vittorini felt naturally constrained from spelling out the deadening actualities of fascist experience. But the thinness of the plot produced a thickness of action. And through the journey south of the disaffected Linotypist, Silvestro; through his encounters en route; through his reunion with his sturdy, handsome, aging mother, Signora Concezione, and his perambulations with her about the Sicilian mountain village in the December cold; through the various conversations that reach their climax in a graveyard dialogue (words exchanged, as it were, in the very land of the dead)—through all this we are steadily exposed to an archetypal movement from death to life. That movement is dramatized, here, in the specific form it has taken in the representative literature of Vittorini's European generation: as the recovery of life through the achieved human relation, through conversation, and by means of the human dialogue.

If the first phase of the threefold action I am trying to describe is the initiation of the sixteen-year-old into the tribal life, and if the second phase carries the nearly thirty-year-old man away from the delicately registered sense of death which that kind of initiation made inevitable and toward a restored reality, then the third phase, no less inevitably, ought to conclude the action in an image of the heroic, even godlike death and departure of a very old man. This, of course, is precisely the action of *Il Sempione strizza l'occhio al Frejus*. This brief novel has practically no plot, no *stòria*, at all, which may be why Vittorini persistently regards it as his most successful work of fiction: it most clearly illustrates his novelistic aims. The *stòria* is made up of conversations in an indescribably impoverished Italian peasant household; but the household is very indistinctly seen, and the conversations, though they beat to rhythms of felt intensity, remain almost inaudible. Attention is focused throughout on the single silent figure, the ancient grandfather, the majestic wreck of what had been an immense personality, a heroic builder of tunnels and domes. He is the elephant of the book's English title; and in the last pages he wanders off in all his grandly collapsing dignity to seek, as elephants do, the proper place wherein to stretch himself out for death. The action is invested with—is partially accomplished by—distinct but elusive religious tremors, as befits a work that touches at all points on the higher reality. The old grandfather is a kind of god: he is blindly worshiped, and he is fiercely resented, the way gods are; and to him, in daily tribute, the family sacrifices most of its one resource, its miserable portion of bread. At the end he disappears, like Oedipus at Colonus; but the vast reality he had once embodied is thereby transmitted to his family and may restore them once more to life. So at least the mother of the family—his daughter—implies when, in the final lines of the book, she tells the children, smiling: "You don't understand a bean. It's not the beginning of night. It's the end." One major reason that

Elio Vittorini has written or completed so little since *The Twilight of the Elephant* may well be that with it he rounded out his fictional effort to repossess and to make perceptible in the form of action that whole reality, the disruption of which through historic and public events his sensibility had so notably recorded.

(1960)

Plans and Products, 1949–1966

The record of Vittorini's fiction-writing ventures and his actual publications, as revealed in the years *following* the date of the article above, comprises a remarkably suggestive, if disconcerting, tale of the creative and the self-editing life in the middle decades of this century.

We can begin with the long novel he published in 1949, *Le donne di Messina*. Vittorini almost immediately expressed dissatisfaction with the work, refused to allow it to be reprinted, and withheld permission for an English translation. A considerably revised version appeared in 1964, at which time Vittorini, looking back at the original, declared it to be "old-fashioned, and here and there false." *Le donne di Messina* (translated finally as *The Women of Messina* in 1973) is a complex saga, or rather a complex interconnecting cluster of stories. Set in the postwar Italy of the later 1940s, it gives us the travels of Uncle Agrippina in (unsuccessful) search of his daughter Siracusa; the troubled relation between Siracusa and Ventura, a penitent ex-fascist; and the efforts of a group of dispossessed Italians to build a new community in a valley in the Appenines, below Bologna. Ventura joins the latter enterprise, and becomes an inspirational leader in it.

But then a character named Carlo il Calvo (Charles the Bald), a former fascist turned government agent, sends a pack of "Hunters" to round up Ventura and any others in the area who can be charged with crimes against the people in the Mussolini period. In the first version,

Ventura confesses his shameful past to Siracusa; and, unable to bear her horror and revulsion, he murders her. He gives himself up and is executed, managing, just before the bullets pierce him, to exhort his fellow workers not to abandon their ideal community. In the later version, the Hunters grow bored with their assignment and depart for the greater attractions of Bologna and Modena. The novel proper ends at that point, with the lovers staring at each other. In an epilogue, the narrative carries us forward cinematographically over a dozen years: "Time passes and has passed, autumn has come and then winter, then March, June, August, and autumn again, '47 and '48, the cold war, the Marshall Plan, April 18, the Christian Democrat government, the Berlin airlift, Rita Hayworth has come and gone, *The Third Man* with Orson Welles has come and gone. . . ." Participating in the brilliant filmic sequence are Carlo il Calvo, now a respectable government representative, and Uncle Agrippina, still looking for his daughter: two figures who loom up recurringly, meeting one another as they step on and off trains in stations all over Italy, year after year, exchanging the news.

The community has lost its identity, blurring into the bourgeois world of jukeboxes and ice cream advertisements created by the "economic miracle" of postwar Italy. "The land," says Carlo, "has lost its importance." The women of Messina, who came north so hopefully, grow fat and spend their time planting grapevines. As to the lovers, they survive and marry; Siracusa is renamed Teresa. She is a conspicuous individual, but Ventura is nearly forgotten. "Ventura? Ventura? You have to say the husband of Teresa before they understand you." He is reduced to a nullity, without any interest in life, lying on his bed all day smoking cigarettes. And Teresa herself is simply a housewife, selling her milk, making her jam, putting up provisions for the winter. Thus drifts to its conclusion Vittorini's rueful parable of what happens to the generous socialistic vision—in the Vittorini vocabulary, what happens to "reality"—when the seemingly irresistible enticements of American-style capitalism take over.

Le donne di Messina also reflects a related, more purely literary disillu-sion, a hardening skepticism about the possibility of making a novel of conventional scope out of contemporary historical materials. By the time he had completed the rewriting for the second version of *Le donne* in 1964 (the author's note tells us that he had worked on it intermit-tently in 1952, 1957, and the year of publication), Vittorini, as we will see, had pretty well disavowed the long novel as a viable form, though he persistently gathered his creative strength to attempt one. But to make sense out of Vittorini's almost allegorically irregular course, we must ourselves take a step backward, to 1950 and the story later known as *La garibaldina*. This novella of a hundred-odd pages would appear, both in its brevity and its cheerful game playing with history and the actual, clearly more suited to Vittorini's natural bent.

The work made its first appearance in the journal *Il Ponte* in 1950, under the title of *Il soldata e la garibaldina*. It was published in book form as *La garibaldina* in 1956, together with *Erica e i suoi fratelli* (the two were translated by Frances Keene as *The Dark and the Light* in the New Directions volume of 1960).

The original title is entirely accurate. The novella introduces us to a youthful Italian soldier, a *bersagliere*—from Italy's most celebrated troop—who, journeying by train down to his seaside Sicilian home for a few days' leave, meets up with an imperious woman of uncertain age but evident wealth, who claims to have been an intimate of Giuseppe Garibaldi. Most of the tale is given to a dialogue between these two as the Garibaldina, whose name is Leonilde, takes charge of the young man, beats off the ticket collector and other importuners, and regales him with anecdotes of the grand old days. She had enlisted in Garibaldi's service in 1869, she says; and in the privacy of their bed she had spurred him on to greater efforts in his campaign to liberate Rome. She had also fought with Garibaldi's volunteers across Europe (though she muddles her dates and battles a little); but she feels she has "filled her place in history" as a woman rather than a soldier: in the manner of Lucretia, the wife of Brutus, rather than Camilla, the warrior maid.

Leonilde, like her inventor Elio Vittorini, is partial to opera; and with Leonilde leading the way, the narrative amplifies winningly into comic opera, with choral chantings and reprises, antiphonies of invective, rhythmical repetitions of speech, and recitatifs of high eloquence. The story, to be sure, is packed with realistic detail of southern Sicilian life and landscape, and even Leonilde's memoirs may have a basis in fact (she must be very old, but the time of the story's action is left vague, and her age is a subject of lively debate among her townspeople). The narrative method and language, nonetheless, invest the goings on with what Vittorini, speaking of Italian opera, called the resonance of larger significations. And the point about Leonilde is that she *is* an outsize creature, a female larger than life in her enthusiasms, her rages, her gusts of humor, her sexual hospitality.

The atmosphere grows murkier, while yet remaining comical, when the pair descend in the town of Terranova. The *bersagliere* loses sight of the Garibaldina; and as he wanders through the darkened streets carrying her bags and trying to find out where she lives and who she really is, the American reader may think of Hawthorne's tale "My Kinsman, Major Molineux." (Vittorini had read and meditated most of Hawthorne, as he had nearly every other American writer from the beginnings to 1960; he had written perceptively about "Rappaccini's Daughter" and "The Minister's Black Veil," and thought that *The Scarlet Letter* was "perhaps a more powerful book than *Karamazov*.") There the naive young countryman Robin wanders through nighttime Boston seeking both to locate and to identify his kinsman, the major. Like Robin, the *bersagliere* encounters shouts of enigmatic laughter, human grotesques and beings other than human, sly insinuations about the missing person's true moral and sexual character; and in *La garibaldina* as in "My Kinsman, Major Molineux," the hallucinatory mingles with dramatic images of national history. The Garibaldina reappears at the end, astride a black and white horse, full of promises to make the young man's fortune for him (she has renamed him Fortunato). Then she rides away, and the soldier starts down the hill toward the sea and his home, singing aloud an old campaign tribute to the Garibaldina, the capricious *biondina,* the bright star of the poor soldiers as they marched.

However one interprets this tale with its diversity of enchantments, one is likely to see it, in the way of its first commentators, as a superbly rounded story, coming at its own pace to its beautifully appointed end, written at a stroke (so one scholar has put it, summarizing the reactions), with a stylistic felicity perfectly in accord with its original semifantastic *donnée.* It comes, then, as a shock to learn what almost no one noticed at the time: that Vittorini intended *Il soldato e la garibaldina* of 1950 to be no more than a single episode, presumably the opening episode, in a novel he had begun work on that same year. The new novel, he announced, would be "full of Sicily but also of all the rest of the world," with elements drawn from his own life and also from the life of everyone else. The title of this awesomely ambitious work, which Vittorini reckoned would take six years to write, would be *I diritti dell'uomo (The Rights of Man).* All he actually succeeded in writing, before he quit this fictional affair once and for all toward the end of 1951, was another thirty pages about Leonilde. She is now seen quarreling with her coachman Cuordileone (Lionheart), and forgetting to send word to the soldier until his leave has run out and he has gone back to his troop. In early 1952, Vittorini moved on to another and very different novel called *Le città del mondo.*

Le città del mondo (The Cities of the World) is an extraordinary performance; and not less extraordinary is Vittorini's performance as its author, in interviews and published notations, during and after the two years he worked on it. In its definitive edition by Mondadori in 1974, the novel—we can continue to call it a novel, though its genre is exactly what is most problematic about it—runs to forty chapters of about 200 pages, followed by 100 pages of "unnumbered chapters" carrying forward the several main narratives at differing lengths, and a few pages of fragments. What Vittorini has done is to set various twosomes moving across Sicily, mostly in the mountainous area in the north central part of the island (the towns of Enna and Agira are mentioned). Four pairs may in fact be made out crossing our line of vision: a shepherd and his young son Rosario, escorting a flock of sheep, with the aid of a sheepdog; a second paternal figure, this one given to philosophical ruminations and literary allusion (he has written a sequel to *Macbeth*), and his young sprig of a boy, Nardo; a honeymoon couple, Gioacchino and Michela, on a seemingly endless bridal journey; and two prostitutes—Odeida, a woman of mature years and ripe experience, and Rea Silvia, a girl just out of adolescence who has fled her repressively boring community in Milazzo (near Messina) and is willing to take up the profession if it will ensure her independence.

These stories touch on one another, flow through each other, are tantalizing half-echoes and incipient reversals one of another. And the characters in them—parents and children and *sposi* and prostitutes—all seem to be participating in the same pageant-tale; all are pilgrims in the gently mythic Sicilian countryside; each couple, with whatever slight imbalance or tension, is seeking the good place, the "city" of fulfillment. The narratives, like the wanderings, can continue forever, one feels; or they can come to a rest anywhere. This is Vittorini's own fulfillment as a writer of fiction.

Vittorini himself came to think altogether otherwise. Between the summer of 1952 and the spring of 1955, he saw to the publication of large portions of the ongoing novel, including two major segments: the decidedly modern fairy tale in which Rosario kisses a young maid during a blindfold game and is then nearly torn apart, Maenad-style, by her female playmates; and the growing companionship between the veteran siren Odeida and the willing neophyte Rea Silvia. Then he came to a dead stop. As almost always with Vittorini, there was a crisis of reality. In a letter to a friend in February 1956, Vittorini remarked that after working for two years on a novel *(un romanzo),* he had of a sudden found himself "caught up in a reality far different" from the one he had been trying to depict in the book. This new reality was the illness and then in December 1955 the death of his firstborn son, Giusto. While still preoccupied with this event, Vittorini was further unsettled by the tragic events of 1956 in Hungary. We can now see that it was about the abandonment of *Le città del mondo* that Vittorini was talking when he made the statement quoted at the start of this essay: "Any large public event can unfortunately distract me and provoke a shift of interests just as much as can a personal misadventure or adventure."

It was at this time too—that is, in the wake of the distractions—that Vittorini began to voice grave doubts about the long novel as a genre. In an interview of August 1957, he spoke again of having worked for two years on "a long and complex novel," and of having to set it aside because of the illness of his son. When he took it up again, he now said, he found himself experiencing "aversion and antipathy for the long novel, the novel of complexity and careful construction." The long novel with its interweavings was "not modern," he declared. In the case of *Le città del mondo*, he had sought to interweave three principal themes; but the connections made were artificial (in his new view): they derived from the traditional compositional mode of the novel, and not from the actualities of life.

So he decided to divide the manuscript into three *short* novels. These would deal with Rosario, Nardo, and their fathers (thematically, a contrast of father-son relationships); with the honeymooners, Gioacchino and Michela (as reflecting the curious contemporary fear of society in their inability to choose any stopping place in their restless onward journeying); and with the open-eyed experiment in whoredome of Rea Silvia, under the tutelage of Odeida. It remains unclear whether Vittorini ever in fact did separate *Le città del mondo* into three novellas, or simply entertained the idea of doing so; and anyhow, as time passed he could be heard referring only to *two* fictional books-in-progress. "I am working on two books," he said in February 1959, "though not of course on both of them each day." The honeymooners had apparently been cast out, with the fathers-and-sons and the two prostitutes remaining.

By 1962, Vittorini had given up on those two tales as well. They struck him, so it seems, as arising from an outdated conception of human personality (as fixed and firm) and narrative possibility (straightforward realism). He was into a completely new fictional experiment, he told an interviewer: something to do with industrial upheavals in Milan. Nothing came of this one either (it was "just another Vittorini," the author wryly informed his friends after he quit work on it). But he made a public promise, in December 1964, not to destroy the surviving remnants of *Le città del mondo*—if merely "out of cowardice. One always thinks at certain moments: what if this were the right road?" And elsewhere: "They tell me I am not a good judge."

We can look at one last example of Vittorini's characteristic creative intentions before venturing some judgments of our own in the whole matter.

The history of *Il Sempione strizza l'occhio al Frejus (The Twilight of the Elephant)* is much like that of *La garibaldina*. The narrative has seemed to its readers for forty years to be beautifully whole and intact, and to arrive unerringly at its denouement. Yet in a note appended to the text in 1947, Vittorini said explicitly (though this too was not widely noticed):

> When I wrote the story, I did not intend to end it where I did. I had in mind a second part in which we would search the woods around the city, looking for the old man who had gone away. This is not to say that I won't take up the work at some other time. It is a motif dear to my heart. So perhaps we may meet again, with "my grandfather," and it doesn't matter much if it's not in the book that immediately follows this one.

The book following was *Le donne di Messina,* and after finishing the long first version of that novel in 1949, Vittorini does seem to have gone back to *Il Sempione.* On this occasion, he wrote nine pages of a fragment known among scholars as *Il barbière di Carlo Marx*—the reference being to a barber whom we meet on the first page, a familiar character in the village of the tale, who keeps a picture of his idol Karl Marx in his shop and tells everyone that it is his uncle. Vittorini began the new segment where the previous sequence left off, and as though starting the next chapter of a far-extending narrative: "In a house of poor folk, the empty place of someone who has died fills up quickly. It's the same with someone who has gone away." But commitment to the story or belief in it faded almost instantly. In September 1952, running through an inventory of novels he had begun and quit work on, Vittorini said: "And *Il Sempione* too is only the first episode of a work that had to be interrupted"—by implication, for keeps.

These creative histories suggest several things about Vittorini. One is that at any given moment a short fictional text could, for him, be complete in itself and also susceptible of enlargement and change of status. The phenomenon is anything but unique. We come upon it with mystery writers who expand a short story of, say, a decade earlier into a full-scale novel; and we observe it in a writer of genius like Faulkner. For Faulkner, as for Vittorini, stories already published, and the characters they brought into being, never ceased to grow and change in his straining imagination. And for both of them, if a text could thicken, it could also contract. To take one Faulknerian instance: *The Bear* in its first form was a slender story in a popular magazine; then it was developed into a five-part masterpiece; then it was published (in *Big Woods*) with its long, visionary fourth part deleted. Something not dissimilar occurred with Vittorini's *Le città del mondo,* swelling at one moment to five centers of interest, then shrinking to two.

Vittorini's difficulty—and here he differed from Faulkner—was that he was uneasy with this lack of fixity, and distrustful of it. One part of him, so to say the conventional part, believed that a work of fiction should be a self-enclosed totality, where everything connected up. But another part believed in multiplicity, in openness of form, in avoidance of what today is called narrative closure. There was no truce to this internal quarrel. Both *Il Sempione* and *La garibaldina* are profoundly satisfying as self-completing poetic and aesthetic wholes; but something in Vittorini urged him to push ahead with them into new adventures and terrains. In an opposite way, *Le città del mondo* is a glowing display of fictional variety and the aesthetically unbounded, a potential source of refreshment for the reader fatigued by conventional forms; but Vittorini felt obliged to cut it up into recognizable smaller wholes. It is good to record that the best of Vittorini won out, though only posthumously and in the complete edition of his fictional writings published in 1974 (see below). Here he takes his place as one of the most accomplished literary artists in what is still, all told, the greatest generation of fiction writers Italy has yet known.

(1989)

Conversations in Milan

We had the happy chance, Nancy Lewis and I, of several conversations with Vittorini in Milan in the early and late 1950s. These invariably took place, at his suggestion, in an upstairs sitting room of the Hotel Manin (on Via Manin, as it angles north from the old city gate that marks the end of Via Manzoni), which is why this is still our hotel of choice on visits to Milan. We remember a tall, friendly man, supple of movement, dark-haired though graying a little, with a small, dark moustache; he was soft-spoken, gentle, and even diffident in manner, with a humorous tug in his expression and a quiet intensity of literary and political opinion. The talk, mostly in Italian, ranged over a good deal of American literature, a subject in which Vittorini was enormously well versed. In 1939 he had produced an anthology of American writing (it was immediately suppressed) in which he discussed and represented a staggering array of writers from the seventeenth century through the nineteenth century and via the modernists—Eliot, Pound, Stein, Hemingway, Faulkner, and others—to the likes of Steinbeck, Caldwell, Saroyan, and James M. Cain; and with the novelist Delfino Cinelli, he translated the stories of Edgar Allan Poe. In our talks, Vittorini spoke of Hemingway, with whom he enjoyed a correspondence and who had written a brief introduction to *In Sicily* ("Elio Vittorini is one of the very best of the new Italian writers," it began); of Nathanael West, who had caught Vittorini's fancy in the late 1940s; of the short stories of Sherwood Anderson and the myth making of Faulkner. We also shared our admiration for the stunning translation of *Moby-Dick* by the sorely missed Torinese novelist Cesare Pavese (his co-editor on the anthology), arguably the best translation into a European language ever made of Melville's epic-romance.

As we looked out at the burgeoning Italian literary scene at these meetings, Vittorini had keenly appreciative words for the tense domestic dramas of Natalia Ginzberg, with their small burdens of horror, just then becoming known (we had seen her husband, Gabriele Baldini, a warm-spirited professor of American literature, in Rome). Vittorini spoke affectionately of Vasco Pratolini, author of *A Chronicle of Poor Lovers* and other superior novels; Pratolini had been one of his best friends since the Florentine days. We exchanged high opinions about Ignazio Silone, both the writer and the man, and agreed that in conversations with him one had to learn to remain silent, while Silone's mind circled slowly about—as it were in ex-Abruzzese-peasant style— in search of the right word or more likely the right anecdote with which to continue. Vittorini was a trifle restrained about Moravia, we felt; genuine professional admiration but limited personal enjoyment (my own view of Moravia and his writings was almost unequivocally favorable).

Vittorini informed us that he turned down Giuseppe Tomasi di

Lampedusa's *Il gattopardo* (*The Leopard*) for the Einaudi publishers, of which he was a senior editor. Vittorini seems to have felt (this was in 1957) that the novel, with its conventionalism of plot and character portrayal and drama of manners, went threateningly against the grain of the fictional experimentation in Italy that he, Vittorini, was supporting and seeking to practice.*

At the last of our meetings, Vittorini mentioned a young writer of (he said) astonishingly original imagination, Italo Calvino; Vittorini was about to launch a new journal called *Il Menabò* with him. In retrospect some years afterward, we could see that Calvino was the natural literary heir of Elio Vittorini, making the very life of the fiction-making impulse the comic hero of his tales—as Vittorini had made gestures toward doing. During the same final gathering in the Hotel Manin, Vittorini spoke with a kind of smiling excitement about a novel of 1957 by Carlo Emilio Gadda that bore the arresting title *Quer pasticciaccio brutto di via Merulana*. The title is cast in the Roman dialect which, with a medley of other regional dialects, flavors the entire composition: *Quello pasticcio*—"that mess"—is the basic phrase, before *quello* became *quer*, and the hissing additional syllable intensified the messiness. The events of the story take place in the 1927 Rome of Mussolini's Italy; the narrative, with artfully deepening obscurity, follows the investigation into a hideous murder and a possibly related jewel theft.

The English translation, done superlatively by William Weaver, carried the title *That Awful Mess on Via Merulana* (the latter a nondescript thoroughfare in Rome), and an introduction by Italo Calvino,

---

*We found out later that *Il gattopardo* had also been rejected, on similar grounds, by Mondadori publishers, before the novelist Giorgio Bassani came upon it and saw to its publication by Feltrinelli. After that, of course, it became a sensational best-seller in Italy and internationally, and led to a film of vast proportions and great elegance, directed by Visconti and starring Burt Lancaster and Claudia Cardinale. The novel also stirred up violent ideological and aesthetic dispute in Italy; Vittorini was far from alone in his adverse (and, many of us would now think, mistaken) opinion.

also translated by Weaver. Calvino, writing as always out of a depth of intelligence (and as a follower of Vittorini), remarks that the solution of the two crimes, of the *pasticciaccio,* becomes ever less important; it is rather "the seething cauldron of life, the infinite stratification of reality, the inextricable tangle of knowledge . . . [that] Gadda wants to depict." Carlo Gadda, Milanese born and Florentine resident, was sixty-four when this novel appeared; unknown outside Italy, he was a cult figure in corners of the Italian literary world and familiar to the habitués of the Giubbe Rosse restaurant in Piazza Repubblica in Florence. International honors and acclaim succeeded in the wake of *Quer pasticciaccio;* and although he is perhaps still not sufficiently recognized, Gadda is now regarded in some quarters as one of the masters of modern fiction.

Elio Vittorini died in his home on Viale Gorizia in Milan in February 1966, at the age of fifty-seven. His collected fictional writings, *Le òpere narrative,* were published by Mondadori in 1974, in two volumes of about 2,070 pages in all. This splendid production was edited by Maria Curti; and it contains some 130 pages of meticulous, exhaustively learned yet thoroughly readable notes on the texts by Raffaella Rodondi. These notes have been extensively and gratefully drawn upon in this discussion. The two volumes offer the full text of the 1964 version of *Le donne di Messina* with a complete editorial account of the vicissitudes of that novel; the forty finished chapters of *Le città del mondo* (prior to that novel's planned or actual dismantling), with the unnumbered chapters and the fragments; a brilliant scholarly sorting out of the intricate history of that work; and *La garibaldina* and *Il Sempione,* each in its original intactness, each with its little sequel, and each with total annotation.

For the Italian-language reader, *Guida a Vittorini* by Sergio Pautasso (Rizzoli, 1977) is perhaps the handiest critical overview. The English-language reader can find invaluable discussions of Vittorini's work, and information about it, in Donald Heiney, *Three Italian Novelists:*

Moravia, Pavese, Vittorini (University of Michigan Press, 1968), and Sergio Pacifici, *The Modern Italian Novel: From Pea to Moravia* (Southern Illinois University Press, 1979). The latter is the third volume in the author's consistently excellent tracing of the Italian novel from Manzoni onward. Sergio Pacifici, professor of Italian at Queens College of the City University of New York, is this country's leading authority on Italian literature in the modern era.

(1990)

5   FROM ENGLAND

Abroad: British Literary Travelling Between the Wars,
by Paul Fussell, Oxford University Press

E nglish literary folk, Paul Fussell tells us in this fascinating,
learned, and witty treatise, fairly vaulted out of their
island home the instant the First World War was over;
and they continued to travel as often and in some cases as far as
possible during the next two decades, providing artful accounts of
their journeys which Mr. Fussell is inclined to rank fairly high within
the corpus of modernist literature. One reason for the sudden spate of
travel, beginning in 1919, was the enormous sense of release after four
years of virtual imprisonment in an England strangled by travel
restrictions, or of being stuck in the rain-swept trenches of France. But
another, briskly set forth in a chapter called "I Hate It Here," was a
profound sense of alienation from postwar England. "I do think,"
E. M. Forster remarked in 1922, "that during the war something in this
country got killed." And a few years later Cyril Connolly was writing
a friend that he had turned against England; it was "a dying civilisation—decadent, but in such a damned dull way—going stuffy and
comatose instead of collapsing beautifully like France." The very

impulse to travel thus constituted a theme—the theme of estrangement—that became a staple of the modernist temper.

Mr. Fussell's method of procedure in *Abroad* is similar to that in his well-designed and deservedly prize-winning study of five years ago, *The Great War and Modern Memory*, to which the present volume may be regarded as a sequel (or perhaps as the second part of a trilogy: Mr. Fussell is currently engaged in a book about the Second World War and its literary consequences*). He circles around his subject, jabbing skillfully at a variety of its aspects; and he pauses periodically to examine at greater length those whom he considers the most accomplished travel writers of the epoch—Graham Greene, Robert Byron, Norman Douglas, D. H. Lawrence, and Evelyn Waugh. Of these, D. H. Lawrence would seem best to fill the bill as the quintessential literary traveler, with his hateful and alienating wartime experience in England, his feeling (voiced by Rupert Birkin in *Women in Love*) that England resembled one's dying parent, his congenital tendency to head south for the sunny places; but for a reason to be touched on, Mr. Fussell makes rather less of Lawrence than one might expect.

In the course of his circling, Mr. Fussell has many lively and telling things to say about the different modes of travel; the cost of it ("abroad" was a good deal cheaper than "at home" in these years); the cult of the sun (the English weather, formerly a source of ironic native pride, had now become intolerable to the literary sky watchers, a personal affront); travel and sex, or the real meaning of the shipboard romance; the English eccentric as the "natural" among travelers, never more outrageously himself than in a foreign situation. Moving toward the writing about travel, Mr. Fussell offers a checklist of texts between the wars that dealt with travel or, like the popular play *Outward Bound* and Yeats's "Sailing to Byzantium," took travel as a metaphor of human destiny. Any work with a place-name in its title gets caught up in the listing, and as Mr. Fussell speeds ahead he makes an occasional and

Wartime: Understanding and Behavior in the Second World War (1990).

unimportant mistake: John O'Hara's *Appointment in Samarra* is not, as it happens, about Iraq but about Pottsville, Pennsylvania (the allegorical title coming from a Near Eastern legend in which a frightened slave, seeking to escape death, flees to Samarra, where Death is waiting for him by appointment). But the technique works: Mr. Fussell is persuasive in suggesting that, for a long moment, reality itself, for the British imagination, was almost equivalent to the notion of travel.

A major distinction in Mr. Fussell's light-fingered but beautifully informed historicocultural analysis is between travel, as a splendid and demanding act of stretched-out human inquiry, and tourism, the contemporary phenomenon of organized group movement to which travel (in this book's perspective) has wretchedly degenerated. For Mr. Fussell, travel is a thing of the past, and *Abroad* is a threnody. "I am assuming," he writes, "that travel is now impossible and that tourism is all we have left." Mr. Fussell is at his virulent and articulate best in vivisecting tourism. He has been chided elsewhere for snobbery in deploring "the disappearance of virtually all passenger ships except cruise ships (tourism with a vengeance) and the increasing difficulty of booking hotel space if one is not on a tour." But up to a point (which I'll return to), he is dead right. Tourism, as here defined, is indeed a matter of mindless uniformity, and the kind of travel it entails, for tourists and fellow passengers alike, is today uncomfortable, undignified, maddeningly undependable; and it can even be dangerous.

In my own experience of trans-Atlantic and transcontinental air travel over a number of years, I reckon that my plane has been seriously late—up to fourteen hours late—more than half the time; and once, outside Heathrow, I, with the other passengers, had to leave the plane hurriedly by sliding down a foam rubber chute to sprawl on the English earth and then run for what I was told was my life; it was feared that the ship was about to catch fire and explode. Luggage goes astray, far astray, much more often than it should, and all this despite the bragging by travel bureaus about the joy of transportation, as in the slogan "Getting There Is Half the Fun." Eleanor Clark, the finest travel writer of our time, has been heard to mutter recently that she is planning an article called "Travel—Where Does It Get You?"

The old travel element of study, the acquisition of new knowledge, has pretty well vanished from tourism, as Mr. Fussell declares. How could it not? In Florence I have seen busloads of tourists being driven slowly through the city without a single stop, faces peering vaguely through the windows at the Badia and the Duomo; they were due to pass through Siena by mid-afternoon and to be in Rome for cocktail time. In the Brancacci Chapel of the Carmine, likewise in Florence, I have watched groups of tourists staring fixedly, not at the extraordinary frescos of Masaccio, but at the face and moving lips of the tour guide. What has been lost in particular is any feeling for place, which one would have supposed indispensable to the travel experience. Real places, Mr. Fussell says pointedly, have given way to pseudo-places, like the Costa del Sol, or non-places, like the interiors of airports and airplanes. Ships and especially cruise ships are simply "moveable pseudo-places," in Mr. Fussell's formula. There comes to mind the cogent query of Janet Flanner when, crossing the Mediterranean on a large steamer, she dropped by the purser's office to ask: "Does this place stop in Naples?"

The special interest of *Abroad* for many readers will be Mr. Fussell's gathering argument about the relation between traveling in the twenties and thirties and the growth of the modern sensibility. (In a similar but gloomier vein of cultural commentary, he also spots later parallels between the replacement of travel by tourism and that of coffee cream by pale powder, glass by lucite, fish by fish sticks, eloquence by jargon, and motoring by driving.) It all began, Mr. Fussell proposes less than half-whimsically, with the introduction of the passport in Great Britain during the First World War, and even more with the provision of Regulation 14c of the Defense of the Realm Acts that required a photograph of the bearer to be attached to every such passport. Given the shame-making quality of passport photographs, then as now, Mr. Fussell is on anything but infirm ground when he finds in them one source, at least, of "that anxious self-awareness, that secret but overriding self-contempt, which we recognise as attaching uniquely to the world of Prufrock and Joseph K. and Malone." Along with passports and in the wake of the war, there came into being new frontiers, new barriers, the shifting outlines of nation-states. The literary corollary is now made emphatic:

> Fragmenting and dividing anew and parcelling-out and shifting around and repositioning—these are the actions implicit in the redrafting of frontiers. All these actions betray a concern with current space instead of time and tradition. All imply an awareness of reality as disjointed, dissociated, fractured. These actions of dividing anew and shifting around provide the method of collage in painting, and in writing they provide the method we recognise as conspicuously "modern," the method of anomalous juxtaposition. Think of *The Waste Land* and the *Cantos* and *Ulysses* and their reliance on disjointed "quotations" from others or from one's self.

It is a breathtaking, enjoyably arguable (*do* the redraftings of frontiers really "imply an awareness of reality as disjointed"?), and highly provocative diagnosis; and it is the carefully planned basis for the later contention about Robert Byron's *The Road to Oxiana* of 1937 that "what *Ulysses* is to the novel between the wars and what *The Waste Land* is to poetry, *The Road to Oxiana* is to the travel book." Robert Byron is the literary hero of *Abroad*, and *The Road to Oxiana* is its sacred text, exactly because Byron's technique of composition so much resembles Joyce's and Eliot's: "as if obsessed with frontiers and fragmentations, [the book] juxtaposes into a sort of collage the widest variety of rhetorical materials."

Robert Byron (1905–1941—he died early in the Second World War) is almost entirely unknown in this country, Mr. Fussell acknowledges; he was certainly unknown to me, except as an occasionally, affectionately, and admiringly remembered name in the memoirs of Sir Harold Acton and others. He was a contemporary at Oxford of Acton and Evelyn Waugh, was suitably outrageous in manner and speech, and was suitably idiosyncratic (he found Rembrandt's great reputation disgusting, and thought Shakespeare terribly overrated and *Hamlet* a hoax). But Byron had the makings of an authentic scholar; his book *The Byzantine Achievement* (1929), a tracing of the history of Byzantium from antiquity through the Renaissance, is evidently a remarkable study, in Mr. Fussell's opinion the work of a "fully professional if largely self-taught historian of art and architecture." *The Road to Oxiana* was the last and, it is said, the most mature and aesthetically dazzling of a series of travel writings. Having explored Russia, Tibet, India, and Europe in previous sallies, Byron now followed a road that led from Venice through Beirut into Iraq and Persia (as it then was) and across Afghanistan to Oxiana, the area of the Oxus River. The climax of the journey was the confrontation, near Shahi in Persia, of Gumbad-i-Kabus or the Tower of Qabus, a startling and awesome Islamic construct (Byron provides a photograph), 167 feet high, all thrust and vigor, eerily resembling a surrealistic rocket at the instant of takeoff. Byron, in retrospect, held it to be among the great buildings of the world.

But it is with *The Road to Oxiana* as a literary text, rather than with its architectural findings, that Mr. Fussell seeks to engage us; and I have to confess—not without a sense of guilt, as of a failure in sensitivity—that I am not wholly convinced. It is clearly a showpiece of those attributes which Mr. Fussell declares essential to travel writings that aspire to literature. Generically, it is a fiction, with dates and incidents shuffled about, dialogues invented, materials selected and arranged thematically, and much of the daily diary rewritten long after and elsewhere, with an eye to comic or dramatic effect. It partakes of the quest myth, the end in view (as it is slowly revealed) being the mysterious, archetypal tower of Shahi. It has vestiges of pastoral romance. It is a mixture of the comic and the hallucinatory. The prose writing often has a tremendous vitality; Robert Byron, a remote kin of Lord Byron, can be a superb manipulator of the words of our speech. But the many passages that Mr. Fussell quotes for our inspection may do the book a disservice: these fragments of an organized work of fragmentation are not in themselves (verbal virtuosity apart) very compelling. Byron's recorded rudeness to strangers lacks charm; and there is little more than schoolboy humor in a long (invented) exchange with some Teherani about Gibbon, wherein the pope of Rome is identified as the Foof of Rum.

I need myself at this stage to introduce a distinction, something which is inevitably implicit in Mr. Fussell's discourse, but which tends to get glossed over. It is a distinction between two kinds of superior and cultivated travel writing: between what might be called "journey-books" and "place-books." (I am anything but happy with those phrases; there is a built-in illogic and semantic confusion to the whole business.) The former do in very fact give accounts of journeys, however skillfully rearranged; of pressing forward from one locality to another; of plunging into the unknown. Motion, adventure, misadventure, and the thirst for arcane knowledge belong to the journey-book; and under a certain kind of creative pressure it may well take on the contours of the quest myth. But the place-book is more stationary; it is the evocation of a milieu, a territory (a city, a country, a landscape) that the author has lived into, and the atmosphere of which he discloses from within. Not journeying but strolling about remembered streets; not adventure but increasingly familiar human intercourse; not questing but an openness to impressions—these are among the attributes of the place-book.

Of the five writers Mr. Fussell chiefly examines, three—Graham Greene, Byron, and Evelyn Waugh—wrote journey-books, as their titles typically indicate: *Journey Without Maps, The Road to Oxiana, A Tropical Journey Through British Guiana and Part of Brazil* (the weighty subtitle of one of Waugh's volumes). Norman Douglas appears to have written in both modes, but D. H. Lawrence was primarily a poet of place: *Etruscan Places, Twilight in Italy*. About Lawrence, I am hardly telling Mr. Fussell anything he doesn't know; his title for the chapter on this author is "The Places of D. H. Lawrence." But it says something perhaps about Mr. Fussell's lesser regard for the literature of place (as against movement) that in this excellent and critically alert chapter he does not pursue Lawrence's continuing dialectic of north and south into *Women in Love*, where it is the central structuring motif, nor does he allude to Lawrence's brooding essay "The Spirit of Place" in *Studies in Classic American Literature*.

Moving further afield: Henry James's *The American Scene*, like his *Italian Hours*, is a place-book; James's train trips up and down the American eastern seaboard are no serious part of his story (in fact James rather disliked train travel), which has to do with cityscapes and manners in Boston, New York, Philadelphia, and points south; and in Siena, he reports unforgettably, he had scarcely deposited his luggage at the inn before he hurried out—*this* was what he was after—to stand in the great piazza and "receive impressions." The title of Edith Wharton's *A Motor Flight Through France* (a flight, incidentally, on which she was for a time accompanied by James) speaks for itself, as, in the other variety, does *Italian Backgrounds*. In the present day, Richard de Combray, in *Caravansary*, has written a journey-book and a very good and lively one, with interspersed leaves from a place-book (the subtitle is *Alone in Moslem Places*). Eleanor Clark has added to the brief list of distinguished place-books with *Rome and a Villa* and *The Oysters of Locmariaquer;* and so has V. S. Pritchett with *The Spanish Temper* and *New York Proclaimed*.

It is Mr. Fussell's eloquently stated belief, as has been said, that travel in the old manner has had its day, and by extension travel writing, too. I should suppose, though, that it is journeying and the journey-book that are inhibited by contemporary circumstances and fashions, with a rarity like *Caravansary* (a romp across North Africa and into the Middle East) as an encouraging exception. But the place-book is alive and well, not only with Ms. Clark and Sir Victor, but on other registers with Mary McCarthy, M. F. K. Fisher, and Hugh Honour, to name only a few. Theirs are travel writings in the root sense that travel was a prerequisite: they departed from their native lands and made their way to some foreign corner where they lived for months if not years, before conjuring the place into imaginative existence. Getting there was not the point or the fun. They are concerned with what it meant to live there; with the special, perhaps deprovincializing experience to which the responsive foreign-born resident may be exposed; with the impact on identity of an environment that, be it ever so intimately known, remains subtly alien. The sense of otherness, which we all crave and fear and which the older kind of traveling used to provide, is still accessible to the sufficiently curious.

(1981)

An Afterword on Paul Theroux

Several years before the above review was published, and unbeknownst to its author, a writer then in his mid-to-late thirties, Paul Theroux, was effectively disproving one of its main theses. The thesis, as formulated by Paul Fussell, was that "travel is now impossible and . . . tourism is all we have left," with the corollary that travel *writing* is a thing of the past. I modified this view into the proposition that "it is journeying and the journey-book that are inhibited by contemporary circumstances." Paul Theroux's *The Great Railway Bazaar* (1975), about a train trip clear across Asia, and *The Old Patagonian Express* (1979), about train travel through the Americas, were more than enough to demolish any such pronouncements; and their successors—among them *The Kingdom by the Sea* (1983), a tour of coastal Britain, *Sailing Through China* (1983), *Riding the Iron Rooster: By Train Through China* (1988), and *Happy Isles of Oceania: Paddling the Pacific* (1992)—demonstrate that in Paul Theroux we have not only a travel writer in the great Anglo-American tradition, but one who is carrying the genre both literally and figuratively into astonishing new areas.

Theroux is prolific almost beyond arithmetical reckoning. From the time of his first book, *Waldo: A Novel* in 1967, he has published at a rate of slightly more than a volume a year; and before *The Great Railway Bazaar* appeared, he had already brought out seven novels, a collection of short stories, and a critical study of the West Indian novelist V. S. Naipaul. To date, Theroux has written nineteen works of fiction (plus a two-act play, *The White Man's Burden,* in 1987), along with seven books of travel. The fictional work arises from a dark, surrealistic, and darkly comic vision. It can move into the apocalyptic or neo–H. G. Wellsian future, as in *O-Zone* (1988), where the Ozarks, contaminated by nuclear waste, have been declared the off-limits O-Zone, visitable only by weekending rich eastern folk ("the Owners") flying out in their jet-roters, but which conceal new forms of perhaps salvational humanity; or, as in Theroux's most recent novel, *Chicago Loop* (1991), it can provide a strangely gentle, even gently funny account of a man, a Chicago businessman, driven by wildly contradictory impulses to kill himself.

The fictions also arise out of Theroux's happily incurable planetary restlessness. They reflect the personal experience of a Massachusetts-born individual who, during ten years out of his native country, traveled and taught school (English) in Italy, Malawi (a southeast African republic dating from 1964), Uganda, and Singapore. Stories are set variously in a new east African country *(Fong and the Indians),* Kenya *(Girls at Play),* Singapore *(Saint Jack),* Honduras *(The Mosquito Coast),* London *(The Family Arsenal),* Chicago.

While the novels and tales are enriched by the travel, the travel writing is invigorated by the story-telling skills acquired in years of fictional practice. Theroux must be the most widely traveled person on earth: a traveler in the grand manner of Alexander von Humboldt (1769–1859), the heroic German scientist who, in addition to lesser forays, journeyed two thousand miles across South America and ten thousand miles across Russia. What should be stressed in this immediate context is that Theroux's travel books really are, emphatically and persistently, about travel: most often by train ("Ever since childhood, when I lived within earshot of the Boston and Maine, I have seldom heard a train go by and not wished I was on it"—so runs the opening sentence of *The Great Railway Bazaar*), though sometimes by boat (as in the first of the two China books). The very chapter titles, volume by volume, comprise a poetic litany of travel, of movement as stated times toward specified places:

The 15.30—London to Paris
The Teheran Express
The Khyber Mail to Lahore Junction
The Mandalay Express
The Golden Arrow to Kuala Lumpur
The Hikari ("Sunbeam") Super Express to Kyoto
                    (*The Great Railway Bazaar*)

The 11.33 to Margate
A Morning Train to the Isle of Wight
The 20.20 to Llandudno Junction
The Boat Train to Ulster
The 15.53 to Belfast
The 14.40 to Aberdeen
The Last Train to Whitby
                    (*The Kingdom by the Sea*)

The Train to Mongolia
Night Train Number 90 to Peking
Train Number 324 to Hohhot and Lanzhou
The Slow Train to Changsha and Shaoshan
The International Express to Harbin: Train Number 17

The Shandong Express to Shanghai: Train Number 124
The Train to Tibet

(*Riding the Iron Rooster*)

"I sought trains," Theroux recalls early on in *The Great Railway Bazaar*, "I found passengers." That is, he found people: human beings of every imaginable variety, of all different races, nationalities, cultures, historical experiences, folklores, languages, habits. Landscapes and people, vistas and anecdotes: this is the stuff of Theroux's travel writing. Theroux was a veteran of genuine—*lived*—multiculturalism long before the fashion came; no one is more truly "multi" in this respect than he.

One of the more memorable characters we meet, with Theroux, is a mysterious elderly Englishman named Duffill, who shared a compartment with Theroux on the then shabby and ill-serviced Orient Express from Paris to Istanbul. At Domodossola on the Italian frontier one morning, Mr. Duffill went off to buy food and was left standing on the platform when the train pulled out. His name "became a verb" for Theroux: "to be duffilled was to be abandoned by one's own train." Ten years later, Theroux made a little side trip to Barrow, near Hull on the east coast of England, where Duffill had said he lived. The old fellow was dead, Theroux discovered, but he learned many of the facts of his English acquaintance's life: particularly his long employment in the international accounting firm of Price, Waterhouse. And, yes, a neighbor told Theroux, Mr. Duffill had eventually collected the luggage the train had carried away and which Theroux had consigned with a note to the *controllare* in Venice. Thinking about it all, Theroux decides that Duffill had been a most unusual person: "brave, kind, secretive, resourceful, solitary, brilliant"—and almost certainly a spy.

Paul Theroux's travel writings form a part of our contemporary American literature, in the most exact, that is to say the most honorific, meaning of that final term. And for this reason it is impossible, in a brief afterword, to do justice to the accomplishment. But some sense of the characteristic texture may be gained from the following passage in *The Kingdom by the Sea*. A main attraction throughout the writing is the forcefulness of opinion, both positive and negative, that Theroux is always willing to proffer. Here, in a summing up about Aberdeen, we have an instance of both sorts.

> Aberdeen was not my kind of place. But was it anyone's kind of place? . . . The food was disgusting, the hotels overpriced and indifferent, the spit-and-sawdust pubs were full of drunken and bad-tempered men—well, who wouldn't be? And it was not merely that it was expensive and dull; much worse was the selfishness.

At the station, as they waited for the train to Dundee, a local acquaintance asks if there wasn't *anything* he liked about Aberdeen? What about the cathedral, the university, the museum? No, Theroux didn't think much of them either.

> [Mr. Muir] looked appalled.
> I said, "But I liked the bakeries. The fresh fish. The cheese."
> "The bakeries," Mr. Muir said sadly.
> I did not go on. He thought there was something wrong with me. But what I liked in Aberdeen was what I liked generally in Britain: the bread, the fish, the cheese, the flower gardens, the apples, the clouds, the newspapers, the beer, the woolen cloth, the radio programs, the parks, the Indian restaurants and amateur dramatics, the postal service, the fresh vegetables, the trains, and the modesty and truthfulness of people. And I liked the way Aberdeen's streets were frequently full of seagulls.

> (1991)

PART TWO

Americans

> *Mr. L——l was so kind as to accede to my desire that he would take notes of all that occurred; and it is from his memoranda that what I now have to relate is, for the most part, either condensed or copied verbatim.*
>
> "The Facts in the Case of M. Valdemar"

One of the important recurring games in American literary history has been that of revising the received human image of Edgar Allan Poe. Something about Poe's personality and the spasmodic circumstances of his short life (1809–1849), especially when linked with the wayward quality of his tales and poems, has periodically convinced literary scholars that he has never hitherto been understood. Over a number of decades the revisionary process has become standardized. It begins by positing as fundamentally false the image perpetrated by earlier biographers. More often than not, this image partakes of a romantic legend wherein Poe rather resembles the haunted figures that stalk through his most horrific tales—feverishly brilliant, tormented, doomed, sexually askew almost beyond mortal comprehension, betimes a murderer and a necrophiliac. Then, as against that version, there is brought into view the "real" Poe, a person whom the ascertainable facts disclose to have been quite humanly recognizable. This Poe is a man among men, even a social being, who shifted about between Richmond and Philadelphia and

New York, and who suffered terribly from poverty, illness, and an intolerance for alcohol; who nonetheless produced fiction, poetry, and criticism at an incredible rate—some of it, at least, among the wonders of our literature—and performed with striking success as magazine editor; who married his thirteen-year-old cousin Virginia Clemm and late in his life courted a dizzying series of widows of uncertain years; and who died, somewhat mysteriously, in Baltimore at the age of forty.

Such, in essence, was the biographical procedure of Arthur Hobson Quinn, whose life of Poe in 1941 did indeed set the record straight in many valuable particulars; of Edward Wagenknecht, the title of whose *Edgar Allan Poe: The Man Behind the Legend* in 1963 announced the familiar intention; and, among several others, of Robert W. Beyer, in an ambitious, unpublished study. Such also was precisely the procedure, almost a century ago, of George Edward Woodberry in his *Edgar Allan Poe* of 1885.*

George Woodberry, in 1885, was a thirty-year-old aspiring scholar and poet; a few years later he would become professor of Comparative Literature at Columbia, and in the course of time he would compile an impressive oeuvre of critical biographies, literary essays, and poems. He was a gentlemen-scholar of the old school—not a bad school, seen in retrospect; and if its graduates displayed a sort of cultivated and well-mannered shrewdness rather than any genuine drive of insight, they possessed an utter integrity of scholarship. This was why Woodbury was so shocked by his findings; everyone had *lied* about Poe, he came to believe; all the witnesses disputed and quarreled with each other. The moment his *Poe* was in print, Woodberry fled to Europe to recuperate amid the old Mediterranean humanities. Writing a friend from Capri and referring to John Ingram, whose life of Poe had appeared in 1880, Woodberry remarked a bit dazedly: "Ingram did an

*Woodberry's *Poe* was reprinted in 1980 by Chelsea House, the occasion for this article.

extraordinary amount of lying about Poe, and I still wonder about it."
In the preface to his own book, after listing his sources, Woodberry
summarized: "The statements of facts in these sources are extraordinarily conflicting, doubtful, and contested; and in view of this, as well
as of the spirit of rancor excited in any discussion of Poe's character,
the author has made this, as far as was possible, a documented
biography."

One of the worst of the liars Woodberry had to contend with was
Rufus N. Griswold, the former Baptist minister and failed poet who
somehow managed to become Poe's literary executor, and who, in that
capacity, exhibited a positive genius in the defamation of Poe's character and behavior. Griswold accomplished this masterpiece of black-
guarding, in his edition of Poe's works, by wholesale lying and
invention, by groundless assertions, and in particular by the systematic
forgery of Poe's letters. It was a performance rooted, it seems, in a
psychopathic hatred of Poe (no one has really explained it); and
although Griswold was quickly denounced, and Poe defended, by the
more knowing and well-disposed, Poe's enduring reputation in many
quarters was that of a drunkard, debauchee, drug addict, and madman.
George Woodberry, however, showed a sturdy reluctance to be taken
in. He was unaware of the extent of Griswold's fraudulence—it would
not be fully revealed until Arthur Hobson Quinn's meticulous exposé
in 1941—but he regarded Griswold's rancorous statements as typical of
the argument over Poe's character that occurred at the time. "An
unsupported statement by Griswold regarding Poe is liable to suspicion," he tells us mildly and typically; Woodberry's Poe is anything but
the libertine lunatic depicted by Griswold.

But the first liar Woodberry was faced with was, of course, Poe
himself. Woodberry seems not to have come upon the yarns Poe took
to spreading about his life during the late 1820s, tales of adventuring
and dueling in Europe (in no other respect does William Faulkner so
resemble his Southern literary ancestor as in this business of creative
autobiography). But he spotted enough wilful misstatements by Poe

to lead him, early on, to advance the customary formula: "It may as well be confessed at once that any unsupported assertion by Poe regarding himself is to be received with great caution."

Woodbury does not pause to meditate on Poe's habit of falsification, or to observe any connection between it and certain characteristic tactics in Poe's fiction. He informs us, shifting the evidence, that Edgar Poe was born on January 19, 1809; that for a period after his adoption he was called Edgar Allan; that when he enlisted in the United States Army in 1828, he gave the name as Edgar A. Perry and his birthdate as 1806; and that when he entered West Point in 1830 he changed his birthdate to 1811, having said publicly not long before that he was not yet twenty. Despite all that, Woodberry gives no sign of being struck by Poe's evasiveness, in his fiction, about names and dates—by the narrator of "Berenice" flatly refusing to tell us his family name; by the narrator of "Ligeia" saying that he can no longer remember when he first met the Lady Ligeia and that he never did get to know her last name; and even more suggestively, by the narrator of "William Wilson" confiding that his real name is not William Wilson but something quite like it (as Edgar A. Perry, one thinks, is like Edgar A. Poe) and that his birthdate, like that of his double and namesake at the English school, is January 19, 1813.

If Woodberry fails to remark on these recurrences, it is partly because he resolutely refuses at any moment to read from the life to the writing. In this, to be sure, he would have been warmly applauded by W. H. Auden and no few others, since Woodberry's time, who regard all biographical interpretation as impertinent and risky; and it is to be admitted that Woodberry's noninterventionist policy allows the reader to have all the fun of tracing the connections. At the same time, Woodberry appears blind to those many occasions when Poe sought slyly to fob off as a true story, thoroughly vouched for, some palpable and incredible fiction—as in "The Facts in the Case of M. Valdemar," which purports to tell how a dying man's body was kept alive for seven months by a mesmeric spell and instantly decomposed when the spell was lifted; and for which the narrator claims a documentary veracity almost identical to that claimed by George Woodberry for his biography of Poe.

Even so, working his way through his network of historical and literary fibs and misrepresentations, Woodberry came astonishingly close to establishing all the significant facts in the case of Edgar Allan Poe. His biographical report has of course been corrected in a host of minor details; new facts have been uncovered (for instance that Poe, making his way to Boston on a coal barge in 1827, briefly assumed the name of Henri le Rennet*); we know a good deal more now about Poe's erudition, both actual and spurious, and several persons of importance in Poe's life have been more fully identified—most notably, Mrs. Charles Richmond, to whom Woodberry refers simply and discreetly as "Annie." But the basic story is all here, and it does not differ very much from the one laboriously arrived at by later generations of scholars.

Woodberry, moreover, may be said in a certain perspective to have had an advantage over those later generations. In his far-off age of innocence, he did not have to struggle through the miasma of the Freudian interpretation of Poe that grew thickest with Marie Bonaparte's study (1933, and still damnably fascinating). And so, for example, Woodberry is able to remark accurately that nothing whatever is known about Poe's father, the young actor David Poe, after the summer of 1810—without indulging in speculation as to whether David Poe "rejected" his wife and children and what the effect of such "rejection" might have been upon the infant Edgar.

To move to the very end of the story (or "the end of the play," as Woodberry appropriately calls it), Woodberry passes on the rumor that Poe's death in Baltimore, in October 1849, was brought on by his having been dragged about the city in a sick and intoxicated state and forced to vote in a succession of polling places. But, says Woodberry,

*On Henri le Rennet, see the Afterword to this essay.

"the basis of this tradition is now lost." The "tradition" caught hold and for a long time provided the concluding episode in the Poe legend. The most recent scholarship, peeling away the speculation about Poe's father and the alleged melodrama of Poe's death, has been content to leave these and other matters almost exactly where Woodberry left them.

Woodberry obviously lost patience with Poe the man before he completed his work—"really," he told his correspondent from Capri, "it became a very unwelcome task before I was at the end"—and his final summing up is moralistic and scolding. Still, his biographical account holds firm. And indeed, the truly telling change regarding Poe in the past decades has been not a major clarification of his life but a radical reassessment of his imaginative intentions and his literary achievement.

As to the latter, Woodberry is extremely sound within the limits of a cultivated impressionism. He is eloquent in describing the *effect* of Poe's tales and poems (notice his remarks about "Ligeia" and "Ula-lume"), something that would have gratified Poe, who said that a particular effect was what he invariably aimed at in his writing. On the whole, Woodberry discriminates acutely (to our modern judgment) between the best, the second best, and the trifling in Poe's work—his most striking lapse being his failure to appreciate "The Purloined Letter." Woodberry, in 1885, could hardly have foreseen Poe's contribution to the immense future of the English-language detective story—the first Sherlock Holmes tale, A Study in Scarlet (in which Holmes refers to Poe's Dupin as "a very inferior fellow"), did not appear until 1887; but taken by itself, "The Purloined Letter," with its tantalizing echoes and secret quotations, might have stirred Woodberry's curiosity more than it did.

As an instance of Woodberry's critical common sense, we can cite his treatment of the story, put forward by John Ingram, of the composition of "The Bells," and the alleged part in it of Mrs. Mary Louise Shew, a friend of the Poe family in the latter 1840s. Claiming to draw on Mrs. Shew's diary, Ingram had written that Poe arrived at the lady's home one day, tired, dispirited, totally lacking in inspiration. Through the open windows there came the sound of church bells; and when Poe declared that he was not in the mood for bells, Mrs. Shew thrust a piece of paper in his hands. Woodberry's paraphrase continues:

> Mrs. Shew then wrote, "The Bells, by E. A. Poe," and added "The little silver bells;" on the poet's finishing the stanza thus suggested, she again wrote, "The heavy iron bells," and this idea also Poe elaborated, and then copying off the two stanzas, headed it, "By Mrs. M. L. Shew," and called it her poem.

This preposterous account of how a possibly great poem got written is received courteously by Woodberry, but he suggests that the origins of "The Bells" were far more plausibly to be found in Poe's lifelong fascination with bell ringing and in his careful reading (documented by Woodberry) of a book by Chateaubriand that spoke of the emotions aroused by varieties of bell sounds.*

But common sense, as we have gradually learned, is not the most trustworthy guide to Poe's imaginative landscape. Richard Wilbur in a series of essays (the most accessible being his full-scale introduction to the Poe section in the anthology *Major Writers of America,* 1966) and Daniel Hoffman in *Poe Poe Poe Poe Poe Poe Poe* (1972) have argued convincingly, if somewhat differently, that the characteristic action of Poe's best tales is nothing external or "realistic" but rather an allegorical

---

*What might be called the Ingram theory of creativity has been exemplified in our time by a scene in the film *Night and Day.* Cole Porter (played by Cary Grant) is seated at the piano in his Foreign Legion uniform (Porter in fact was never in the Legion) waiting for inspiration. From outside, he hears the sounds of drums, and the first line of a song immediately presents itself: "Like the beat beat beat of the tom-toms." He hears a clock ticking in the room, and the second line arises: "Like the tick tick tock of the stately clock." Raindrops are espied on the window: "Like the drip drip drop of the raindrops"; and then Porter, hands moving swiftly and confidently over the keyboard, is in full swing into the chorus of "Night and Day."

dream-journey. Within the dream, one part of the psyche goes desperately in search of that other part of himself from which he has been disjoined in some metaphorical childhood. Thus the narrator of "Ligeia" is separated from the maternal and godlike Ligeia at the instant of her death; the narrator of the more complex "Fall of the House of Usher" had been Roderick Usher's closest boyhood friend before their ways parted; and even William Wilson, contemplating his double at the English school, has the strong belief of "having been acquainted with the being who stood before me, at some epoch very long ago—some point of the past infinitely remote."

The dream-journey toward reunion may be beset by horror, loss of reason, premature burial, and even murder—but these (the argument runs) are necessary phases in the escape from the fallen earthbound state, the imprisoning world of prosaic fact and banal morality. The climactic re-encounter, however terrifying in any normal viewpoint, may accordingly be a kind of triumph within Poe's unique vision. Speaking of the moment in which Madeline Usher "in her violent and now final death-agonies, bore [her brother Roderick] to the floor a corpse," Wilbur contends that "grisly as their death-embrace may seem, it actually symbolizes the momentary reunion of a divided soul; and . . . the final restoration and purification of that soul in the life to come."

Wilbur's thesis is the following:

> The typical Poe story is, in its action, an allegory of dream-experience; it occurs within the mind of the poet; the characters are not distinct personalities, but principles or faculties of the poet's divided nature; the steps of the action correspond to the successive states of a mind moving into sleep; and the end of the action is the end of a dream. Sometimes, as in "William Wilson," the narrative will have a strong admixture of realism and of credible psychology; elsewhere, as in "The

Fall of the House of Usher," there will be no such admixture, and the one available coherence will be allegorical.

Daniel Hoffman, deploying his own vocabulary, would essentially agree; and the rest of us can find our own terms of interpretation. But that Poe's stories variously enact the effort of a psyche to regain a lost primal harmony seems to me incontestable. The thesis serves to explain, as nothing else does, Poe's contempt (referred to earlier) for factual truth, and his imaginative involvement with criminality and violence—the psyche, en route to transcendent beauty, must as it were conceive itself to be blasting through and beyond the dullness of the true, as humanly understood, and the drabness of the good. Poe's most interesting poems—including "The Raven," "Ulalume," and "The City in the Sea"—can be freshly grasped by means of the thesis; and his most elaborate hoaxes, especially when they describe spectacular journeys, can be seen as huge parodies of the persistent intention—products of the same imagination in its season of jocosity.

There are definite hints that George Woodberry would not have been altogether shocked by this reading of Poe. He says about the Lady Ligeia, after all, in clear pre-Wilburian terms, that she "has still no human quality. . . . She is, in fact, the maiden of Poe's dream, the Eidolon he served, the air-woven divinity, in which he believed; for he had the true myth-making faculty, the power to make his senses aver what his imagination perceived." But Woodberry's New England temperament would scarcely have approved the correlative impulse to violate truth and outrage morality in the course of the visionary enterprise. It was, apparently, a lingering sense of something equivocal, something ethically flawed, in Poe's achievement that led Woodberry, in his final verdict, to withhold his highest critical accolade. Faced with the present-day reading of Poe, Woodberry might have reconsidered that verdict, though it is doubtful. There is not much else, in all fairness, that he should have felt called on to reconsider.

(1980)

Afterword: The Poe Biographer

In the fall of 1991, there appeared *Edgar A. Poe: Mournful and Never-Ending Remembrance* by Kenneth Silverman, whose biography of Cotton Mather won the Pulitzer Prize in 1984. The life of Poe may or may not be "definitive": a cluster of accomplished biographers at a daylong session in New Haven in the early spring of 1992 could be heard agreeing that there could never, really, be a definitive biography of anyone, and for all sorts of reasons; but it is authoritative to the last degree. It is certainly, as the publishers claim, "the first comprehensive Poe biography in English in half a century," that is, since Arthur Hobson Quinn's book. But it is much more than that, in the range and richness of its detail, in the constant alertness of the authorial eye, and in the intimacy displayed both with American literary currents in the last century and with literary quality in any time.

George Woodberry's biographical tact, meanwhile, is reconfirmed. As regards Edgar's father, David, for example, Professor Silverman tells us succinctly (on page 7) that at a certain moment the twenty-five-year-old failed or failing actor simply disappeared from the theatrical company and "apparently from the lives of Eliza and of his two children." The reasons for his disappearance are said to be unknown, nor is anything known of where he went or what became of him. And that is that. In a similar vein, Professor Silverman so little credits the old yarn about Poe's death in Baltimore that he does not even pause to mention it.

The tone and method of this account in all such places may be suggested by the author's comment at an early stage: where he is reflecting on Poe's extraordinarily ambivalent responses to death and loss and especially the death of a woman, with the death of his mother, Eliza, when Edgar was three, in the background.

> The inability of young children to mourn the death of a parent seems but one of many ways, if any are needed at all, to account for Edgar's odd, intent imaginings about death. As

this biography is not an argument but a narrative, no attempt will be made to "prove" that the psychoanalytic prototype of the bereaved child applied to him, still less to examine by its light his every word and action.

The Poe story, retold in that spirit of perceptive sanity, has a powerful double effect. It seems more "normal," more humanly familiar, than in either the Gothic or the psychoanalyzing versions; but at the same time, it seems, subtly and increasingly, more incredible. A wildness *within the life,* and antedating the stories, is made gradually evident, without any authorial need to press or emphasize. There is after all a wholeness to Poe, the biography persuades us: a wholeness so to say of the lunatic, the lover, and the poet interweaving.

Here is a final instance of the kind of thing the new Poe biographer must absorb into his weave. In the winter of 1827, Edgar Poe departed from Richmond, taking to himself the name Henri le Rennet and putting about a report of exotic and adventurous wanderings. This name, it is explained, was "a Frenchifying of his brother's middle names," the brother's full name being William Henry Leonard Poe. The pseudonym was intended to confuse his foster father, John Allan, and to mislead Edgar's creditors; and the "false trail of maritime roving"—Edgar in fact had merely gone north to Boston—was in imitation of William's real-life travels in South America and elsewhere. But the matter did not end there; matters rarely do end tidily in the Poe saga. Brother Henry before long performed in kind by naming the hero of one of his own tales Edgar Leonard, and by giving him a history not unlike Edgar's. Henry's poem "Original," moreover, repeats almost verbatim three stanzas of a poem in Edgar's volume *Tamerlane,* nor is it easy to determine which came first. Doubles and doublings proliferate almost casually in the Poe family experience; more generally, the uncanny has a habit of appearing as a commonplace of the clan. Or so Kenneth Silverman's biographical art brings us at last to feel. It is a life portrait altogether worthy of its subject.

(1991)

I n this new foray into American cultural history by the author of the exemplary *Virgin Land,* Henry Nash Smith proposes to explore a series of American fictional master-pieces in the context of the social processes and popular taste of their time. There is something old-fashioned about the book, just as there is something old-worldly about the author's style of discourse—his unfailingly good (and charming) intellectual manners. Professor Smith is an unreconstructed humanist: and at a moment when much of the critical talk about American literature is getting as far away from humanism as it can manage. Cultural environment counts for nothing in the newest critical talk; texts are purified of association with external reality to a degree that would have left the *old* New Criticism dizzy; and novels and poems are seen as concerned largely with the internal convulsions attendant upon their own begetting. The result, to say the least, has been uncanny.

Not that Professor Smith, a canny hand if ever there was one, is entirely averse to some of the current critical proceedings. He can decode a text and point to rhetorical modulations and blurrings with the best of his younger fellows, and can observe with an air of tolerance instances of a novelist trying to hoodwink his reader or battling covertly with some intransigent aspect of himself. He is conversant with the most "sophisticated" recent scholarship and criticism and can bring it aptly to bear, though without feeling the need, which one senses elsewhere, to belittle or forget the contributions of an older day by F. O. Matthiessen, Constance Rourke, and others. If *Democracy and the Novel* is in some sense old-fashioned, it is in no sense outdated. It seeks at every turn to build bridges between the literary-critical past and the literary-critical present: a profoundly humanistic endeavor.

Since Professor Smith, in his quiet graceful way, delivers suggestive ideas at the rate of about one per sentence, it is not easy to do any sort of justice to the book, short as it is (some 160 pages). It might be helpful, as a beginning, to modify or reverse the subtitle, "Popular Resistance to Classic American Writers." For one thing, hardly more than a quibble, only two of Professor Smith's authors, Hawthorne and Melville, are "classic" in the customary meaning of the term, which, deriving from D. H. Lawrence's *Studies,* refers to American literature before the Civil War. His other novelists—Henry Ward Beecher (who is included for contrast, almost for parody), William Dean Howells, Mark Twain, and Henry James—belong to a later and different literary age. To chart a path from the classical to the postwar figures is exactly Professor Smith's intention.

At the same time, the subtitle appears to have things wrong-way round. In the case of Hawthorne and even more of Henry James, Professor Smith does offer disheartening evidence of popular resistance to their work. Hawthorne skewed the relation between the external world and the perceiving mind; the world, hitherto thought to be instantly and easily knowable, thereupon grew unsteady and mysterious under the brooding, symbolizing eye of guilt-ridden observers like Reuben Bourne and Hester Prynne. For this, one reviewer categorized *The Scarlet Letter* as "mentally diseased." Another expressed a well-grounded alarm at Hawthorne's "awful probing into the most forbidden regions of human consciousness." An English novelist, Margaret Oliphant, berated Hawthorne for snobbishly addressing himself to the intellectual few rather than to "the common people."

Professor Smith's survey of the unending flow of hostile reviews that greeted Henry James's novels over a quarter of a century is a cautionary tale. In almost perfect innocence of what James was up to, reviewers denounced book after book as cold, excessively analytical, and even, astonishingly, slipshod and slovenly. James "analyses too much," said a reviewer of *Washington Square* in 1881; and *The Portait of a Lady* was thought to be "a cruel book in its dissection of character and exposure of the nerves and sinews of human actions." Reviewing rhetoric grew yet more garbled and anxious with the awareness that James was highly regarded in certain narrow, elitist circles. One comment on *The Bostonians* wound its way through ponderous metaphors to conclude that "Mr. James may nowadays be looked upon as the head of a certain college of savants, a man delighting in writing what to the majority of flesh-and-blood men and women has no excuse for being so praised. . . . This long, prosy carefully written book was not worth writing and is unreadable." When H. G. Wells in 1914 declared that James reminded him of a hippopotamus trying to pick up a pea and that his narratives were "tales of nothingness," he was merely saying with a more practiced and professional snidery what American reviewers had been saying for many years. Only an "obstinate finality," as James allowed himself to be, could have withstood and (such are the strategems of the creative impulse) even battened on such critical adversity.

Even so, what Professor Smith is really telling us about more often than not is the resistance of American *writers* to their cultural setting—to the popular taste, the currents of belief, and sometimes the institutions of their age. That resistance took the form of a succession of fictional modes: successive attempts, by the resources of fiction, to combat or outflank the attitudes and assumptions of the American book-reading public. The long, twisty effort—and this is the heart of Professor Smith's story—produced the romance novel of Hawthorne and Melville; then the realistic fiction of Howells and others; Mark Twain's vernacular "lowbrow" stories; and James's achievements in what might be called semimodernism.

The cultural enemy was the post-Calvinist American ideology, something compounded of prudery and money grubbing, a watered-down religiosity, and a vague optimism about progress and the American destiny. I am here oversimplifying Professor Smith's somewhat oversimplified account of the American cast of mind from the 1850s onward. The national temper was not always or wholly undisturbed; in the 1880s, for example, segments of upper-middle-class American society suffered notable attacks of the jitters, due partly to a felt sagging of genuine religious faith and a sense that "modern" America was getting quite out of hand. But what the majority of Americans *believed* they believed in were in fact technological advance, liberal Christianity, virtue of character, and happy endings. The literary embodiment of this jumbled doctrine was the sentimental novel, which made its first important appearance in 1850 with Susan Warner's *The Wide, Wide World*. *The Scarlet Letter* came out the same year and *Moby-Dick* a year later; but the moment for recognition and acceptance of the romance form had already passed, and its extraordinary possibilities would not be explored again until the epoch of William Faulkner.

The Scarlet Letter sold five thousand copies in six months, but Maria Cummins's *The Lamplighter* in 1854 sold forty thousand copies in eight weeks; and by that time *The Wide, Wide World* was on its way to an eventual sale of more than half a million. No wonder that Hawthorne, who made his living by his pen, spoke wincingly of the "d——d mob of scribbling women." Anyone who thinks that the publishing industry has only in our time, and as it were suddenly, become a greedy and calculated affair should read these pages of Henry Nash Smith, and the scholarship that lies behind them. Almost every trick of the publishing trade, every lure to bigger and bigger readership, had been established before the Civil War was over. What is new today is not greed and pliable popular taste, but rather the huge publishing conglomerates, the refusal of certain publishers and bookstores to take on any serious but predictably low-selling work of fiction (prediction, in such cases, being about as accurate as that of the weather bureau), and the slick tailoring of paperback originals for the mass market.

But perhaps that last development is not altogether new either. Witness Professor Smith's chapter on Henry Ward Beecher's *Norwood*, a novel of 1867 written by invitation, and written to measure, for the New York *Ledger*. The paper, which paid Beecher $30,000 for the serial, had a circulation of 300,000; and Beecher, the most popular preacher in the country's history and one of the most esteemed men of his generation (Whittier kept a portrait of Beecher in his study), could be counted on to provide a preachy novel that would swell the sales even more. Professor Smith is to be admired for sticking to the end with this package of sententious rubbish: the fine young man afflicted by religious doubt; the tender young woman from whom he is separated through a misunderstanding; and the trio of male conversationalists who swap garrulous sermons on morality and religion. "Genteel" is scarcely the word for it all. Most reviewers, as a matter of fact, remained cool toward *Norwood;* but Beecher had taken expert bead on popular longings, and the novel made an enormous splash.

It was a troublesome time for writers of more grasping literary intentions. Mark Twain, by a crafty maneuver, bypassed the middlebrow, or *Norwood*-loving, audience completely; he gave his work to a firm that peddled its wares by house-to-house and farm-to-farm canvassing in outlying districts across the nation. To hang on to this vast and generally unlettered new readership, Twain perfected the vernacular style he had inherited from southwestern humorous writing; the most famous and influential idiom in American literary history was thus, to a thought-provoking extent, an accident of the marketplace. Henry James deployed the opposite tactic: he fictionalized the sentimentalists by making them a satirical element in his subject matter; in one of his most wryly delightful tales, "The Next Time" of 1895, James traced the gallant effort of a gifted novelist to write a book so bad, so vulgar, that it would make his fortune. He fails in the effort, the narrator says, because "You can't make a sow's ear out of a silk purse."

These and others of Professor Smith's findings are eminently worth the mulling, but I want to linger a bit over the chapter on William Dean Howells. It is the pivot of *Democracy and the Novel* and is the most arresting, the most original, and, in my view, the most debatable section of the book. It is gratifying to see so accomplished a critic taking Howells seriously; Howells is still insufficiently honored, though an essay appears every twenty years or so lamenting the fact, and though one can encounter little pockets of enthusiasm for him here and there. But Professor Smith does not, perhaps, take Howells seriously enough. He rests his challenging case on a series of utterly brilliant analyses of ten passages from Howell's novel of 1881, *A Modern Instance*. The writer that emerges from these dazzling exercises believed that "moral principles are immanent in all experience," so that a straightforwardly realistic (as against an idealized) portrait of men and women would reveal those principles as a matter of course; but he then, along about Chapter XXXII of the novel, took fright when he saw the kind of principles that were revealing themselves, and reverted in the final stretch of the narrative to the pious moralizing he had set out to undermine.

For anyone who has not been through *A Modern Instance* slap-bang just lately, I offer a brief summary. It deals mainly with Bartley Hubbard, an initially amiable but morally tone-deaf journalistic hack; his marriage to Marcia Gaylord, the wilful daughter of an agnostic old lawyer in the village of Equity, Maine; and the breakup of their marriage, in Boston, after a number of quarrels, reconciliations, and charges of ill-conduct. Bartley takes off for the Midwest and disappears. Narrative attention now shifts to other characters, in particular to Ben Halleck, the twitchy son of a Boston tradesman, and an elegant lawyer named Atherton. In intervals between lurches of plot, these two agonize together as to whether it had been sinful for Ben to fall in love with Marcia Hubbard, a married woman, and after news of Bartley's death filters back to Boston, whether it had been so very sinful that Ben is now precluded from proposing marriage to the widow.

Professor Smith detects a creeping authorial religiosity in these last chapters, and seems to take it for granted that Atherton, in his ferocity of recitude, speaks for Howells himself. (Atherton says things to Ben Halleck like "You don't *look* like one of those scoundrels who lure women from their duty, ruin homes and destroy society. . . . Do you propose to defy the world, to help form within it a community of outcasts with whom shame is not shame, nor dishonor, dishonor?") At issue here is not simply the interpretation of one portion of one novel, but Howells's entire relation to gentility—as a key representative case, a paradigm of the cultural history of the era. It is far from easy, I would agree, to reach an accurate judgment on Howells in this regard. He can be quoted, as he was in his lifetime, as resolutely in favor of virtue triumphant, in fiction, and as abiding cozily within the smiling aspects of life. But those statements look a little different in context; and anyhow, Howells was a much wilier and more self-conscious literary manipulator than he is usually given credit for.

He may well have believed that moral principles were immanent in all experience; so, in another formulation, did Henry James. But Howells knew that the resolutions of moral dilemmas are almost always ambiguous and unsatisfying; life, for Howells, had a mean habit of letting you off the moral hook, especially by refusing to display real alternatives. The point about Ben Halleck is that he is no less a moral cripple than Bartley Hubbard, whose initials he shares; he is, indeed, Bartley's artfully conceived and hopelessly neurotic double (and an example, incidentally, of the disturbed state of mind, or jitters, mentioned earlier). And the point about the moral maunderings of Halleck and Atherton is that *this* is what constituted so much of the foggy moral atmosphere through which Americans groped their way in the 1880s. Similarly, in the opening chapters of *A Modern Instance,* and intermittently thereafter, Howells provides a devastating picture of the liberalized, socialized, cheerleading religious element of the day. At this sort of thing, Howells was without peer. Howells grew dismayed to the edge of panic, according to Professor Smith, when he saw, by Chapter XXXII, that he had made Bartley and Marcia Hubbard seem doomed from the start "as if by a Calvinist inevitability." On the contrary, it seems to me, Howells has all along been describing what happens to two young people of disastrously inadequate upbringing in a morally fogbound world. The last chapters of *A Modern Instance* conclude the presentation of that world; and far from reflecting a cop-out to sentimentalism, they constitute Howells's most telling subversion (I had almost written "deconstruction") of the piety they give voice to.

Arguing with Henry Nash Smith is a treat, and privilege. I would like to prod him, for instance, on his occasional observation that this or that novel of Hawthorne or Melville or Mark Twain looks forward to modernist and even postmodernist fiction: the longest of the book's bridges. He is dead right, of course, but the phenomenon deserves larger meditation—the premature modernity, so to speak, of earlier American fiction. But let us, as my wife's mother used to say, take the biscuits while they're passing; *Democracy and the Novel* is a feast of them. Though Professor Smith suggests modestly that the work deploys what are essentially "hit-and-run tactics," it has its own kind of wholeness. It is a book that sorts things out and puts them together, and it does so with wisdom and humanity, and a range of vision rarely attained these days.

(1978)

8

One phase of American writing in the mid-nineteenth century at its best and strangest is something that the reader, a century and a half later, might uneasily label "modernist." Hawthorne's *The Blithedale Romance* belongs in the category, and so do a number of the poems of Emily Dickinson: works that seem to break through and beyond the contemporary literary manner in fiction and poetry. It is as though they were trying to accomplish something for which the resources were not yet fully available, or perhaps for which the readership was not yet prepared. For whatever reasons, these writings might be seen as elements in a kind of premature modernism; and the most striking example of the genre is Melville's romance novel of 1852, *Pierre; or, The Ambiguities.*

The first and most obviously modernist aspect of *Pierre* is the problematic nature of its plot—certain crucial facts and relationships are exactly what can never be fully determined. What we are given essentially is the tale of the youthful Pierre Glendinning, scion of a wealthy upstate New York family at Saddle Meadows; Lucy Tartan, his sometime fiancée; and Isabel Banford, a youngish woman who announces herself to Pierre as his half-sister, the daughter of Pierre's father in the latter's bachelor days. Despairing of having Isabel accepted by the Saddle Meadows community, Pierre departs with her to New York, and there attempts to make a living by his pen. The two are eventually joined by Lucy Tartan. Lucy's brother Fred and Pierre's cousin Glendinning Stanley arrive in hot pursuit, and after an exchange of threats, Pierre shoots and kills his cousin; he is arrested and jailed. Pierre is visited in prison by Lucy and Isabel. Lucy dies, apparently of shock, and Pierre and Isabel commit suicide by drinking poison.

This, then, is the novel that Melville—with a cynicism or a naïveté unmatched in the history of literary genius—described to his English publisher as "very much more calculated for popularity than anything you have yet published of mine—being a regular romance, with . . . stirring passions at work, and withal, representing a new & elevated aspect of American life."

I want to touch on four or five aspects of the novel, but feel impelled to offer a couple of cautionary observations. For one thing, the aspects I have chosen do not, obviously, exhaust the bizarre richness of this extraordinary novel, and may not even include those matters that some would consider primary (words like "psychology," "the unconscious," and "symbolism," for example, will scarcely cross my lips). For another thing, I can only deal with these aspects seriatim, whereas in the actual text, as against my squinted reading of it, they interweave, modify, overlap, and undermine one another. The ideal critic of *Pierre* would be someone like Mycroft Holmes, of whom his younger brother, himself a master of the problematic, once said: "Mycroft's specialism is omniscience. We will suppose," Sherlock continued, "that a minister needs information as to a point which involves the Navy, India, Canada and the bimetallic question; he could get his separate advices from various departments upon each, but only Mycroft can focus them all, and say offhand how each factor would affect the other."

Let me look first, then, at the temporal dimension. "The question of Time occurred to Pierre," the narrator tells us partway through the story, and the same question occurs to the reader from start to finish; *Pierre*, in what would be one of the modernist fashions, is a time-drenched novel. It is not only that the narrative begins in the summer and ends in the winter—begins, moreover, at sunrise and ends in the midnight dark. This is a familiar inversion of the traditional rhythm of the old romance form, though it has rarely been so underscored. Early on, the narrator informs us (grimacing, we later feel, at our innocence if we should believe a word he says) that "The first worlds made were winter worlds; the second made were vernal worlds; the third, and last, and perfectest, was this summer world of ours." But this turns out to be one of the great lies of which the author-hero of Pierre's abortive novel speaks when, giving voice to Pierre's own savage disillusion, he writes in his manuscript: "Oh! blessed be the twenty-first day of December, and cursed be the twenty-first day of June."

That, however, is the least of it. More interesting is the element of narrative pace: the way the novel manipulates psychological or, as it might be said, pre-Einsteinian time. This is a novel of some four hundred pages in a normal edition, and it covers a period of seven months. But the narrative account of the first day, from dawn to midnight, occupies one-quarter of the entire book; that of the first three days, a full half of the book. The fourth day then hurries by in a series of staccato episodes and lightning leave-takings that require only a relative handful of pages to describe; but time stretches out again into gray reaches as the party makes its way to New York and, over three or four days, settles in lodgings in the decrepit old building known as the Apostles, and while Pierre and the novel brood over his situation and his literary prospects. The final sixty pages compress nearly seven months of life in New York before the story catapults itself into the fast-moving climax of murder and suicide. Melville, in *Pierre*, wrenches time asunder and rearranges it according to his own perception of the vital punctuations of experience: time not as measured by clocks and calendars but as humanly experienced. Such would be the aim and the achievement, though often in a more knowing and crafty manner, of a variety of modernist writers.

Even more intriguing is the problem of the different *ages* of the central characters. Very much in the fashion of Faulkner (though, again, less sure-handedly), Melville simultaneously stresses the matter of age and sheds a mist of uncertainty over it. We are urged to keep tabs, but are not allowed finally to do so. Indulge with me in a little arithmetic.

Mary Glendinning, we are told flatly at the story's outset, is forty-nine years old; and since Pierre is first presented as "a boy of 19," Mary, at the time her first and only child was born, must have been thirty years of age. As to Pierre, his mother (or the narrator) seems to be trying to throw dust in our eyes when she tells her son over dinner one evening that he is "scarcely twenty"—which I take to mean that he has just passed his twentieth birthday. But it is said repeatedly elsewhere that he is only nineteen: part of the point being that Pierre cannot hope to receive his inheritance for two more years. Mary Glendinning is also our source for thinking that Lucy Tartan, Pierre's fiancée, is barely seventeen when we first meet her. But if so, Lucy ages with incomprehensible speed; for by the time she joins Pierre and Isabel in New York a few months later, she is going on nineteen: she is "of age by the law," it is twice proclaimed about her; that is, the law of New York state, according to which a young woman came of age at eighteen.

These are mild perplexities, however, compared to the problem of the age of Isabel Banford. It is indeed about that very problem that Pierre is speculating when "the question of Time occurred" to him; he is sure that Isabel is some years older than himself, but is unable to decide how many. Isabel's age, while of capital importance, is problematic indeed, and the question is further complicated by the most problematic of all the novel's issues—whether Isabel is or is not the daughter of Pierre's father, Pierre Glendinning II. Let us assume for the moment that she is.

The successive ages of Pierre II are much to the point. Mary Glendinning, that undependable witness, tells herself on one occasion that Pierre II was thirty-five when he married her—that he "was turned of five-and-thirty," which suggests that he might have been rather older. Allow a few years before the couple produced an heir: they do not strike us as being unduly hasty in such matters. Pierre II was thus thirty-eight or thirty-nine when young Pierre was born. The father was also about fifty-one when he died; or rather (for this is how the information is given us, in one of Melville's sly, slightly obfuscating disclosures), young Pierre was twelve at the moment of his father's death.

But how old was Pierre II when, if ever he did, he sired Isabel Banford? At this stage of his calculations, a dim apprehension begins to set in upon the arithmetician. One piece of testimony is offered by the so-called "chair portrait" of Pierre II, painted by his Cousin Ralph during the days when Pierre II was allegedly courting the French lady, Isabel's presumptive mother; and in the description of that portrait, the emphasis is overwhelmingly on youth—with a rhythmic repetition anticipatory of D. H. Lawrence. It is the "portrait of a fine-looking, gay-hearted, youthful gentleman . . . with a peculiarly bright and carefree, morning expression"; the sitter was "so trim and young"; the portrait "painted a brisk, unentangled young bachelor . . . charged to the lips with the first uncloying morning fullness and freshness of life."

How old is a youthful gentleman in the morning freshness of life? Melville insists that we ponder the question and withholds or dissolves the clues by which we might answer it. If we turn to Isabel, in her autobiograpical account of herself in the first meeting with Pierre, we get tantalizingly little help as to her own *or* her "father's" age. In an atmosphere permeated by the temporal element, as its first reality, Isabel has a singularly infirm grasp upon time; she lives, dreamily, within a private world of time slippages. "I must have been nine, or ten, or eleven years old," she tells Pierre, when she was removed from the madhouse of her childhood to the farmhouse of her adolescent years and later. In the farmhouse "weeks and years ran on." She is visited by a gentleman with a wonderful face, a face that bafflingly resembles her own as she sees it in the water. He whispers the word "father" in her ear. "He came to see me," Isabel says, "once every month or two." Over how long a period of time?—Isabel seems not to be aware that so concrete a question might even raise itself. Some indeterminate amount of time passes, and Isabel learns that the gentleman has died. "I was a grown girl now." How old is a grown girl to *this* girl's hazy understanding? The arithmetician now realizes with a distinct *brivido* that Isabel Banford may quite possibly be old enough to be Pierre's mother. This would in fact be the case if Pierre II, that carefree young bachelor, had been no more than twenty-two or twenty-three when he pursued the French lady, and pushing forty when Pierre III was born. One cannot but wonder whether the narrator may be at once hinting at and holding back some large and terrible secret, which might explain certain things that are otherwise darkly mystifying in the novel's atmosphere; and the wonder is made to recur later on in the story.

That possibility, anyhow, thickens the theme of double incest that has already been sounded in the relation between Pierre and the handsome mother whom he addresses as his sister. I want to get on to that theme after a bit, but I think we should turn first to yet another general motif in the novel: I mean the motif of madness.

We may recall, as we bore into that motif, that no few of the first reviewers of *Pierre* pronounced the book, its author, and the conduct of its hero to be nothing short of lunatic. "The craziest fiction extant," wrote one critic in August 1852: a book that "might be supposed to emanate from a lunatic hospital rather than from the quiet retreats of Berkshire." "A mad mosaic," wrote another; and a third concluded that Herman Melville had gone "clean daft" and ought to be locked up. A century later, commentary would voice a comparable opinion. Newton Arvin, on balance the calmest and steadiest of Melville's critics, wrote in 1950 that "Pierre is presented to us as an Enthusiast to Duty;

well and good; we are wholly prepared to believe in his acting in an ideal, absolute, self-abnegating, intolerant, and even destructive manner. We are not prepared to believe in his acting like a madman." By the time Pierre has outraged and insulted everybody, Arvin goes on to say, "he has conducted himself generally like a psychopath."

All of this—and one could cite more of the same—strikes me as curiously unfair. Critical hackles have never been raised by other stories about mad folk in Melville's literary generation; and of these there was no shortage—derangement being another of the phenomena by which that generation unknowingly announced its affinity with the modernist imagination and its sense of the unhinging nature of human life and relationships. The man who calls himself William Wilson in Poe's tale has plainly abandoned his reason; the narrator of *Ligeia*, as has been said, is certifiably insane; and Roderick Usher—to judge from the poem "The Haunted Palace," which serves as a musical version of his experiences—almost literally has bats in his belfry. Hawthorne encourages us to entertain grave doubts about the sanity of Wakefield, the self-begotten outcast of the universe, and about the black-veiled minister and young Goodman Brown. Nor has much opposition been expressed to the mad prophets and whaling captains, the lackwits and men of paralyzed mind, and the mentally agitated naval officers that show up in Melville's other writings.

In any event, the behavior of Pierre Glendinning, even if we allow it (as I do not) to be judged psychopathic, would be entirely in keeping with the recurring psychic condition within the novel's evoked social world. When Pierre, devastated by the revelation of his father's youthful misstep, declares, "I will be a raver," he is no doubt recalling that Pierre II, as it had been put, "died a raver," died raving madly about some daughter or other. People go mad in this book with appalling regularity. Pierre's mother, soon after her son's departure, takes abrupt leave of her senses and dies insane. Lucy Tartan, after she has been waked up by Pierre one morning with the news that he is marrying another girl, is for a spell anything but in her proper mind. Seated silently in the dim New York lodgings, Pierre is haunted by his memory of a story involving a schoolmate of Lucy's: a sort of triangle of madness. The fiancé of this girl was persuaded that a second lady was going out of her wits for love of him; whereupon, "his conscience insanely upbraid[ing] him," as Pierre formulates it, "the demented youth" married the second lady, and Lucy's jilted friend consequently "came to a lunatic's death on his account." When Fred Tartan, seconded by Pierre's cousin Glen Stanley, comes to New York in pursuit of his sister Lucy, the two have it in mind to declare before the world that Lucy has been driven hopelessly mad and is hence no longer protected by the law; "the sweet girl is mad," Glen Stanley shouts as he tries to carry Lucy off bodily from the Apostles. And brother Fred, in Pierre's image of him, is "a noble soul made mad by a sweet sister's shame," a person capable of the kind of "murders [that] are done by maniacs."

The fact is, the whole world of the novel *Pierre* has been invaded by madness. The deranged scheme of things is synecdochically imaged by two successive milieus, two instances of what Kenneth Burke might call the act-scene ratio. The first is the strange large house in the country—somewhere in America, Isabel thinks—a place where, to her dim remembering, she spent "five, six, perhaps seven years." It is a house full of "strangely demented people," Isabel faintly recalls. Incoherent human noises could be heard at all hours: "shrieks, howls, laughter, blessings, prayers, oaths, hymns, and all audible confusion issu[ed] from all the chambers of the house." To her childlike gaze, some of the occupants seemed "composed of countenance, but wandering of mind"; others were haranguing the walls or sticking their tongues out at the air and trying to strike it. In context, this rural lunatic asylum—or, in the reviewer's phrase, "lunatic hospital"—becomes a grotesque metaphor for the deranged setting in which children, in this novel's vision, are given their first taste of adult life.

And the second is like unto it: the police station, or "watch house," where, on their nighttime arrival in New York City, Pierre leaves Isabel and the servant Della in safekeeping for an hour while he goes off in search of his cousin Glen Stanley. When he returns, the watch house has been transformed into a scene of "indescribable disorder, [in which] frantic, diseased-looking men and women of all colors, and in all imaginable flaunting, immodest, grotesque, and shattered dresses, were leaping, yelling, and cursing around him": all of them, to the stunned Pierre, seemingly caught up in "some crazy and wanton dance." What had happened during Pierre's absence was that a detachment of police had herded into the station the drunken denizens of a "notorious stew," which they had raided in the midst of "some outrageous orgie." But, again in context, the insane spectacle takes on even more ominous contours: the maniacally disordered environment in which young manhood and young womanhood must attempt to chart a way; the place of institutionalized safety, the watch house, become a scene of madness and terror. Herman Melville's intention, in *Pierre*, we gradually make out, was precisely to create what the exasperated critic called a "mad mosaic." Upon such a scene, Pierre's behavior, while undeniabley eccentric and inconstant, has at least a measure of nobility and idealism. It can even be argued, though it would take a lot of arguing, that Pierre, like the navigator in *Catch-22*, is the one truly sane figure in a senseless world, and that the mosaic has been designed to make this evident.

Modernist fiction, heaven knows, is sufficiently populated by the demented and the estranged—by the likes of Mr. Kurtz, Septimus Smith, Benjy Compson, Adrian Leverkuehn, and more others than one can name. But it is hard to think of any later American novel that portrays the human condition itself as afflicted by madness. (I say "American," since in Melville's own lifetime a comparable image was maneuvered into view in the last large segment of Dostoyevsky's *The Possessed*.) Even in the Bowery of Stephen Crane's *Maggie*—where outbursts of murderous rage are the order of the day, and where the hallucinated air, like that of Isabel's madhouse, is filled with a "confused chorus" of "howls and curses, groans and shrieks"—it is warfare rather than madness that is the norm of behavior. Melville, in *Pierre*, goes beyond such modernist recordings of intermittent derangement to suggest that our entire human world has become a planetary home for the insane. Nor has postmodernist fiction, for all its consciousness of the radically disjointed, really caught up with him yet: Ellison's *Invisible Man*, Heller's *Catch-22*, and Pynchon's *The Crying of Lot 49* are, on various orders of achievement, comically inspired efforts to do so.

Melville's mad mosaic, I venture, was built on the supposition that the great traditional sources of order and control in human life—the family, social cohesion, the Christian ethic, the potent philosophies, literature itself—had pretty much lost their authority; and that what was being ushered in (so felt this supreme American master of the apocalyptic) was the age not of reason but of the loss of reason. I shall push on to these matters in a moment, but at this stage I should enter a mild demurrer, in part to explain the recurring postponement of topic from which this discourse inevitably suffers.

It is true that *Pierre* abounds in instances of derangement, but the novel does not always remember that this is so; it has too many other things that claim its interest. The very richness of *Pierre* is troublesome to its nature. It is a distracted novel, a novel that tests, abandons, and returns to a series of fictional motifs and possibilities. If these various aspects, as I have said, at once thicken and modify, they also jostle against and displace each other. The same might be said of the novel's figurative language, which is now maritime, now military, now pastoral, now supernatural: a wild disorder of imagery, some of it overpowering, and all of it reflecting as in a crazy house a human landscape that is flying apart. We can recognize the intention and honor it; in our contemporary moment of affection for artistic disunity and the explosion of form, we may even be tempted to idolize it. But we can also regret, or at least I can regret, that this towering genius was working without literary precedents or companionships relevant to his purpose. I will risk the outrageous proposition that *Pierre*, as a work of fiction, would have been even grander if Melville had had before him such disparate examples as Nietzsche and Henry James, Conrad and Faulkner.

Be that as it may. Another source of the pervasive moral disorder in *Pierre*, so it seems, is the nearly intolerable pressure and the unhealthful closeness of the human relationships. This aspect, at its most intense, takes the form of incest; but incest (there is an analogy here to the treatment of madness) is only the condition to which all other involvements appear to be tending. If, in reading Jane Austen's *Emma*, we have the sense that everyone is everybody else's brother-in-law, in reading *Pierre* we have rather the impression that all the characters are close blood relations and bear a disturbing physical resemblance to one another.

Pierre Glendinning is beset by family. He seeks to define himself in—and to escape from—a context composed of parents, cousins, second cousins, aunts, an alleged half-sibling; no hero or heroine in a Victorian novel was more smothered by kinship. Connections proliferate, or try to. Pierre's fiancée, Lucy Tartan, is the daughter of his father's oldest and closest friend. The minister Mr. Falsgrave is his would-be stepfather, and Mrs. Tartan his would-be mother-in-law. When Pierre breaks with Lucy, he is succeeded in the role of fiancé by none other than Cousin Glen. And when Lucy enters the ménage at the Apostles, she does so in the guise of Pierre's cousin, even claiming that there actually was "some connection between our families" traced out by her mother, "some indirect cousinship." Melville does not even scruple to inform us that the elderly person who delivered the chair portrait to the adolescent Pierre at Saddle Meadows was a former suitor of his Aunt Dorothea and now her chatty neighbor. There are no *strangers* in this oppressively confined world, no new and unrelated individuals who appear along the way, bringing with them fresh human options. (The exception, if you will, is Plotinus Plinlimmon, a phantom figure borrowed in advance, so one feels, from *The Crying of Lot 49*, and the deviser of a moral doctrine that simply enlarges the novel's continuing distinction between fixed time and relative time.)

Little wonder that Pierre laments to Isabel about "the myriad alliances and criss-crossings among mankind, the infinite entanglement of all social things." In *Pierre,* as Richard Brodhead has remarked, society is the adversary of all human effort.

Familial closeness announces itself, as Melville never wearies of pointing out, in family resemblances. Almost the first thing we hear about Pierre is that he looks very much like his mother; but his Aunt Dorothea, gazing at the boy's features, finds in him "the likeness, the very soul" of his father. Yet Isabel, too, we recall, detected in her mirrored face a strange likeness to that of the gentleman who whispered "father" to her. On the old axiom about things equal to the same things, we may wish to imagine that Pierre and Isabel are also to a degree look-alikes or doubles. The doubling process reaches a climax in the novel's penultimate chapter, when Pierre, dreaming of the incestuous titan Enceladus, suddenly sees in the fury-driven giant of his dream not the face of Enceladus but "his own duplicate face and feature magnifiedly gleam[ing] upon him with prophetic discomfiture and woe." We are still working out the implications of this nightmare self-reflection when in the succeeding sequence the entire pattern of resemblances is both dizzyingly congested and cast into irresolvable doubt.

Pierre escorts Isabel and Lucy to a New York gallery that is displaying some recently imported European paintings. One of these is a copy of the portrait of Beatrice Cenci by Guido Reni, before which Lucy stands motionless for many moments; and though Melville's prose remains silent about the possibility, the face of Beatrice, as best we can determine, is very like that of Lucy Tartan; Lucy may be thought to be staring, with unspoken reactions, at her own image. But it is a second painting, meanwhile, that separately agitates Pierre and Isabel, a painting that so exactly faces the Cenci from an opposite wall that the two portraits seem (Melville says) to be in secret communion with each other—as though (this is the reader's guess) they might be the likenesses of a brother and a sister. This second painting is listed as "No. 99. A stranger's head, by an unknown hand." Has Melville, after all and at the last minute, introduced a stranger to open up the atmosphere? Hardly; or rather, not quite; or rather, no and yes. For to Pierre, the stranger resembles nothing so much as his youthful bachelor father in the chair portrait; to Isabel, his is the face of the mature gentleman who used to visit her. It might be added, in parentheses, that, to the harried reader, the unknown has a good deal in common with the exotic and Europeanized face of Glen Stanley.

But just as we are feeling permanently trapped inside a hall of mirrors, Melville opens a way out for us. The very fact that the painting is that of a stranger, and a European at that, brings Pierre to question the likenesses; they are probably a matter of pure coincidence, he reflects, especially since (here the reader experiences a lurch of reason) the painted face may be altogether imaginary, a piece of invention. The whole business of resemblances seems suddenly dubious; the reader, doing his share, realizes that Lucy Tartan, whatever the physical similarity may be, has nothing whatever in common with Beatrice Cenci and her burden of "incest and parricide"; and it seems quite fitting to us that Pierre, beginning to question everything, now questions the relationship for which he has staked his life and sacrificed his fortune. "How did he *know* that Isabel was his sister?" Pierre asks himself.

The final spasmodic pages of *Pierre* enact a process of inexorable thematic demolition. "Deconstruction" is too weak a word for it. The motif of incest, which had gained a seemingly overpowering momentum, is shredded before our eyes. The narrative had begun with the stressed and somewhat shy-making suggestion of a double incestuous relation between Pierre and his mother. The erotically disturbed atmosphere of the house at Saddle Meadows may well, it appears in retrospect, have prepared Pierre to accept Isabel with open arms as his half-sister and to have excited in him a strong sexual desire for her—a desire that, as I read the self-erasing prose of the account, was fulfilled in the New York lodgings. And it may thereafter be the relation consummated over many a winter evening that arouses in Pierre's sleeping mind the dream of Enceladus: Enceladus, who (in Melville's homegrown mythology) was the product of a pattern of incest unbroken through three generations. "Old Titan's self was the son of incestuous Coelus and Terra . . . and Titan married his mother Terra, another and accumulatively incestuous match. And thereof Enceladus was one issue. So Enceladus was both the son and grandson of incest." To this the narrator adds, in language whose implication we try hard not to accept, that the dream "generated there the doubly incestuous Enceladus within him," within Pierre. Half a dozen pages later, the multileveled incestuous framework is rendered hopelessly problematic, if not utterly shattered.

More largely, it comes to us, the spreading family network is dissipated: in those last pages we attend to the accented fall of the house of Glendinning. When Pierre shoots and kills his cousin Glen Stanley, the narrator observes that "his own hand had extinguished his house in slaughtering the only unoutlawed human being by the name of Glendinning." Pierre II, Aunt Dorothea, second cousin Ralph, Mary Glendinning, and now Cousin Glen: all are dead, and outlawed Pierre that same evening will die of poison, preceded by his "indirect cousin" Lucy and followed by his maybe half-sister Isabel.

Pierre is, in the end, a novel that systematically subverts the Victorian model. The habitual movement of that model was to disclose and also to create an intricate network of family relationships: a community of parents and children, of uncles and aunts and cousins, of relatives by law, of spouses about to become new parents. *Pierre* works in quite the opposite direction. The great dramatic gestures are aimed not at strengthening but at dissolving the family ties: Mary Glendinning disavows her son, and Mrs. Tartan her daughter; Glen Stanley disavows his cousin Pierre, and Pierre forthrightly disavows him back. Marriages do not take place, cousins are murdered, families are wiped out. Melville's imaginative purpose in this regard—his essentially anti-Victorian vision both of human life and of the novel as a genre—

would be shared by D. H. Lawrence, who saw to the extinction of the Crich family and the sundering of the Brangwens in *Women in Love* as one way of declaring the demise of Victorian fiction, and by Faulkner, who obliterated the Sutpen clan, except for Jim Bond, by violence and disease in *Absalom, Absalom!*

Melville's revealed and strenuous aversion to the forms and conventions of the traditional family narrative brings me to the final aspect of *Pierre* that I want to consider. This is, exactly, its novelistic aspect: along with Melville's conception, at this stage, of the novelistic mode, Victorian, American, and otherwise, and the profound contempt for the cultural environment that informs the story at every moment. I can touch only briefly on these concerns, though it is here that *Pierre* is most markedly modernist and most courageously premature in its modernist reachings.

Lionel Trilling, in one of his most elegant essays,* spoke of "a certain theme which appears frequently in modern literature—so frequently, indeed, and in so striking a manner, that it may be said to constitute one of the shaping and controlling ideas of our epoch. I can identify it," Trilling continued, "by calling it the disenchantment of our culture with culture itself—it seems to me that the characteristic element of modern literature, or at least of the most highly developed modern literature, is the bitter line of hostility to civilization that runs through it." If we rummage among modernist novels we will find every confirmation of Trilling's proposition, and *Women in Love,* with its large-scale image of a moribund industrial civilization, is probably the supreme example, more so, I should say, than *Nostromo* or *The Magic Mountain* or *Absalom, Absalom! Pierre* goes beyond all of these in the wholeheartedness of its cultural loathing; and doing so, it may beget more problems for its author than he can easily handle.

Two young college students, calling upon Melville in 1859, found him in a state of absolute disgust with "civilisation in general, and our

---

*"On the Teaching of Modern Literature," in *Beyond Culture* (1965).

Christendom in particular." *Pierre* was written out of that disgust of spirit, in a series of what might be termed cultural disavowals that parallel those of the family kind. Pierre has no sooner concocted a design to have Isabel accepted at Saddle Meadows when he realizes, with an inward groan, that his mother is simply a well-cushioned bigot, inflexibly conventional; his already battered filial piety expires on the spot. As his mind ranges and rages onward, anticipating (even before he has heard Isabel's story) the obdurate resistance his design will meet elsewhere, Pierre comes swiftly to deplore and despise not only the family institution but the entire fabric of social morality— what he now sees as "the heart-vacancies of the conventional life." He instructs himself, fairly stammering in an alliterative paroxysm: "Eternally this day deface in me the detested and distorted images of all the convenient lies and duty-subterfuges of the diving and ducking moralities of this earth."

He turns in despair to the local religious resource, the Reverend Mr. Falsgrave, in the hope that Falsgrave in his "Christian character" might give him honest and sincere advice. But Falsgrave, though the representative of that ideal of Christian gentlemanliness which Pierre's father had sought to inculcate in him, has no answer for Pierre and asks to be excused. Pierre departs quite civilly (he is not nearly as rude to Falsgrave as Newton Arvin indicates), saying simply: "Thou hast no earnest and world-disdaining counsel for me." So much for Christendom and the worldly church. The great philosophers are next excoriated. Riding the stagecoach to New York and confronting the monumental question of how to reconcile the experienced world and his own soul's yearnings, Pierre is seized with hatred of that philosophic "guild of self-impostors"—Plato, Spinoza, and Goethe are singled out—who claim to have found the secret of reconciliation. Later, in the pages of Pierre's novel, Plato and Spinoza have become reduced to chattering sophomoric apes, and Goethe has become an "inconceivable coxcomb."

As children of modernism, we confidently expect that, after all those cultural rejections, *literature* will emerge as the last best possibility for the seeker after truth and understanding. And indeed, it is at about this point that the narrator makes the stupefying disclosure that Pierre was a writer, has been one all along, and had in fact "written many a fugitive thing" that had won him credit and compliments and the applause of "the always intelligent and extremely discriminating public." Some of that applause is quoted by the narrator as an index to the literary taste of the time, the reverence for the genteel and traditional, the rejection of anything astonishing or new or vigorous. In New York, Pierre decides to take his hitherto unsuspected writing talent seriously, and begins on a novel—a book that, like the novel *Pierre*, will be written out of a radical disillusion with the entire civilized world, including the intelligent and discriminating public.

We are once again inside a hall of mirrors. The novel that the novelist Melville tells us Pierre is writing is about a novelist named Vivia who is writing a novel: a premature species of that infinite literary regression introduced into modernism by André Gide and brought to culmination in John Barth's funhouse of fiction and more recently in *Letters*. But for Pierre Glendinning, there is one insurmountable obstacle: the more he complicates the novel-writing process, the more he is aware that by its very nature fiction is incapable of telling the truth about life. He had realized as much after listening to the first half of Isabel's story when he perceived that the plot of her life could never be unraveled; and moreover that all novels, pretending as they do to unravel "the complex web of life," were a tissue of lies. They were "false, inverted attempts at systematizing eternally unsystematizable elements." In one of those characteristic Melvillian displays of verbal firepower, Pierre then deposes that

> not always doth life's beginning gloom conclude in gladness; that wedding-bells peal not ever in the last scenes "of life's fifth act"; that while the countless scribes of common novels laboriously spin vails of mystery, only to complacently clear them

up at last; yet the profounder emanations of the human mind . . . never unravel their own intricacies, and have no proper endings; but in imperfect, unanticipated, and disappointing sequels (as mutilated stumps), hurry to abrupt interminglings with the eternal tides of time and fate.

So Pierre—speaking, I should say, for the Melville of 1852—has even been brought to repudiate the literary art, the art of fiction.

Pierre's novel about Vivia does end up as a series of mutilated stumps—or rather (from the bits we get of it), anguished little cries of a lacerated spirit. But the same cannot be said of Melville's four-hundred-page novel about Pierre Glendinning. There is a gathering critical opinion, these days, that what Melville undertook in *Pierre* was to confront and lay bare not only the falseness and fictionality of all novels and of literature in general, but the fictionality as well—the inveterately lying and self-deluding nature—of human life and speech and conduct. In this view (which to a real extent I share), the early sunlit scenes at Saddle Meadows, for example, are not only a parody of sentimental fiction and its lisping neo-medieval mode of dialogue, but also representations of the rosy, false, and fictional vision of life entertained and acted on by Pierre and Lucy. Similarly, Isabel's memoirs can be seen not only as a parody of Gothic romance but as expressing Isabel's self-Gothicizing personality, her Gothic fictionaliz-ing of experience. And so further. The most preposterous stretches of narrative rhetoric, it might be argued, are not signs of Melville's loss of control or contempt for control, but rather efforts to convey the flailing absurdities of Pierre's inward language of thought. *Pierre,* in this reading, is not a novel that moves from fictions and lies to truth and understanding, but that replaces one fiction by another: Pierre as Isabel's champion and would-be novelist in New York is playing no less a self-created fictional role than when he was romancing with Lucy in the hills above Saddle Meadows.*

*This interpretation of *Pierre* is vigorously argued in an essay by Professor Bryan Mihm, to whom I am much indebted.

What is appealing about this view of the novel is that it discovers a significant and coherent (if unorthodox) movement through the successive phases of the action, and at the same time goes far to rescue the narrative language from the charges that have been brought against it ever since a wittily inimical reviewer in early 1853 held that in *Pierre*, "Language is drunken and reeling. Style is antipodical and marches on its head." There is indeed a strong central strain of satire in the narrative, at times a kind of ferocious playfulness; any discussion of *Pierre*, in my opinion, does well to reflect in some degree the novel's wilful comicality of treatment. The point can be made more forcefully: *Pierre* is satirical or it is nothing—nothing bearable at least, nothing readable. It is parodic, teasing, cunning, subversive, or, as Newton Arvin implies, it is a literary and psychological disaster. For a writer disgusted with the range of inherited and contemporary culture and who had lost faith even in the art of fiction as then practiced, both in America and in England, what recourse was there except satire first and last—satire bitter and extravagant by turns?

And yet the account just cited, I venture, indicates what Melville *wanted* to accomplish, and what, if he had undertaken to write *Pierre* seventy or eighty years later, he would have accomplished. The author of *Pierre*, like the author of *The Blithedale Romance*, had an extraordinary premonition of how narrative strategies might be deployed in a situation of radical disrepair. It is only to acknowledge Melville's imaginative boldness the more if we say that he was up to something for which the novelistic program had not yet been worked out, and would not begin to be really until, to pick a date at random, Conrad's novel of 1904, *Nostromo*.

Let no note of critical condescension be audible here. *Pierre*, clotted though it may be, is much more than an honorable experiment; it is a unique and staggering work of fiction. It looms well above most of those modernist novels which, with similar strategies for similar purposes, had a happier literary atmosphere to grow in.

(1981)

E dith Wharton's long life—1862 to 1937—passed through and well beyond the great age of letter writing in America. In one perspective, that age may be seen as coming to an end with the death of Henry James in 1916 and of Henry Adams two years later. A different portent of the art's demise was offered by Edith Wharton herself in a letter of early 1914 to Corinne Robinson, the sister of Theodore Roosevelt, apologizing for not writing during a recent visit to New York and explaining that she had become so addicted to telephoning and telegraphing that she had lost the ability to express herself on paper. She soon recovered the ability, needless to say. Edith Wharton belongs to the American company of prolific and eloquent letter writers; and there are special qualities, special intensities of personal involvement and exposure, that set her letters apart from those of most others in that company.

Scarcely a day passed, in her maturity and in good health, when she did not compose and dispatch half a dozen letters, many of them carrying forward ongoing conversations. (Returning once from a short trip, in 1924, she found sixty-five letters awaiting her: the incoming mail over three days.) There are extant about four thousand letters from Edith Wharton that might be suitably drawn upon for a published collection. At least as many more exist and are accessible—mainly in Beinecke Library, Yale—but these deal largely with routine business matters, and were dictated to and in some cases probably written by one or another of Mrs. Wharton's secretaries.

Of the usable four thousand, we have after an elaborate and always fascinating process, chosen a little fewer than four hundred, about one in ten. We could well wish the number were higher, and could in fact, without much difficulty, have included up to one hundred more, but at some risk of repetition and perhaps an occasional slackening of appeal. The letters selected are intended to show Edith Wharton at her epistolary best and most characteristic, and in the striking variety of her voices, her changeable states of being, the modes and phases of her major relationships. One source of frustration to us, it might be added, was Edith Wharton's habit, in her later years, of embedding a passage of great charm or wit in an otherwise rather desultory letter. An anthology of these gemlike moments might be in order at some future date.

The largest surviving correspondences, as it happens, are those beginning in 1893 with the several editors at Charles Scribner's Sons (now held at Firestone Library, Princeton), and with Bernard Berenson, the distinguished Italian Renaissance art connoisseur and historian, and Mary Berenson. There are more than six hundred of the latter: happily for the rest of us, Berenson, with the help of his longtime associate Nicky Mariano, kept and catalogued every letter ever written to him by anyone of importance over the better part of a century. There are also about 360 letters, from the early 1900s, to Gaillard Lapsley, the astute Rhode Island–born don of medieval history at Cambridge, who would eventually be Edith Wharton's literary executor and the initiator of the Wharton archive at Yale. To swell the archives unexpectedly, there came into view a few years ago at the University of Texas in Austin—we will look more closely at this event—three hundred letters from Edith Wharton to her sometime lover, the Paris-based American journalist William Morton Fullerton.

The survival of letters is a chancy affair. Edith Wharton was thirty-eight years old, had been publishing fiction for nine years, and was the author of a book on house decoration and a well-received volume of short stories before someone other than her Scribners editors thought her letters worth retaining. This was Sara Norton, the literate and discerning daughter of Charles Eliot Norton, Harvard professor and scholar; among the 240 letters held on to—and, where necessary, dated—by Sara Norton are some of the finest Edith Wharton wrote before the First World War. Some correspondences known to have existed have vanished: like that with Percy Lubbock, the gifted English writer with whom, after years of friendship and patronage, Edith had a falling-out; and with Geoffrey Scott, the author of *The Architecture of Humanism,* who was, unwittingly, one of the causes of the falling-out.

Henry James burned all but a handful of the many letters (170?) Edith Wharton wrote him between 1902 and 1915. But Edith Wharton was the one to destroy her letters to Walter Berry, the American lawyer who was her adviser and companion for thirty years. She went to Berry's apartment in Paris after his death in 1927, retrieved her letters to him, and burned them. At a reasonable calculation, there must have been four hundred letters and more to be consumed. Most collections of letters in the modern period suffer from deprivations of this sort, and it is well to remember that the self-portraits emerging in the letters are inevitably limited or distorted by the simple phenomenon of what has survived, not to mention what has been editorially selected therefrom.

Edith Wharton's family clan—Stevenses, Rhinelanders, Joneses, New Yorkers all—were not themselves much given to letter writing as a serious exercise. In this they differed, for example, from the Jameses

(William, Henry, Alice), who were brought up with a high regard for the practice and who regularly congratulated one another on the brilliance or vivacity of a letter just received. The American ancestry of Edith Jones reached back to the early eighteenth century, to Ebenezer Stevens, a gallant artillery commander and a fellow officer of the Marquis de Lafayette during the Revolutionary War, and to William and Frederick Rhinelander, who built a flourishing business in sugar and shipbuilding in the 1780s. It included assorted wealthy and influential Schermerhorns, among them Edith's second cousin Caroline Schermerhorn, who married William Backhouse Astor and managed to establish herself as *the* Mrs. Astor. What it did not include, as far as one make out, was anything like a literary or artistic energy, any sustained interest in letters in both the broad and the literal meaning of the word.

The closest one gets to such an interest is with Edith's father, George Frederic Jones, a Columbia College graduate of upper-middle-class background whose comfortable income derived from city land-holdings. George Frederic read with some diligence in history and philosophy, and he had a genuine if baffled fondness for poetry—a tendency, so his daughter was to feel, that had been stifled by her mother, Lucretia Rhinelander Jones. "I imagine there was a time," Edith Wharton wrote, looking back, "when his rather rudimentary love [of poetry] might have been developed had he any one with whom to share it. But my mother's matter-of-factness must have shrivelled any such buds of fancy." It was George Frederic, anyhow, who taught Edith to read, led her at a very young age to memorize and recite *The Idylls of the King,* and encouraged any symptom she might display of literary enthusiasm.

But the prevailing atmosphere in the Jones household and in the society—the old guard, the "good old families" of lengthy lineage and cautious habits—to which the Joneses belonged was one of indifference to literary expression and even suspicion of it. Edith's mother apparently did see to the private printing of her daughter's verses in

1878, but this was a solitary gesture. Neither Lucretia nor Edith's brothers—the remote Freddy, the kindly but unimaginative Harry— seem to have lent any significant support to Edith's shy efforts at literary composition in any form.

All the more, in after years, did Edith Wharton respond with pleasure if anyone spoke admiringly of one of her letters. In the winter of 1912, Bernard Berenson, writing from his Villa I Tatti outside Florence, remarked casually that he had received a "good letter" from her. Edith was much gratified. Her "epistolary art," she wrote in reply, had "never before been commended"; and as one result she found herself consciously striving to emulate the praised performance. "Beginning a letter to you," she went on, "has the excitement of a literary adventure as well as the joy of communicating with a friend." In typical fashion, she then deprecated; "Unluckily for literature, I always forget the former, and only remember the latter pleasure when I'm under way." As though to illustrate the point, she veered off into an inquiry about some trifling accident Berenson had suffered, and wondered whether he had incurred it while trying to scale a wall.

Early and late, the letters of Edith Wharton oscillate between the literary and the friendly: between the more or less consciously composed and the gracefully expressed at one moment, and the gossipy, the querying, the commiserating at another. One of her last letters, to Mary Berenson, concludes a lyrical outburst about her unabated pleasure in "this wonderful adventure of living"—"I'm an incorrigible life-lover & life-wonderer"—with a sympathetic reference to the illness of a sister of one of Berenson's Italian associates. In this respect, the letters mirror the life. A comparable alternation was indicated in a remark to Sara Norton in September 1902. "Zwei Seelen wohnen, ach, in meine[r] Brust," Edith said, quoting from Goethe's *Faust* ("Two souls, alas, do dwell within my breast"); "& the Compleat Housekeeper has had the upper hand for the last weeks." Stories and articles by Edith Wharton were appearing everywhere in American periodicals;

her novel *The Valley of Decision* was winning accolades on all sides and was selling briskly (thirty-five thousand copies by the end of the year); she had just finished the translation of a play by the German dramatist Sudermann. But her literary life had to slow down for a period while she devoted her energies to settling herself, her husband, Teddy Wharton, and the staff of servants and gardeners in The Mount, the new home in Lenox, Massachusetts.

The reflection of the two souls in the shifting rhythm of Edith Wharton's letters suggests what has been argued elsewhere, that letters by American women, and among them the literarily gifted, tend to give much more attention to the human concerns of daily life than do those of their male counterparts. For the attuned reader, this is always part of the attraction: in this case, the spectacle in letter form of Edith Wharton moving between a vigorous play of mind and imagination or of highly charged feeling and the horde of demanding and sometimes harrowing practical problems, professional and domestic, with which she had to cope virtually unaided.

Edith Wharton, as one might say, was nothing if not a dialectical personality. In the fall of 1907, she received from Robert Grant, the Boston judge and a novelist whose work she esteemed, a long and balanced analysis of her novel *The Fruit of the Tree*. She was happy, she replied, that he had liked the construction of the book, but agreed with him that in the interest of firm construction, she had allowed her characters to remain little more than "mere *building-material*." She then drew a distinction—a trifle muddled in formulation, but clear and compelling in essence—between *conceiving* a novelistic subject like a man, "that is, rather more architectonically & dramatically than most women," and *executing* the subject like a woman, via a marshaling of "small incidental effects" and a technique of "episodical characterisation."

One could go far into Edith Wharton's fiction writing by tracing within it the deployment of these two narrative modes: the masculine and the feminine, the dramatic and the accumulative. In her letter writing as well, we can observe the alternation and the mingling. A letter to Berenson from North Africa in April 1914, as an example, moves naturally from the evocation of an atmosphere like that of an "unexpurgated page of the Arabian Nights" and the delineation of "effeminacy, obesity, obscenity or black savageness" in the native populace to a moment of almost shattering drama: the sheer sexual terror Mrs. Wharton experienced when she awoke in the darkness of her Timgad hotel room to find a strange man bending over her. The letters to Henry James about visits to the battlefronts in the winter of 1915 are dramatic enough in all truth, and at the same time are enlivened by a succession of incidental effects. In the 1920s and later, as Edith Wharton's taste in fiction grew to favor less the tightly composed Jamesian mode and more the Victorian novel, and especially the gossipy narratives of Anthony Trollope, her letters became looser, more leisurely and spacious, more filled with solicitous inquiries, reports about friends, random anecdotes and musings.

The "masculine" and the "feminine" sides of Edith Wharton in her letters can be detected in other ways, but a clarifying word should be offered in advance. It is, of course, woefully misleading to say of her, as one or two onlookers have been tempted to do (for example, Janet Malcolm in a New York *Times* article on the Library of America volume of Edith Wharton's fiction), that she hated, feared, and distrusted women. Such an idea could derive only from an ignorance of her character and personal life, and from a doctrinaire misreading or simple nonreading of the work. As to the work, one could compile a list of female characters, from Fulvia Vivaldi in *The Valley of Decision* to Laura Testvalley in the posthumous novel *The Buccaneers*, whom Edith Wharton depicts with a sad and protective admiration. Among her personal relationships, one does remark the unrelenting and deepening rancor toward Lady Sybil Cutting, after her successive marriages to Geoffrey Scott and Percy Lubbock. But this was without parallel elsewhere, and it always had a touch of the darkly comic and hyperbolic.

On the other hand, it would be hardly less misleading to suggest that Edith Wharton was a feminist, at least in the current understanding of the term. She had no interest or belief in institutional reform, and rather shied away from literary women who did, like the English novelist May Sinclair. The latter, almost exactly Edith Wharton's age, was indeed an active supporter of women's suffrage as well as an intelligent propagandist for psychoanalysis. Mrs. Wharton managed twice not to meet May Sinclair, despite pressing invitations, during the London social whirl of December 1908; and on a later occasion she alluded to May Sinclair's recent novel as pantingly didactic.

What Edith Wharton did, obviously, as a superb and intuitive social historian, was to dramatize the condition of women, which usually meant the repression and the entrapment of women, in the social worlds she lived in. Narrative after narrative culminates in the settled pathos or, as sometimes, the tragedy of that condition; but, again, the letters also testify to the informing vision. To Sara Norton, who wrote in October 1908 to ask whether she might not have done more over the years for her father, then on his deathbed, Edith replied in a gust of impatience: "Alas, I should like to get up on the house-top & cry to all who come after us: 'Take your own life, every one of you!' " A few months later, when her English friend John Hugh Smith spoke severely about a play, recently seen, which (he thought) weighted its plot too heavily on the side of the discontented wife, Edith Wharton rallied to the cause. She mentioned "a few other neurotic women who were discontented with their husbands & relations," naming Clytemnestra, Phaedra, Iseult, Pia Tolomei (in Dante's *Purgatorio*), and Anna Karenina; and went on to contend that "among all the tangles of this mortal coil," none contained "tighter knots to undo" and suggested "more tugging, & pain, & diversified elements of misery, than the marriage tie." Her point claimed to be literary: that the marriage tie with its tugging and pain was peculiarly " 'made to the hand' " of the dramatist; but the expression was of a woman whose compassion for the marital misery of women in general had been sharpened by her own wretched marriage and her adulterous relationship with Morton Fullerton.*

So much being said, it can be remarked that Edith Wharton had a decidedly masculine strain in her, even if the adjective be taken in a largely metaphoric and associational sense. Witness her keen interest in science and her self-declared role as the priestess of reason. During the early days in Paris, her letters are sprinkled with allusions to books on Darwinism, heredity, new developments in biology. She denounced William James's skepticism about the scientific mentality and what she called (it is wittily unfair) his "psychological-pietistic juggling." The phrase occurs in a letter to Sara Norton in February 1906, after she had read a philosophical tome "with a 'foreword' by le dit James." With the first page, she said, she was in the midst of "the familiar jargon," and she quoted a sentence: " 'Humanity will never be satisfied with scientific knowledge to explain its inward relation to reality.'— What other kind of knowledge is it capable of receiving? Oh, dear— oh, how slowly the wheels turn."

Edith Wharton's view of William James was no doubt colored by a possessive resentment at Henry James's devotion to his older brother. The feeling erupts when she writes to Morton Fullerton in 1910, after visiting with the suicidally depressed Henry James, that all the James family had been "the victims of the neurotic, unreliable Wm James," and that Henry's breakdown was "very different . . . from the chronic flares and twitches of the other brother—William o' the wisp James."

*The victimization of women continued to be an important theme in Edith Wharton's fiction to the end; but the compassionate attitude rather disappears from the *letters* in the later years. Occasionally, indeed, an acerbic note can be heard creeping into her comments in this area. Elizabeth Ammons, in her sensitive study *Edith Wharton's Argument with America* (1980), suggests that it was the overwhelming impact of the war and its threat to the traditional values she cherished that brought on Edith Wharton's conservatism—in general, and with regard to women—during her final decades.

But along with the jealousy, there was a more purely intellectual aversion: the Enlightenment side of Edith Wharton was offended by William James's modernist philosophical flexibility.

Something of the same found expression in the message of warning she sent to Berenson in February 1922, when her young friend and protégée, the delightful Philomène de Lévis-Mirepoix, was about to join the Berensons for a trip to Egypt. They would both like Philomène, she said, and they could help greatly in the mental training she so badly needed. Her "charming eager helpless intelligence" had been filled with "third-rate flashy rubbish." Above all, Mary Berenson was not to befuddle Philomène "with Freudianism and all its jargon. . . . What she wants is to develop the *conscious*, & not grub after the subconscious. She wants to be taught first to see, to attend, to reflect."

All this bespeaks the aspect of Edith Wharton that Fullerton took cognizance of when he slyly addressed her as "Cher Ami." But the opposite aspect was always present, or always ready to be summoned up: what we may perhaps define as "the feminine-mystical mind," borrowing the phrase from *le dit* William James, who (in an essay of the 1890s) contrasted it with "the scientific-academic mind." And this aspect, this mind, was never more evident than in the letters to Morton Fullerton.

The very existence of these letters is a cause for astonishment, it having long been assumed that Fullerton yielded at last to the entreaties of his former mistress and burned the lot of them. Morton Fullerton died in 1952, in Paris, at the age of eighty-six. Some time before his death, he sold twenty-two letters from Edith Wharton (and a great many from Henry James) to Houghton Library at Harvard; these date from 1916, at least five years after the end of the love affair proper. It was the letters known to have been written during the peak of the affair, in 1908–1910, that were thought to have been destroyed. (A sizable batch of Fullerton documents from other sources, including passionate communications from the ranee of Sarawak, turned up in the late

1960s, but it contained nothing from Edith Wharton.) Then, in 1980, some three hundred letters from Edith Wharton to Morton Fullerton—written between 1907 and 1915, and the great bulk of them during the critical period—were offered for sale by a Dutch firm of booksellers acting for an antiquarian bookdealer in Paris.

The collection was purchased by the Harry Ransom Humanities Research Center at the University of Texas in Austin. The university's *Library Chronicle* devoted a special issue in September 1985 to this new holding, printing twenty-six letters selected and splendidly edited by Professor Alan Gribben. This is the only instance, before the present volume, of the publication of letters by Edith Wharton. But precisely where the precious Fullerton papers lay hidden or forgotten for nearly three decades, and how and why they happened to come into sight just when they did: these questions remain shrouded in the intriguing mystery that attends other aspects of the Fullerton story. The Paris antiquarian, be it said, seems not to have had the letters in his possession very long, nor to have quite understood what they amounted to.

The relationship with Fullerton, as we watch it being enacted in the letters, passed recurringly through several distinct phases. The first cycle, to call it that, covered about eleven months, from February through December 1908. The friendship had begun the previous spring in Paris, when Fullerton, working out of the Paris office of the London *Times* and drawing on his extensive knowledge of the Paris literary world, helped secure magazine publications for a French translation of *The House of Mirth*. It deepened appreciably during Fullerton's visit to The Mount in October 1907; and soon after the new year, in Paris again, it moved into intimacy. The affair was sanctified, so to say, by a quotation from Emerson: "just the phrase for you—and *me*," Edith wrote: " 'The moment my eyes fell on him I was content.' " There were carefully arranged assignations: "at the Louvre at one o'c, in the shadow of Jean Gougon's Diana"; at 7 P.M. in the Invalides station, but *inside* the station, so that Cook, her chauffeur, would not espy them meeting. There were hangings back ("At first—yes—I hesitated, because I thought it, for you, not very real") and surgings forward ("And if you can't come into the room without my feeling all over me a ripple of flame . . ."). There were occasions of great happiness, like the one signaled after a visit to Beauvais by the underlined phrase from the *Paradiso: quella allegrezza;* and others of despair, like that recorded two weeks after the Dante quotation: "Sometimes I feel that I *can't* go on like this: from moments of such nearness, when the last shadow of separateness melts, back into a complete néant of silence, of not hearing, not knowing." But when she left Paris in late May to return to The Mount, Edith Wharton, to paraphrase her own words, was almost beside herself in the excitement of her love.

Her first letters to Fullerton from Lenox are the most vibrant and openhearted she was ever to write. The one dated over three days from June 8 to ii, in fact, may almost be reckoned a masterpiece; it is certainly brilliant, and it reveals an evolving form, if only a half-conscious one—something approaching Emerson's "frolic architecture"; and it can be scrutinized and enjoyed as if it were a wholly imaginative literary text. It begins with a ripple of happy memories, among them their first lunch together in Paris, "with the kindly prognathous lady-in-waiting, & the moist hippopotamous American with his cucumber-faced female." That memory contrasts with the dismal mood she had just barely overcome, and during which she almost cabled him a single word: *"Inconsolable."* (But had she done so, Fullerton might have cabled back; telegrams to The Mount were telephoned from the village, and Teddy might have been the one to answer the phone. "Si figuri!") She is better now, and has finished three more chapters of her new novel, *The Custom of the Country,* an announcement she compares to a casually bragging message from the king of Spain to the queen, his wife, in Hugo's *Ruy Blas.*

The images of the slant-jawed waitress at Duval's and the two American diners, affiliated respectively with the animal and the vegetable kingdoms, lead to (as they were probably evoked *by*) her current reading in studies of ancient forms of life, evolution, and Mendel's theories of heredity. She confesses to being dumbfounded by some of the phenomena described—the biophors and determinants (units of germ plasm that convey heredity, and units made up of these); but she gains control by converting them into comic cartoon figures: "the biophors . . . small and anxious to please, the determinants loud and domineering, with eyeglasses." More awesome to her inventive imagination is "that monstrous animal the heterozygote," a hybrid form she had encountered in a text on Mendelism. "Oh, dear—what nonsense to send three thousand miles."

She turns from the playfully literary and intellectual to the more than friendly; to the closely personal. "Do you want to know some of the things I like you for?" She lists Fullerton's capacity for discrimination in people and things, and his concern for the important trifles, the "green worms" of life—a waitress being deprived of a tip, a taxi driver of a fare. Most of all, she likes Fullerton for something that (she says) she and Fullerton are virtually alone in sharing: "a 'radiant reasonableness.' " She describes this paradoxical quality as talent for feeling "the 'natural magic,' au-delà, dream-side of things," even while insisting on "the netteté [clearness or sharpness] . . . in thinking, in conduct—yes! in feeling too!" In a superb small literary maneuver, and by way of concluding the June 8 portion of the letter, she quotes Milton's *Comus* on "that poor dear maligned Goddess of Reason":

"How charming is divine philosophy!
Not harsh and crabbèd, as dull fools suppose,
But musical as is Apollo's lute."

With the Miltonic notion of musical philosophy, Edith Wharton has in effect married the *netteté* and the *au-delà,* dream-side, the scientific and the "feminine-mystical."

Taking up the letter two days later, Edith Wharton proceeds, with a certain hardening of tone, to castigate the sorry familiar tendency of lovers "to bargain and calculate, as if it were a game of skill played between antagonistics." A phrase from an obscure text thought to be by Pascal is drawn upon: "Il faut de l'adresse pour aimer"—*adresse* being skill or dexterity; a noble saying, she argues, if it means the exercise of sympathy and self-effacement; but "the most sordid of counsels if it appeals to the instinct to dole out, dissemble, keep in suspense." For herself, she wants no gaming, no winning: "I want to lose everything to you!"

The tone modulates again the next day, from the impassioned to the gently lyrical, with the news that against all belief she had heard a cuckoo calling from the woods near her garden: a sound thought to be unheard in New England, sweet and insistent, bringing back the birdsong she and Fullerton had listened to in Montmorency.*

The entire letter is an expanding dance of opposites: Paris and Lenox, inconsolable and high-humored, the anxious biophor and the domineering determinants, love as gaming and love as self-giving. Finally, in an afterthought, Edith offers a contrast between novelistic possibilities: the ability "to do justice to the tender sentiment in fiction"—a quality she suspects that Fullerton's fiction-writing sister would accuse Mrs. Wharton of lacking—and her own "low & photographic order of talent qui a besoin de se documenter." So ends a letter that has been sufficiently documented and photographic, and which has not been remiss in the language of feeling, both tender and intense. Fusing and harmonizing the diverse aspects of Edith Wharton's nature, the letter has indeed made her during the time of its utterance a fully, one could say joyfully, integrated being.

*This is one of several moments when one wishes ardently that Edith Wharton had known the poetry of Emily Dickinson—in particular, here, "The Robin's my Criterion for Tune." That poem continues: "Because I grow—where Robins do—/ But, were I Cuckoo born—/ I'd swear by him—. . ." The only indication of an interest on Edith Wharton's part in her New England predecessor comes in July 1934, when she sent a $7.00 check to the *Yale Review* for one year's subscription and (as the bonus) *The Life and Letters of Emily Dickinson*, by Martha Dickinson Bianchi.

In retrospect, we recognize the letter of June 8–11, 1908, as marking a moment of well-nigh perfect poise and balance in Edith Wharton's sense of the affair. The moment did not outlast the summer, partly because it was to a dangerous degree self-deceptive, and it would never be entirely recovered. A nakedly personal voice is heard in letters like that of August 26, 1908—a scant ten weeks later—which begins: "Dear, won't you tell me soon the meaning of this silence?" and goes on to say "how I dreaded to be to you, *even for an instant,* the 'donna non più giovane' who clings and encumbers"; it ends: "My last word is one of tenderness for the friend I love—for the lover I worshipped." Needless to say, it was not the last word. His silence remaining unbroken, Edith Wharton wrote icily to "Dear Mr. Fullerton" from London, in December, asking him to return to her at once "a few notes & letters of no value to your archives," but which could fill a lacuna "in those of their writer."

Over the next two years, the pattern repeated itself at intervals, with Edith Wharton constantly moving from the exhilarated to the apprehensive, from the hopeful to the wretched. A peak of erotic consummation and emotional fulfillment was reached in the summer of 1909, beginning with a "long secret night together" (in Edith's poetic account of it) at the Charing Cross Hotel in London and going on through a month of traveling in England. "During that month," Edith writes on August 12, "I have been completely happy. I have had everything in life that I ever longed for." A fortnight or so after that, she is saying how impossible it is that "our lives should run parallel much longer," and how much she dreads that her love may blind her to the facts when the time of separation arrives. In November, she again solicits the return of her letters.

Early in 1910, she starts to press for an end to the sexual part of their relationship—for "an easy transition to amitié," as she puts it in one letter—now calmly, now with a touch of frenzy beseeching Fullerton to take the step that she in herself seems not ready to take. Along with these confusing messages are expressions of pain and incomprehension at Fullerton's cavalier forgetfulness, his small-minded deceits, his erratic behavior. It is a humiliating period, lightened by only an occasional declaration that she—that "a woman like me"—deserves something rather better. Things come to a head after her return from a visit to London and Henry James. Fullerton writes her regularly while she is away, and, one gathers, in a most outspokenly loverlike manner; in Paris, he subjects her to the old familiar treatment, arriving on her doorstep unannounced, then disappearing, to leave her without a signal for days. The experience draws from her a statement at once desperate and forceful about the intolerable ambiguities of desire and identity that afflict them. "I am sad & bewildered beyond words": such is the opening of the mid-April letter. "Ballottée perpetually between one illusion & another . . . I can't any longer find a point de repère. I don't know what you want, or what I am! You write me like a lover, you treat me like a casual acquaintance!"

She begs him to send her no more false or misleading letters like those she received from him in England, and comes to what is intended as an ending once and for all.

> I have had a difficult year—but the pain within my pain, the last turn of the screw, has been the impossibility of knowing what you wanted of me, & what you felt for me. . . . My life was better before I knew you. That is, for me, the sad conclusion of this sad year. And it is a bitter thing to say to the one being one has ever loved d'amour.

The affair continued in a sporadic manner for another season or two (perhaps half a year more than had been thought before the letters to Fullerton showed up), but, on Edith Wharton's part, with diminishing conviction and dwindling passion. By 1911, they had become "companions," in Edith's oft-invoked word, and were acting as one another's literary advisor. A note of astringency enters Mrs. Wharton's letters of counsel to Fullerton, as in the one of October 1912 about his work-in-progress, in which the professional writer tells her friend that, while the argument ought to be couched in a manly, energetic style, he had "hung it with all the heavy tin draperies of the Times jargon—that most prolix & pedantic of all the dead languages. . . . Read Emerson," she enjoins him, "read Tyndall, read Froud[e] even, read Arnold—get away from . . . all the scientific-politico-economic charabia [gibberish] of your own specialists into the clear air of the born writers."

The recurring expressions of subservience in the letters to Fullerton, with what seems to be a felt need for sexual nagging, cannot but strike a disquieting note for a reader in the late 1980s; and especially when, *through* these letters, we receive a clearer and far less appealing picture of Morton Fullerton than had hitherto been available. He was loved by many women, and liked and thought well of by a number of men. Theodore Roosevelt, for example, is quoted as having a high opinion of him. He had undoubted graces of mind and speech; and for a space of time, as we know from other sources, the sexual relation between the lovers was vigorous and imaginative. But Fullerton was curiously insubstantial on the human side; he seems to have had almost no impulse to engage another person to the full of the other's being, no capacity for genuine human love. The slackness of conduct that caused Edith Wharton such torment derived, one comes to think, not only from a kind of smiling selfishness, but from a sheer slackness of nature. In allying herself to Fullerton, Edith Wharton (though she was slow to realize it) was acting out a theme she had dealt with in her earlier fiction, in *The Fruit of the Tree* and in novellas like *The Touchstones* and *Madame de Treymes:* the larger and finer spirit subdued and even defeated by the smaller and cruder one.

At the same time, the record of that poignant process, in the letters, is quite remarkably human. It is the disclosure of enormous emotional arousal and then of emotional bruising and grief not easily matched in our epistolary annals. Nor is Edith Wharton's revealed vulnerability limited to the Fullerton papers. This woman, whose public image was that of the austerely self-contained (and who could be exactly that in her formal correspondence), was in fact extraordinarily open to experience, immediately responsive to the here-and-now of life. She lived so close to the quick of things, was so urgently caught up in them, that sometimes, reading her letters, one feels that the prose is about to break through the page. This was true whether she was speaking of the vagaries of a lover, the dangerous illness of a friend, the exhilarating view from a mountaintop in Sicily, the march of the German armies, or the street riots in Paris. In her most personal communications, she was surprisingly unguarded; and so, she was vulnerable to a degree. We may think of the winter and spring of 1913, when she was nearly brought down by a series of unsettling events: a grave though short-lived misunderstanding with Henry James ("I can never get over this," she told Lapsley in the course of it); an estrangement from her brother Harry; the ugliness of the divorce proceedings.

She testified to her own grief at these times; and she was invariably responsive to the grief of others: of Sara Norton during the last illness and after the death of her father; of Dr. Beverley Robinson, on the death of Anna Robinson, his wife of forty-six years and a friend of Edith Jones in her Newport days. The last letter Edith Wharton wrote, a week before her own death, was a message of loving condolence to Matilda Gay on the loss of her husband. Death is a major element in these letters because it was accepted as such, as a central event in human experience, by Edith Wharton in her life. Among her finest and most touching letters are those about the deaths of Henry James and Walter Berry, and later of Catharine Gross, her lifelong friend and housekeeper; and to these one must add the obituary, in June 1908, of the Norton family's dog Taffy:

> His artless but engaging ways, his candid enjoyment of his dinner, his judicious habit of exercising by means of those daily rushes up & down the road, had for so many years

interested & attracted us that he occupies a very special place in our crowded dog-memories.

The learning displayed in Edith Wharton's letters—the close acquaintance with texts literary, artistic, scientific, historical, philosophic, religious, in five languages, from medieval to modern, from European to American—is of sometimes awesome proportions. The letter to Fullerton on June 8, 1908, with its range and variety of allusions and quotation, is far from exceptional. To the same correspondent, and writing in May 1911 from the tedious confines of the spa at Salsomaggiore, she listed some of the books she had brought with her to while away the hours: Richard Wagner's *My Life* (which had saved *hers*, she said), a posthumous work by Victor Hugo, a historical essay by Ernest Renan on Averroës, the twelfth-century Arabian philosopher and commentator on Aristotle, an early novel by Flaubert *(Novembre)*, a history of philosophy by George Henry Lewes ("which I love & haven't read for years"), some Emerson, Sir Joshua Reynolds's *Discourses on Art* ("*such* a mixture of drivel & insight"), Dostoyevsky's *The Idiot*, Melville's *Moby-Dick* ("do you share my taste for Melville?"), an account of Germans in France, a French translation of *Leaves of Grass* ("'When lilacs last' is unbelievably well done"), and a life of Whitman by the translator. She did not often roam quite so broadly; but typically, in a letter to Berenson from Hyères just before Christmas 1920 as she was about to take possession of her new Riviera home, she mentioned a recent life of Blake, a reminiscent essay by Max Beerbohm about a visit in 1899 to the London home of Algernon Charles Swinburne and the lawyer-writer Theodore Watts-Dunton, Santayana's *Character and Opinion in the United States* ("oh, what a tone, what standards!"), a book ("brilliant yet impartial") about Mme. de Maintenon—the mistress and then the extremely influential wife of Louis XIV—by Edith Wharton's friend Mme. St.-René de Taillandier, a "dull & laboured" study of George Sand, Barrett Wendell's *The Traditions of*

European Literature from Homer to Dante ("terribly pre-masticated and primaire"), and a review of a new biography of Goethe.

Only the accessibility of one of the world's great libraries, that of Yale, and of a great humanities faculty, made it possible for us to track down many of these references. But it was as desirable as it was necessary to show Edith Wharton forth, whenever the occasion demanded, in the full panoply of her remarkable cultivation. What one discovers, after this has happened a few times, is not merely that Edith Wharton was learned, but that her learning was for her a vital and shaping presence.

Dante, for example, supplied her not so much with quotations as with ways of focusing herself at key moments: she drew from the *Inferno* to disavow an interest in argumentation (*"Non ragionam"*), the *Purgatorio* to point to a disastrous marital situation (Pia Tolomei), and the *Paradiso* to convey the blessed beauty of her postwar Mediterranean surroundings ("cielo della quieta"). Later in the 1920s, when what she described to Fullerton as "the au-delà dream-side of things" took stronger possession of her, we find Edith Wharton talking to her old friend Margaret Terry Chanler, a devout Catholic, about a life of St. François de Sales and the saint's posthumous *Traité de l'amour de Dieu* (1626), the monumental ongoing work by Abbé Henri Bremond (her "beloved author"), *Histoire littéraire du sentiment réligieux en France,* and Henry Vaughan's poem "The World," from which she quotes: "I saw Eternity the other night."

Edith Wharton read whatever book fell into her hands, from whatever source and of whatever vintage; but what she *retained* from her reading tended to gather into patterns. Her relation to German literature was characteristic. We hear her tell Sara Norton of "rummaging" amid the "metaphysical lumber" of Schopenhauer; and six years later—in the summer of 1908, when she is meditating the import of the affair with Fullerton—of reading Nietzsche's *Beyond Good and Evil* and warmly endorsing its attack on Christian attitudes. A few years after that, as though by a natural sequence, she is reveling in Wagner's autobiography; and in Berlin in 1913, escorted by Bernard Berenson, she attends the cycle of *Der Ring des Nibelungen.*

Meanwhile, in a volume of German poetry given her by Berenson, she rereads the medieval songs of Walther von der Vogelweide, long a favorite of hers, and the verse of Goethe and Hugo von Hofmannsthal. Then, in the winter of 1917, she goes back to Walther and to the Icelandic sagas contemporary to him, the Edda, reading those tales of gods and men in an English version of the German translation from which Wagner drew his materials for the Ring cycle. Commenting on this to Berenson, she tells of quoting—to a hapless dinner companion who did not understand a word of it—a line from the dark story of Helgi and Sigrun: *"More powerful at night are the ghosts of the dead heroes than in the light of day."* All of her German reading and remembering resonated in the stirring passage, and at this somber and perilous moment in the Great War.

"Goethe always Schillered when he wrote to Schiller, didn't he?" The observation was made to Berenson in the letter preceding the one about rereading the Edda. Edith had been going through the correspondence between the two German writers, and she continued: "That's the reason why, generally, transcribed talks are so much more satisfactory than letters. People talk more for themselves, apparently, & write more for their correspondents." The judgment arose from having simultaneously delved into the third volume of *With Walt Whitman in Camden,* Horace Traubel's record of conversations with her favorite American poet. To an extent, Edith Wharton did adjust her letter style to the person she was addressing: a somewhat different voice can be heard talking to Berenson and to Henry James, to Margaret Terry Chanler and to Minnie Jones, to her young English protégé John Hugh Smith and her American academic friend Gaillard Lapsley. Yet it is unmistakably, in every letter, the distinct and recognizable voice of Edith Wharton.

She could write Berenson a painterly letter, as she did from the palace of the Resident General of Morocco in October 1917: "Imagine, after a flight across the bled [hinterland], passing through battlemented gate after gate, crossing a dusty open space with mules, camels, story-teller, & the usual 'comparses,' & passing through a green doorway into a great court full of flowers," and on through more flowers, orange groves, streams, fountains, yellow jasmines, and pomegranate trees. Yet something about Berenson drew from Edith Wharton an impish and teasing strain, as when agreeing to meet him in Rome (in April 1910), she declared her intention *not* to go to the kind of luxury hotel to which Berenson was addicted: "I'm still a slave to the picturesque, & want a Trasteverina dancing the Tarantella in front of a Locanda to the music of a Pifferaro." We find her, in like humor, writing Mary Berenson while traveling across Germany with B.B., that the latter was learning "several useful things" on the trip: among them, "getting out of the motor to ask the way of an intelligent-looking person on the corner, instead of calling out to the village idiot or a deaf octogenarian from one's seat; & abstaining from shallow generalizations such as: 'You'll find it's always safe in Germany to follow the telegraph poles.' "

To Margaret Terry Chanler, she spoke as one who belonged to the same richly be-cousined venerable American society, and to the same community of the extremely well read; to her sister-in-law Minnie, of whom she was enormously fond, her tone was a trifle impatient, as to one whose thought processes were never as rapid or as lucid as they might be. In the early letters to John Hugh Smith, there is an engaging air of flirtatiousness not unmixed with tenderness, of the admired and pursued older woman cautioning the impetuous younger male. With Lapsley she strikes a worldly adult note without the faintest hint of the erotic. Perhaps her most unchanging voice was to her editors and publishers: professional, businesslike, insistent, never missing a trick. In the wake of her first volume of fiction in 1899, she complains with some vehemence at the failure (as she alleges) of Charles Scribner's Sons to advertise the book, though it had (she said) been most favorably reviewed; and a few months afterward, responding to a "kind note" from William Crary Brownell reporting a sale of three thousand copies, she remarks pointedly: "I knew, from the number of letters I have received from publishers, that it must be doing well." Thirty-five years later, she is announcing to her editor at D. Appleton and Company that its advertising of *A Backward Glance* had been so deplorably sparse, and so far behind the practice of all the other major American publishers, that she wishes to be released from the contract for her next novel.

Only a scattered few of Edith Wharton's letters to Henry James have survived: some postcards in 1911, a literary chat in 1912, and a small batch during the early period of the war. The others were presumably destroyed in the ritual bonfire with which James, some time in the 1900s, did away with most of his incoming mail. The loss may well be a major one for literary history. There are about 170 letters extant from James to Edith Wharton, and one may suppose that she wrote that many to him. The few items that have slipped down to us suggest what we have been deprived of.

The two letters written in the winter of 1915 after successive visits to Verdun and neighboring points in the war zone are particularly dramatic and colorful, and made a profound impression on their recipient. From a hotel in Verdun on February 28, Edith Wharton describes some actual fighting she had witnessed.

From a garden we looked across the valley to a height about 5 miles way, where white puffs & scarlet flashes kept springing up all over the dark hillside. It was the hill above Vauquois, where there has been desperate fighting for two days. The Germans were firing from the top at the French trenches below (hidden from us by an intervening rise of the ground); & the French were assaulting, & *their* puffs & flashes were half way up the hill. And so we saw the reason why there are to be so many wounded at Clermont tonight!

After a second little tour eleven days later, Edith sketched a scene on the Meuse River, west of Verdun:

> Picture this all under a white winter sky, driving great flurries of snow across the mud-and-cinder-coloured landscape, with the steel-cold Meuse winding between beaten poplars—Cook standing with Her [the Mercedes] in a knot of mud-coated military motors & artillery horses, soldiers coming & going, cavalrymen riding up with messages, poor bandaged creatures in rag-bag clothes leaning in doorways, & always, over & above us, the boom, boom, boom of the guns on the grey heights to the east.

"Those big summing-up impressions meet one at every turn," she added, as she went on to offer several more. Edith Wharton was well aware that she was addressing the American writer, in her literary epoch, who was the supreme collector, designer, and conveyer of impressions: the chief summer-up, so to say, of places and persons. Henry James was quick to acknowledge the achievement. He regularly treated Edith Wharton's letters with ceremonial enthusiasm, and sometimes provides us with a hint of what the lost missive may have contained. He had "revelled and rioted" in her letter from Munich in December 1909, he told her: "You are indeed my ideal of the dashing woman, and never dashed more felicitously or fruitfully, for my imagination, than when you dashed, at that particular psychologic moment, off to dear old rococo Munich. . . . Vivid and charming and sympathetic *au possible* your image and echo of it all." There, as often, mockery mixes audibly with admiration. The Jamesian response to what Edith had called her *"sensations de guerre"* was unmodified.

He would not, he says, attempt to expatiate on his failure to reply sooner to her "inexpressibly splendid bounties."

> The idea of "explaining" anything to *you* in these days, or of expatiation that isn't exclusively that of your own genius upon

your own adventures and impressions! I think *the* reason why I have been so baffled, in a word, is that all my powers of being anything else have gone to living upon your two magnificent letters, the one from Verdun, and the one after your second visit there; which gave me matter of experience and appropriation to which I have done the fullest honour. Your whole record is sublime, and the interest and the beauty and the terror of it all have again and again called me back to it. . . . I know them at last, your incomparable pages, by heart.

Absorbing the Jamesian voice into her own, Edith Wharton had never expressed herself more handsomely. Henry James's tribute to the epistolary art of his friend and fellow writer ("Chère Madame et Confrère," he had called her), so much more cogent and elaborate than Berenson's, was warmed by a quality that must have made it especially endearing: a kind of generous envy, not only at Edith Wharton's powers of description but at the grand historic adventures that had called them into being.

(1988)

A VOICE OUT OF THE DARKNESS

The period from about 1890 to 1910 is one of the hardest to define, and to appraise, in modern American literature. There was, on the one hand, a genuine vigor in the area of fiction—though one masterpiece, *Billy Budd*, remained unpublished until the late 1920s and another, *Sister Carrie* (1900), was, at the time of its publication, generally ignored. Still, Stephen Crane flared brilliantly, if briefly, and Henry James was passing through some of the ripest years of his career; Sarah Orne Jewett and other gifted women were writing quietly in various sections of New England. But the situation in poetry was a good deal murkier: to the literary historian, figures seem to loom in a kind of cultural fog and disappear; reputations are made overnight and as quickly forgotten. Out of this general darkness, the poetic voice that now comes through to us most clearly is that of Edwin Arlington Robinson.

Literary achievement is always to some extent a matter of luck: the luck, quite simply, to have been born at the right time—a time when one's vision coincides with a vocabulary sufficiently alive (and it is sometimes luckier to have at hand a vocabulary in partial decay) to convey that vision in an enduring manner, and when there is an audience equipped to grasp and respond to the vision. Jacques Maritain has spoken of Dante's great good luck in coming to maturity just as the medieval "synthesis," fully realized in the work of the master theologians, became, on the eve of its dissolution, accessible to poetry. And about Emily Dickinson, Allen Tate has made a similar point: that as the formidable New England Protestant vision of human affairs began to dissolve, Emily Dickinson could seize upon its ingredients as symbols for the poetry of terror and ecstasy. Edwin Arlington Robinson had no such luck.

During his most fruitful years, between 1896 and 1916, he suffered a kind of absolute silence and neglect, something explicable only by the murkiness and the chaos of literary standards of the time. There was little for him to draw upon in his cultural environment except a kind of waning and effete idealism, the thin residue of the transcendental theory (which indeed rather hampered than aided his natural poetic instinct); and there was little for him to appeal *to* in the minds and imagination of readers. It was not only that his lack of readership was the source of pain that led him to the brink of suicide; it was also—his biographer Louis O. Coxe (*Edwin Arlington Robinson*, 1969) has persuasively argued—that the long years of public indifference actually damaged him as a poet. He was a very fine poet; but it is more than possible that he would have been even better if he had been luckier. Considerable success, along with honors and a modest affluence, came to him in the 1920s. But by this time he had virtually abandoned the dramatic and reflective lyric by which he had made his enduring mark in favor of a series of long narrative poems, some of them very popular and prize-winning but not likely, today, to engage many readers. By that time, too, the modern vision, or, as it is sometimes called, "the modern tradition," had taken hold of Anglo-American literary culture, and the important voices in American poetry—Eliot, Pound, and later William Carlos Williams, Wallace Stevens, and Hart Crane—were carrying the art into areas (imagist, symbolist, metaphysical, and in some ways European) from which Robinson was self-excluded. Seen in broad outline, Robinson's career resembles one of his own ironic and compassionate lyrics based on the theme of failure, including the failure of success. Like Miniver Cheevy, he picked the wrong time to be born into.

If Robinson's life sometimes seems a reflection of his poetry, there is no doubt that his finest poems are in part a reflection of his life, and of his darkly troubled family backgroud. He was born in December 1869, in Head Tide, Maine, the third son of Edward and Mary Palmer Robinson; after going nameless for six months, the child was christened Edwin at the suggestion of a lady from Arlington, Massachusetts, who was then rewarded by having her hometown chosen for the middle name. The following September, the family moved to Gardiner, Maine (the Tilbury Town of Robinson's poetry), a burgeoning mill and factory town of some forty-five hundred inhabitants where, except for two years at Harvard, Robinson would live more or less uninterruptedly till 1897, when he moved down to New York ("the town down the river," as Robinson would call it in his wry Yankee way). The Robinsons never quite "made it" in Gardiner, socially or otherwise. Mary Robinson could count the distinguished Dudley family among her ancestry, and Robinson could properly claim to be descended from the New World's first genuine poet, the Mistress Anne Bradstreet who married Governor Dudley. But Edward Robinson, though he amassed a certain amount of wealth through his involvement with local factories and banks and through the manipulation of farm mortgages, and became a citizen of some renown, was known derisively as the Duke of Puddledock and was not invited to the grander mansions on the hill. Still, the years of the poet's childhood were passed in reasonable comfort (though he would later recall that at the age of six he had spent some hours in a rocking chair pondering the question of why he had ever been born) and it was not until late in his adolescence that things began to go, at first mildly, then hideously, awry.

Dean Robinson, Edwin's older brother, had gone to college and medical school and had begun the practice of medicine, a profession for which he was woefully unfitted. He wore himself out at tasks from which he derived no sense of reward, took to morphine to keep himself going, abandoned his practice, and came back to the family home to live out the wreckage of his life. Edwin loved him and admired him extravagantly ("Dean knew more at twenty than I shall ever know," he said later, in sad retrospect); it was his first close experience of desperate failure. The second son, Herman, was to be the financial wizard of the family. He toured the Middle West, speculating in land, mills, railroads, extending his father's resources in a heady effort to multiply them—until the smash came; whereupon he took to drink with bitter and serious determination, became at last a helpless alcholic, leaving his beautiful wife, the former Emma Shepherd (with whom Edwin has been rumored, probably falsely, to have been in love), and their three daughters largely dependent on the very small and very occasional donations from the youngest brother. When Edward Robinson, the father, died in 1892, he was all but bankrupt, an acrimonious old man vainly demanding explanations from a world that had somehow destroyed him. The culminating horror was the death of Mary Robinson four years later. She was strickened by black diphtheria, and no townsman would even enter the house for fear of contagion. The doctor refused to call and the dying woman was cared for by the three sons; the pastor intoned a prayer at a safe distance through an open window; and when told that Mrs. Robinson was dead, the undertaker left a coffin on the front porch and departed in haste. The sons (one of them, Dean, more nearly dead than alive himself) saw to their mother's burial in the family plot of the Gardiner graveyard.

For examples of frustration, defeat, wreckage, and in general of the smitten life, Robinson needed thus to look no further than his own family, though he did in fact look beyond it—for his early poems and for years thereafter—at least as far as other secretively troubled residents of Gardiner. And it was the experience of the devastations wrought upon those dear to him—his brother Dean and, more ambiguously, his mother—that gave him the oddly detached sympathy that is the strength and perhaps also the limitation of his characteristic poems. The note was struck perfectly in "Reuben Bright":

> For when they told him that his wife must die,
> He stared at them, and shook with grief and fright,
> And cried like a great baby half the night,
> And made the women cry to see him cry.

The poem is from Robinson's first volume, *The Torrent and the Night Before*, published in 1896, the year of his mother's death.

His literary education, meanwhile, had been spurred by the two years (1891–1893) he managed to complete at Harvard before financial disaster back home made it impossible for him to continue. The Robinson household was not without books; there was Anne Bradstreet in the background; and Edward Robinson was not opposed to the reading and even the writing of poetry so long as it did not interfere with the serious business of life. But the period at Harvard, though it was not a happy one for Robinson personally, served to introduce him to a larger world and to other young literary enthusiasts—like William Vaughn Moody, of whom Robinson became a friend, admirer, and wary rival (and in celebration of whose highly successful play, *The Great Divide*, Robinson would write a poem called "The White Lights"). He was not a particularly voracious reader (it might be hazarded that most American writers who went to college read rather less than those who did not), nor were his tastes unusual. He enjoyed the Romantic writers, but he was also drawn to Latin poetry (some of which he translated at an early age), and perhaps something of the gravity and solidity of the Virgilian lyric may be felt amid the Yankee idiom and tonality of Robinson's own verse. He was not affected by Browning, whose "men and women" might otherwise be thought to have been an obvious influence upon him; but he did respond to Kipling and, to a lesser degree, Housman.

Still, as more than one observer of Robinson has suggested, it is less to previous poetry than to fiction—especially nineteenth-century American, English, and French fiction—that one must turn for anything like "sources" for his poetry. If there was no powerful ongoing movement in poetry for Robinson to attach himself to in the nineties, there was a strong movement in fiction, both at home and abroad: that is, the development of literary realism. The evidence is inadequate, but one naturally associates Robinson's poems of New York City life more with the novels of William Dean Howells than with the exoticism of his best-known contemporaries in poetry; and "Eros Turannos," one of Robinson's masterpieces, gazes at the nearly hidden desperation of a wealthy married woman in a manner remarkably similar to a short story by Edith Wharton. There is little doubt that Robinson was a serious reader of Henry James during most of his life and that he also seized upon Hawthorne's tales of dark New England passion and human fatality. Even his attachment to Emerson seems to have been mainly to Emerson's effort to restore the pungent everyday language of street and farm to poetry, and what appealed to him in Whitman was the poet's experiments with narrative realism.

All this constitutes a fact of considerable importance. Robinson is not to be reduced to a single lyrical mode; and yet many of his best poems—one picks, almost at random, "Reuben Bright," "The Clerks," "Eros Turannos," "Old Trails," "The Poor Relation," "Mr. Flood's Party"—deal with themes, episodes, individual characters that before Robinson and for the most part after him were dealt with by writers of fiction. What is perhaps more surprising, Robinson scarcely bothered to devise new poetic forms in order to project his little dramas: he preferred to reinvigorate the forms that were available. "Reuben Bright," like "The Clerks," is cast in the form of an absolutely conventional Petrarchan sonnet. The form of the poem constrains and tightens the narrative content, while the narrative movement to some extent loosens and vitalizes the form.

All but one of the poems in *The Torrent and the Night Before* were reprinted in *The Children of the Night* (1897). At least half a dozen of these are very good indeed, and neither volume went entirely unnoticed; but they did not elicit from the literary periodicals any demand for new work. Robinson had a job of sorts at Harvard in 1898–1899 and then moved to New York City, where he would spend part of every year for the rest of his life. He wandered the streets, frequenting bars and, from time to time, brothels, and consorted with the bohemian set. By 1902 he had a new volume ready: *Captain Craig*. On this book he rested his poetic case, so to speak; he presented it to the public as his announcement of himself as a mature poet—particularly in the long title poem, which memorializes a picaresque figure whom Robinson had come to know in New York (and whose actual name was Alfred Louis), and also in "Isaac and Archibald," which is in fact superior to "Captain Craig" and is one of the handsomest and freshest treatments in American poetry of the theme of initiation. When the volume was received with almost total silence, Robinson was reduced to something like despair.

For a time he threatened to follow the alcoholic path to ruin of his unhappy brother Herman and wrote next to nothing. Then, in March 1905, he received a letter from the White House: "I have enjoyed your poems . . . so much," wrote President Roosevelt, "that I must write to tell you so." Roosevelt's son Kermit had drawn his father's attention to *The Children of the Night;* and the president followed up his letter not only by having Robinson appointed to the customs house on Wall Street at the then princely salary of two thousand dollars a year, but also by writing an article for the *Outlook* in which he praised Robinson's poetry as giving off "just a little of the light that never was on land or sea." "I am not sure I understand 'Luke Havergal,' " Roosevelt remarked, naming one of the strangest and best of Robinson's early poems, "but I am entirely sure I like it."

Roosevelt salvaged Robinson's external situation, and Robinson was now able to come in turn to the aid of his sister-in-law and her three daughters. But the president's public support rather hindered than helped Robinson's standing with the literati of New York, nor did it stimulate Robinson to new creative efforts. He spent his days reading in the customs house office before going back to his room to drink heavily and talk till all hours with his few cronies. When Roosevelt left the White House in 1909, Robinson was out of a job—and, miraculously, experienced a sudden recovery of power. In 1910, he brought out *The Town Down the River*.

Though there was little immediate acclaim, Robinson's reputation was at last beginning to grow. In 1911 he was invited to the MacDowell Colony in Peterboro, New Hampshire, a haven for serious, indigent writers; it was here that Robinson thereafter did most of his work. Harriet Monroe's *Poetry* was inaugurated in 1912, and Robinson began to appear in it; other magazines were after him; in Boston the English poet Alfred Noyes proclaimed that Robinson was the best American poet living. When *The Man Against the Sky* was published in 1916, a number of reviewers, and not the least discerning and influential among them, found themselves in agreement with Noyes's estimate.

The Man Against the Sky does contain a group of poems sufficient by themselves to make any poet's lasting reputation—including, "Flammonde," "The Gift of God," "Hillcrest," "Eros Turannos," "Old Trails," "Veteran Sirens," and "The Poor Relation." Yet there was something ominous in the intellectually ambitious meditative poem that gave the volume its title, something ominous too in the fact that this was the work singled out by most commentators for special admiration. The intention of "The Man Against the Sky" is indeed admirable; in one perspective, it is noble: nothing less than to confront, through the resources of poetry, the very mystery of the universe—the mystery, that is, of human knowledge, of man's capacity to perceive his relationship with reality. But here again luck was against Robinson. There was simply not enough in his intellectual background and environment to provide him—as Melville and Emily Dickinson in their time *had* been provided—with the instruments necessary for such an inquiry. The terms from which a poet might draw meaningful symbols and images, the ingredients of his poetic discourse, were lacking. The result is a sort of dignified bombast, an earnest but unsuccessful attempt to resurrect an Emersonianism in which Robinson no longer really believed.

But that may be putting the case too simply, and even (though such is far from being the intention) condescendingly. The fact is that Robinson's relation to Emerson was highly ambiguous. If he was tempted at times to strive after the spiritual freedom Emerson proclaimed, he was also tempted at other times to accept too quickly Emerson's occasional acknowledgment of the element of necessity, or fate, in human experience. Harold Bloom, in *The Ringers in the Tower* (1971), makes the latter point and notes that Robinson read Emerson's essays "Fate" and "Power" as early as 1899, was much struck by them, and said that Emerson walloped the reader "with a big New England shingle," the weapon of fatalism. But however one interprets the matter, one is forced to the conclusion that neither his personal circumstances nor his intellectual environment provided Robinson with the resources to project a persuasive idealism on the one hand, or on the other a vision of what Hawthorne called the "dark necessity."

Robinson's best poems, nonetheless, are glimpses into the darkness. Some of these are among the lyrics in *The Three Taverns* (1920), *Avon's Harvest* (1921), and his *Collected Poems* (also 1921), which won him the first of three Pulitzer prizes. But the cosmic appetite apparent in "The Man Against the Sky" could be sensed even more strongly in *Merlin* (1917), in the two Arthurian stories in verse which followed over a decade, *Lancelot* and *Tristram,* and in the succession of narrative poems beginning with *The Man Who Died Twice.* The Arthurian poems represented Robinson's attempt, stimulated by the First World War, to wrestle with vast problems of history and politics, but to do so through character, dialogue, patterns of relationship. Conrad Aiken was brilliantly right when he observed, in 1922, that *Merlin* and *Lancelot* "give us a Malory as Henry James might have written and enlarged it," and that in both instances the narrative method is strikingly Jamesian: "Merlin and Vivien have here all the dim subtleties and delicate mutual awarenesses of the people, let us say, in *The Wings of the Dove*. The story, the poetry, is precisely in these hoverings and perturbations, these pauses and approaches and flights."

Nothing finer could be said about the Arthurian poems; but at a greater distance in time, *Merlin* and the others strike us as Jamesian only in technique, with not enough of the old master's tough moral substance. As to the other narrative poems, they all now blur together in one's memory, to paraphrase Louis O. Coxe, in one long gray undifferentiated work. There are arresting passages in all of them, especially when, as in *The Man Who Died Twice* (which won the poet his second Pulitzer prize), Robinson seems to be reflecting on the theme of failure as it relates to his own artistic career. And there is some hint that in *King Jasper*, which was published posthumously in 1936 with a curiously grudging introduction by Robert Frost, the then dying poet was attempting a new narrative idiom.

But Robinson's achievement, and it is very considerable, consists finally not in those large poetic enterprises by which, in his later years, he exercised the role of the Great Poet in a recognizably Georgian manner. It consists in a goodly handful of lyric poems, dramatic or meditative or both, as the case may be. When we think of Robinson, we think of Reuben Bright shaken with grief and fright, of Luke Havergal mysteriously summoned to the western gate, of the clerks grown old without fulfilling the vague bright promise of youth, of Miniver Cheevy dreaming and scratching his head, of Richard Cory going home one fine summer night to put a bullet in his head, of the "poor relation" ensconced by her unfeeling family in an apartment perhaps in Yonkers, of old Eben Flood swallowing his drink and singing his quavery song on the hillside at night. We hear a voice, calm and sure, speaking out of and into the darkness, telling us of loneliness, sorrow, defeat, endurance. It may be that Robinson insisted too much on the "light" for which he always waited—that he concealed a little the tragic vision that he really possessed. But the expression of such a vision during Robinson's best years might also have meant a silence on the part of readers even longer drawn out than the one he suffered from. Robinson was a superior poet, but an unlucky one.

An anecdote the critic R. P. Blackmur used to tell about Robinson has a fine symbolic quality. Young Blackmur, himself a native of Maine, had been taken to be introduced to Robinson, in Gardiner. Robinson was sitting on the front porch of his house, and as the shadows lengthened Blackmur could no longer clearly make him out. Finally Robinson asked, in a low voice, "What do *you* want to do?" "I want to be a poet," Blackmur answered. After a silence: "Don't!" said the voice out of the darkness.

(1973)

A Handful of Poems

Luke Havergal (1896)

Go to the western gate, Luke Havergal,
There where the vines cling crimson on the wall,
And in the twilight wait for what will come.
The leaves will whisper there of her, and some,
Like flying words, will strike you as they fall;
But go, and if you listen she will call.
Go to the western gate, Luke Havergal—
Luke Havergal.

No, there is not a dawn in eastern skies
To rift the fiery night that's in your eyes;

But there, where western glooms are gathering,
The dark will end the dark, if anything:
God slays Himself with every leaf that flies,
And hell is more than half of paradise.
No, there is not a dawn in eastern skies—
In eastern skies.

Out of a grave I come to tell you this,
Out of a grave I come to quench the kiss
That flames upon your forehead with a glow
That blinds you to the way that you must go.
Yes, there is yet one way to where she is,
Bitter, but one that faith may never miss.
Out of a grave I come to tell you this—
To tell you this.

There is the western gate, Luke Havergal,
There are the crimson leaves upon the wall.
Go, for the winds are tearing them away,—
Nor think to riddle the dead words they say,
Nor any more to feel them as they fall;
But go, and if you trust her she will call.
There is the western gate, Luke Havergal—
Luke Havergal.

Richard Cory (1896)

Whenever Richard Cory went down town,
We people on the pavement looked at him:
He was a gentleman from sole to crown,
Clean favored, and imperially slim.

And he was always quietly arrayed,
And he was always human when he talked;

But still he fluttered pulses when he said,
"Good-morning," and he glittered when he walked.

And he was rich—yes, richer than a king—
And admirably schooled in every grace:
In fine, we thought that he was everything
To make us wish that we were in his place.

So on we worked, and waited for the light,
And went without the meat, and cursed the bread;
And Richard Cory, one calm summer night,
Went home and put a bullet through his head.

Reuben Bright (1896)

Because he was a butcher and thereby
Did earn an honest living (and did right),
I would not have you think that Reuben Bright
Was any more a brute than you or I;
For when they told him that his wife must die,
He stared at them, and shook with grief and fright,
And cried like a great baby half the night,
And made the woman cry to see him cry.

And after she was dead, and he had paid
The singers and the sexton and the rest,
He packed a lot of things that she had made
Most mournfully away in an old chest
Of hers, and put some chopped-up cedar boughs
In with them, and tore down the slaughter-house.

The Clerks (1896)

I did not think that I should find them there
When I came back again; but there they stood,

As in the days they dreamed of when young blood
Was in their cheeks and women called them fair.
Be sure, they met me with an ancient air,—
And yes, there was a shop-worn brotherhood
About them; but the men were just as good,
And just as human as they ever were.

And you that ache so much to be sublime,
And you that feed yourselves with your descent,
What comes of all your visions and your fears?
Poets and kings are but the clerks of Time,
Tiering the same dull webs of discontent,
Clipping the same sad alnage of the years.

Miniver Cheevy (1910)

Miniver Cheevy, child of scorn,
    Grew lean while he assailed the seasons;
He wept that he was ever born,
    And he had reasons.

Miniver loved the days of old
    When swords were bright and steeds were prancing;
The vision of a warrior bold
    Would set him dancing.

Miniver sighed for what was not,
    And dreamed, and rested from his labors;
He dreamed of Thebes and Camelot,
    And Priam's neighbors.

Miniver mourned the ripe renown
    That made so many a name so fragrant;
He mourned Romance, now on the town,
    And Art, a vagrant.

Miniver loved the Medici,
  Albeit he had never seen one;
He would have sinned incessantly
  Could he have been one.

Miniver cursed the commonplace
  And eyed a khaki suit with loathing;
He missed the mediæval grace
  Of iron clothing.

Miniver scorned the gold he sought,
  But sore annoyed was he without it;
Miniver thought, and thought, and thought,
  And thought about it.

Miniver Cheevy, born too late,
  Scratched his head and kept on thinking;
Miniver coughed, and called it fate,
  And kept on drinking.

Veteran Sirens (1916)

The ghost of Ninon would be sorry now
To laugh at them, were she to see them here,
So brave and so alert for learning how
To fence with reason for another year.

Age offers a far comelier diadem
Than theirs; but anguish has no eye for grace,
When time's malicious mercy cautions them
To think a while of number and of space.

The burning hope, the worn expectancy,
The martyred humor, and the maimed allure,
Cry out for time to end his levity,
And age to soften its investiture;

But they, though others fade and are still fair,
Defy their fairness and are unsubdued;
Although they suffer, they may not forswear
The patient ardor of the unpursued.

Poor flesh, to fight the calendar so long;
Poor vanity, so quaint and yet so brave;
Poor folly, so deceived and yet so strong,
So far from Ninon and so near the grave.

The Poor Relation (1916)

No longer torn by what she knows
And sees within the eyes of others,
Her doubts are when the daylight goes,
Her fears are for the few she bothers.
She tells them it is wholly wrong
Of her to stay alive so long;
And when she smiles her forehead shows
A crinkle that had been her mother's.

Beneath her beauty, blanched with pain,
And wistful yet for being cheated,
A child would seem to ask again
A question many times repeated;
But no rebellion has betrayed
Her wonder at what she has paid
For memories that have no stain,
For triumph born to be defeated.

To those who come for what she was—
The few left who know where to find her—
She clings, for they are all she has;
And she may smile when they remind her,
As heretofore, of what they know

Of roses that are still to blow
By ways where not so much as grass
Remains of what she sees behind her.

They stay a while, and having done
What penance or the past requires,
They go, and leave her there alone
To count her chimneys and her spires.
Her lip shakes when they go away,
And yet she would not have them stay;
She knows as well as anyone
That Pity, having played, soon tires.

But one friend always reappears,
A good ghost, not to be forsaken;
Whereat she laughs and has no fears
Of what a ghost may reawaken,
But welcomes, while she wears and mends
The poor relation's odds and ends,
Her truant from a tomb of years—
Her power of youth so early taken.

Poor laugh, more slender than her song
It seems; and there are none to hear it
With even the stopped ears of the strong
For breaking heart or broken spirit.
The friends who clamored for her place,
And would have scratched her for her face,
Have lost her laughter for so long
That none would care enough to fear it.

None live who need fear anything
From her, whose losses are their pleasure;
The plover with a wounded wing
Stays not the flight that others measure;

So there she waits, and while she lives,
And death forgets, and faith forgives,
Her memories go foraging
For bits of childhood song they treasure.

And like a giant harp that hums
On always, and is always blending
The coming of what never comes
With what has past and had an ending,
The City trembles, throbs, and pounds
Outside, and through a thousand sounds
The small intolerable drums
Of Time are like slow drops descending.

Bereft enough to shame a sage
And given little to long sighing,
With no illusion to assuage
The lonely changelessness of dying,—
Unsought, unthought-of, and unheard,
She sings and watches like a bird,
Safe in a comfortable cage
From which there will be no more flying.

Eros Turannos (1916)

She fears him, and will always ask
    What fated her to choose him;
She meets in his engaging mask
    All reasons to refuse him;
But what she meets and what she fears
Are less than are the downward years,
Drawn slowly to the foamless weirs
    Of age, were she to lose him.

Between a blurred sagacity
    That once had power to sound him,

And Love, that will not let him be
 The Judas that she found him,
Her pride assuages her almost,
As if it were alone the cost.—
He sees that he will not be lost,
 And waits and looks around him.

A sense of ocean and old trees
 Envelops and allures him;
Tradition, touching all he sees,
 Beguiles and reassures him;
And all her doubts of what he says
Are dimmed with what she knows of days—
Till even prejudice delays
 And fades, and she secures him.

The falling leaf inaugurates
 The reign of her confusion:
The pounding wave reverberates
 The dirge of her illusion;
And home, where passion lived and died,
Becomes a place where she can hide,
While all the town and harbor side
 Vibrate with her seclusion.

We tell you, tapping on our brows,
 The story as it should be,—
As if the story of a house
 Were told, or ever could be;
We'll have no kindly veil between
Her visions and those we have seen,—
As if we guessed what hers have been,
 Or what they are or would be.

Meanwhile we do no harm; for they
 That with a god have striven,

Not hearing much of what we say,
  Take what the god had given;
Though like waves breaking it may be,
Or like a changed familiar tree.
Or like a stairway to the sea
  Where down the blind are driven.

Old Trails (1916)
(Washington Square)

I met him, as one meets a ghost or two,
Between the gray Arch and the old Hotel.
"King Solomon was right, there's nothing new,"
Said he. "Behold a ruin who meant well."

He led me down familiar steps again,
Appealingly, and set me in a chair.
"My dreams have all come true to other men,"
Said he; "God lives, however, and why care?

"An hour among the ghosts will do no harm."
He laughed, and something glad within me sank.
I may have eyed him with a faint alarm,
For now his laugh was lost in what he drank.

"They chill things here with ice from hell," he said;
"I might have known it." And he made a face
That showed again how much of him was dead,
And how much was alive and out of place,

And out of reach. He knew as well as I
That all the words of wise men who are skilled
In using them are not much to defy
What comes when memory meets the unfulfilled.

What evil and infirm perversity
Had been at work with him to bring him back?

Never among the ghosts, assuredly,
Would he originate a new attack;

Never among the ghosts, or anywhere,
Till what was dead of him was put away,
Would he attain to his offended share
Of honor among others of his day.

"You ponder like an owl," he said at last;
"You always did, and here you have a cause.
For I'm a confirmation of the past,
A vengeance, and a flowering of what was.

"Sorry? Of course you are, though you compress,
With even your most impenetrable fears,
A placid and a proper consciousness
Of anxious angels over my arrears.

"I see them there against me in a book
As large as hope, in ink that shines by night
Surely I see; but now I'd rather look
At you, and you are not a pleasant sight.

"Forbear, forgive. Ten years are on my soul,
And on my conscience. I've an incubus:
My one distinction, and a parlous toll
To glory; but hope lives on clamorous.

" 'Twas hope, though heaven I grant you knows of what—
The kind that blinks and rises when it falls,
Whether it sees a reason why or not—
That heard Broadway's hard-throated siren-calls;

" 'Twas hope that brought me through December storms,
To shores again where I'll not have to be
A lonely man with only foreign worms
To cheer him in his last obscurity.

"But what it was that hurried me down here
To be among the ghosts, I leave to you.
My thanks are yours, no less, for one thing clear:
Though you are silent, what you say is true.

"There may have been the devil in my feet,
For down I blundered, like a fugitive,
To find the old room in Eleventh Street.
God save us!—I came here again to live."

We rose at that, and all the ghosts rose then,
And followed us unseen to his old room.
No longer a good place for living men
We found it, and we shivered in the gloom.

The goods he took away from there were few,
And soon we found ourselves outside once more,
Where now the lamps along the Avenue
Bloomed white for miles above an iron floor.

"Now lead me to the newest of hotels,"
He said, "and let your spleen be undeceived:
This ruin is not myself, but some one else;
I haven't failed; I've merely not achieved."

Whether he knew or not, he laughed and dined
With more of an immune regardlessness
Of pits before him and of sands behind
Than many a child at forty would confess;

And after, when the bells in *Boris* rang
Their tumult at the Metropolitan,
He rocked himself, and I believe he sang.
"God lives," he crooned aloud, "and I'm the man!"

He was. And even though the creature spoiled
All prophecies, I cherish his acclaim.

Three weeks he fattened; and five years he toiled
In Yonkers,—and then sauntered into fame.

And he may go now to what streets he will—
Eleventh, or the last, and little care;
But he would find the old room very still
Of evenings, and the ghosts would all be there.

I doubt if he goes after them; I doubt
If many of them ever come to him.
His memories are like lamps, and they go out;
Or if they burn, they flicker and are dim.

A light of other gleams he has to-day
And adulations of applauding hosts;
A famous danger, but a safer way
Than growing old alone among the ghosts.

But we may still be glad that we were wrong:
He fooled us, and we'd shrivel to deny it;
Though sometimes when old echoes ring too long,
I wish the bells in *Boris* would be quiet.

11

RALPH ELLISON
AND TONI MORRISON

W hen asked about the origins of *The American Adam,* I think back to a certain literary and critical atmosphere in the late 1940s, when a concern with "myth and ritual" (the three words were usually strung together as though a single, hyphenated vocable) was much in the ascendancy in American criticism. "Myth" was as frequently evoked and as magical a referent in critical discussion then, at least in some quarters, as "deconstruction" would be twenty years later. Or to put it more personally, "myth" was as resonant a term in the vocabulary of the literature faculty at Bennington College, where I taught in those years, as "deconstruction" became in that of the English department at Yale, where I have mostly been teaching since. In fairness to myself, I ought to say that if I was never completely mythicized at Bennington, I have not been deconstructed at Yale. Even so, recent critical fashions, and especially structuralism and its assorted spawn, have had the effect of diverting my gaze from those earlier mythological interests, in part by alienating me from the whole business of contemporary literary criticism and sending me toward literary biography and related matters.

But Bennington College was a wonderfully lively and invigorating place thirty years ago. I had occasion, about a year back, to re-evoke the atmosphere of the campus, and the intellectual and literary doings of Kenneth Burke, Howard Nemerov, Stanley Kunitz, Stanley Edgar Hyman, and the others, along with our sanctifying texts by Joseph Campbell, Lord Raglan, and Robert Graves. I rehearsed all that, not to describe the context in which I wrote *The American Adam,* but to describe the context in which Ralph Ellison brought to completion his novel *Invisible Man,* published in 1952. For Ellison, too, was on the scene, fleeing New York to work in Vermont peace and quiet as the houseguest for weeks at a time of the Stanley Hymans, meeting occasionally with Bennington students, but talking endlessly and exuberantly with Kenneth Burke and the other faculty members. And my suggestion was that *Invisible Man* owed a portion of its mythic dimension to that Bennington critical environment.*

Invisible Man, as I think everyone will agree, is the finest and richest work of fiction by an American novelist since the end of the Second World War. At the same time, it is the central and pivotal text in modern black literature; every discussion of black narrative that I know of rises toward and takes its bearings *from* this astonishing literary achievement. But in our current perspective, three decades after the novel's appearance, we can, so to say, place *Invisible Man* within a much longer and broader tradition of black writing. In particular, we can observe how its mythic elements relate to those of earlier and later texts. This is what I want to do in this essay. For if various critical goings on distracted me from myth study, a growing awareness of the enormous role of black writing in our culture has, at least temporarily, brought me back to it. As regards that mode of study, it is here, I feel, that the really interesting and really new critical action may lie.

The segment of myth I shall be most concerned with is the one

*For a further word on that environment, see the extended note in "Notes on Origins and Other Agenda," at the end of this volume.

implicit in the title of Ellison's novel: it has to do with the problematics of identity. We can begin our inquiry with the autobiographical writings of Frederick Douglass, the former Maryland slave who escaped from bondage in 1838 and went on to become one of the most honored and valuable public figures of his American generation. Douglass published three versions of his life story. The first, *Narrative of the Life of Frederick Douglass, An American Slave,* which appeared in 1845 and runs to only 115 pages, carried that story through the moment of escape and up to an impromptu speech Douglass gave a couple of years later at an antislavery convention in New Bedford, Massachusetts. In 1855 Douglass offered a second edition, called *My Bondage and My Freedom:* it retold his experiences as a slave and added further events and associations during the period intervening. Finally, Douglass composed a six-hundred-page volume, published in 1881 as *Life and Times of Frederick Douglass;* it was revised and completed shortly before his death in 1895. A good third of this version was devoted to another retelling of his slave life, after which Douglass gives a leisurely account of such matters as his postwar role in defense of the rights of freedmen and his services as secretary of the Santo Domingo Commission, as recorder of deeds in Washington, and as United States minister to Haiti.

Throughout these successive renderings of his slavery experience, Douglass presents himself as a man who essentially created his own identity. He could never even be sure of his birth date, he remarks; black slaves had, in any case, a very limited sense of time, which they measured not by years and months but by seasons and such recurring routines as planting and harvesting. Nor, he informs us, is he able "to say much of my family," since "genealogical trees did not flourish among slaves." By way of emphasizing this and stressing one of many contrasts between the human situations of blacks and whites, Douglass builds an increasingly elaborate and detailed genealogy of his white master, Captain Aaron Anthony: wife, children, in-laws, grandchildren, and so on over three crowded generations. In fact, there *was* available to Frederick Douglass a well-stocked black genealogy going back to the early eighteenth century; and reviewing it recently in a brilliant study of Douglass's Maryland years, Dickson J. Preston declares forthrightly that Douglass "had not sprung full-blown out of nowhere. . . . [H]is black ancestors, for a century or more before his birth, had been a strong and closely knit kin group with family pride and traditions that were handed on to him by his part-Indian grandmother Betsey Bailey."

But Douglass, in his personal narratives, almost wholly ignored these ancestral legacies. His grandmother is given no more than a passing sentence in the 1845 volume; by 1881, she is accorded a page, but one devoted mainly to her skills as a fisherwoman and gardener, with no slightest hint of her role as a conveyor of family traditions. Among his other black forebears, Douglass mentions only—and as we shall see, peculiarly—his mother, Harriet Bailey. Douglass's manner of achieving identity, in short, was what I beg leave to call Adamic, though in a moment I shall want to modify that a trifle. I quote a sentence from my book, not at all because of any eloquence of prose, but because of its accidental but suggestive relevance to the case of Frederick Douglass, a person of whom I had scarcely heard at the moment of writing. The new hero on the American scene, I said, was "an individual emancipated from history, happily bereft of ancestry, untouched and undefiled by the usual inheritances of family and race; an individual standing alone, self-reliant and self-propelling," and more of the same. Douglass, it should be insisted, struck no such romantic heroic posture; but the young escapee who emerges from his pages is bereft—is, we come to realize, self-bereaving—along the lines just indicated.

Douglass's treatment of both his presumptive father and his actual mother shifts quite strikingly from one autobiographical version to another, something well remarked on by the gifted young scholar Henry Louis Gates, Jr., in the current *Yale Review*. In the 1845 *Narrative*, Douglass states without equivocation: "My father was a white man"; he twice speculates briefly and inconclusively as to whether the man might have been his owner, Captain Anthony. But in the 1881 *Life and Times,* he says: "Of my father I know nothing. Slaves had no recognition of fathers, as none of families." Period. The father disappears or is obliterated, as Douglass progressively establishes his identity over the years. But the mother, meanwhile, is being brought ever more substantially if disconcertingly to life.

"I never saw my mother, to know her as such, more than four or five times in my life," Douglass writes in 1845; "and each of these times was very short in duration, and at night." She died when the boy was seven, an event, according to Douglass in this first version, that meant little to him. "Never having enjoyed, to any considerable extent, her soothing presence, her tender and watchful care, I received the tidings of her death with much the same emotions I should have probably felt at the death of a stranger."

But ten years would make a great difference. By 1855, in *My Bondage and My Freedom,* Harriet Bailey had become "tall and finely proportioned, of dark, glossy complexion, with regular features, and amongst the slaves was remarkably sedate and dignified." More than that, she comes to her child's rescue at a dramatic moment. As punishment for some misdemeanor, little Frederick is being forced to go without food for a day; and as he is sitting by the fire, starving and tearful, his mother appears, snatches a large ginger cake to give him, and bestows upon him that "tender and watchful care" of the sort that in 1845 she had provided no single example. Lastly, and more arrestingly yet, the mother of 1855 is unexpectedly imbued with an ability to read and "an earnest love of knowledge." Indeed, Douglass is now disposed "to attribute any love of letters I possess, and for which I have got— despite of prejudices—only too much credit, *not* to my admitted Anglo-Saxon paternity, but to the native genius of my sable, unprotected, and uncultivated *mother,* a woman who belonged to a race whose mental endowments it is, at present, fashionable to hold in disparagement and contempt."

How can this transformation of Harriet Bailey be explained? We have here something like a parable about the reality and the mythology of black experience, the moral of which is that for the aspiring black individual there could be no such thing as "pure Adamism." Historical pressure would not permit it, as Douglass can testify. In the years following his arrival in New England, he was warmly taken up by the white anti-slavery agitators led by William Lloyd Garrison, who wrote a prefatory word to the 1845 *Narrative,* as did his associate Wendell Phillips. Douglass, in the modern idiom, was being preempted; and it was even said, especially by *pro*slavery people, that his obviously exceptional intelligence derived entirely from his white owner-father. To counter that slur against his race, in the 1855 volume Douglass ritualistically disposed of the Anglo-Saxon father, and evoked a goddesslike black slave mother from whom, alone, he inherited his "love of letters." The former act emphasized his self-created nature; but the latter at once reinvested him with a black heritage and bespoke the mental capacities of his people even under the condition of slavery. The 1855 version, notably, carried a single preface by a black writer.

The besetting paradoxes would not let up. "Once initiated into my new life of freedom," Douglass wrote in 1881, the "question arose, as to the name by which I should be known thereafter, in my new relation as a free man." The twenty-one-year-old had been known since birth by "the name given me by my dear mother": Frederick Augustus Washington Bailey. On the flight from Maryland, Frederick changed his surname to Johnson to conceal himself, as he says, from the slave hunters. But in the New Bedford neighborhood there were so many other Johnsons that another change proved necessary. His host and protector, who was one of the Johnsons, chose for him the name of a heroic character, Douglass, in Walter Scott's *Lady of the Lake.* In abandoning the name Bailey, Frederick was to a degree dissociating himself from the "dear mother" he elsewhere in the same text apotheosizes and declares his indebtedness and his closeness to;

and he was cutting himself away from the black slave background that he simultaneously proclaimed.

As though to soften the paradox, Douglass describes the question of a new name as "comparatively unimportant"; and it is true that Bailey, before it became a black family name, was that of a white slave owner, perhaps of Douglass's grandparents. But ritual renaming has been and continues to be one of the major themes in black cultural history. Among others, Booker T. Washington, one of the first of Douglass's biographers, has remarked on the special importance of the moment when a freed slave selected a new designation for himself; and Douglass in 1838 must have felt the vibrancy of the occasion, however he would downgrade it later for his strategic and fictive purposes. But long after slavery—indeed, in response to the fresh urgencies of every generation up to the present moment—the act of naming and renaming, of inventing names and discovering names, has been a salient aspect of black mythology.

It is certainly a key aspect of Ralph Ellison's *Invisible Man,* to which, ourselves moving down across those generations, we may now come. What we notice first, and it haunts and teases us from the start to finish, is that *for the reader* of *Invisible Man* the protagonist and narrator of the novel is nameless; and we are never more teased than when, before our very eyes so to speak, he writes down his name and local address in the series of New York offices to which he has been sent as a vindictive joke by his former academic overseer. In the Long Island paint factory, where he is given a job with the man in charge of the basement plant-works, he is again asked his name; he shouts it out, but the word is lost "in the roar of the furnaces." Soon afterward, one of the furnaces blows up in his face. The protagonist is flung violently out of kilter; when he comes to, he is being given electrical shock treatment, and a stranger is thrusting before his eyes a large card that reads: "WHAT IS YOUR NAME?" He realizes that he no longer knows his own name. "WHAT . . . IS . . . YOUR . . . NAME?" the card asks again; and then, "WHO . . . ARE . . . YOU?" "Something inside me," the narrator says, "turned with a sluggish excitement. This phrasing of the question seemed to set off a series of weak and distant lights . . . Who am I? I asked myself." But it was useless. The card probes further: "WHAT IS YOUR MOTHER'S NAME?" "*Mother,* who *was* my mother? . . . You always knew your mother's name." He cannot remember.

The protagonist is thus totally dissociated from his past, his family, his name, his former identity. And this condition, which results initially from a grotesque accident as of a technology gone mad (and in one of the most savagely funny scenes in modern fiction), is confirmed on another level of experience, when the protagonist joins the political organization called the Brotherhood. At the gathering in a luxurious downtown apartment, he is given a white envelope. " 'This is your new identity,' Brother Jack said. 'Open it.' Inside I found a name written on a slip of paper. 'That is your new name,' Brother Jack said. 'Start thinking of yourself by that name from this moment.' " The newly named young black man is likewise commanded to cease all contact with his family.

At this stage, the protagonist's identity is a fictive one, falsely imposed upon him by a scheming and treacherous white world; though we must be careful not to say this too heavy-handedly—for if *Invisible Man* is a nearly perfect marriage of realism and allegory (and not least in its deployment of colors), and if it is shot through with pain, it is also in the great tradition of robust comedy. What the protagonist comes to believe—as, at the end, he prepares to shake off "the old skin" and come forth in search of a truer identity—is what James Baldwin has argued every black man must learn. And this is that the black man, far from accepting an identity, a name, from the white environment, must create a highly flexible self in dialectical opposition to that environment. "To become a Negro, let alone a Negro artist," Baldwin wrote in the aptly titled volume of essays *Nobody Knows My Name,* "one had to make oneself up as one went along. This had to be done in the not-at-all-metaphorical teeth of the world's determination to destroy you." To this purpose, in the closing sequence of *Invisible Man,* the protagonist makes a ritual burning of the slip of paper with his Brotherhood name on it.

Ralph Ellison, of course, is a Negro man who is also a supreme literary artist—in this latter respect, at once Negro, American, male, and human. When he made his major statement about his own experience as a black man becoming a writer in America, he chose to concentrate exactly upon the phenomenon of *naming.* This was an address delivered at the Library of Congress in January 1964 and called "Hidden Name and Complex Fate." Ellison's hidden name was Waldo, for he was named by his father, a great admirer of the Concord sage, after Ralph Waldo Emerson; even as Frederick Douglass was rebaptized in honor of Walter Scott's hero. The name puzzled him in his childhood, Ellison recollected, and intimidated him a little in his young manhood, to the point where, first, he reduced it to the initial W., and then he suppressed it altogether. The ritual of suppression, we are given to understand, was part of the larger effort to create an independent identity as a writer of fiction and a citizen of the world of letters.

Before coming to his personal case, however, Ellison reflects more generally upon the challenge and the energizing power of names, especially the names of black people; and here he warrants quoting at some length, since what he has to say can, in the present context, reverberate both backward and forward. In the writer's struggle to take hold of the protean, the multiply named, nature of reality, he says:

> We must first come into the possession of our own names. For it is through our names that we first place ourselves in the world. Our names, being the gift of others, must be made our own. . . . We must learn to wear our names within all the noise and confusion of the environment in which we find ourselves. . . . They must become our masks and our shields, and the containers of those values and traditions which we learn and/or imagine as being the meaning of our familial past.

You will not have failed to detect a new emphasis getting expressed in these sentences—a beginning suggestion that identity is not something altogether self-begotten, as a mask or a shield, but may have to do as well with the values and traditions that constitute the meaning of a familial past. Identity is only in part *created*, so runs the implication; it is in equally good part *discovered*.

And this is singularly if strangely and painfully true for black persons. Ellison continues:

> And when we are reminded so constantly that we bear, as Negroes, names originally possessed by those who owned our enslaved grandparents, we are apt, especially if we are potential writers, to be more than ordinarily concerned with the veiled and mysterious events, the fusions of blood, the furtive couplings, the business transactions, the violations of faith and loyalty, the assaults; yes, and the unrecognized and unrecognizable loves through which our names were handed down to us.

He acknowledges with deep respect

> the example of the followers of Father Divine, and, now, the Black Muslims, discarding their original names in rejection of the bloodstained, the brutal, the sinful images of the past. Thus they would declare new identities, would clarify a new program of intention and destroy the verbal evidence of a willed and ritualized discontinuity of blood and human intercourse.

Not many blacks in the modern day, Ellison observes, adhere to that older tradition of self-renaming begun by former slaves. Most, he says, rather "take what we have and make of them what we can."

And there are even those who know where the old broken connections lie, who recognize their relatives across the chasm of historical denial and the artificial barriers of society, and who see themselves as bearers of many of the qualities which were admirable in the original sources of their common life.

I can think of no passage more cogent than that to introduce the text I want finally to consider, Toni Morrison's novel of 1977, *Song of Solomon*. This stupendous work of fiction carries as its epigraph the lines "The fathers may soar / And the children may know their names"; and it is a story that culminates in the discovery of "old broken connections," the recognition of "relatives across the chasm of historical denial," and the proud acknowledgment of admirable qualities in the original sources of a common life. I know next to nothing about Toni Morrison's literary antecedents, but I find it hard to believe that both Ellison's essay and Douglass's autobiographical narratives were not among the texts at work somewhere in her imagination.*

This is a most densely plotted narrative, as intricately woven as a Ross MacDonald novel, with which it has otherwise something in common in its aura of mystery, murder, and hidden wealth, and its pursuit of identity into the thickets of family history. At the center is a young black man whose legal name is Macon Dead the Third, but who, as the result of an embarrassing incident in his late childhood, has been rechristened Milkman; "the Negro community," Ellison remarked in that Library of Congress talk, "is deadly in its ability to create nicknames and to spot all that is ludicrous in an unlikely name

*In an insightful article on *Song of Solomon* in 1987, Lucinda H. MacKethan associates the novel both with Ellison's writings and with black slave narratives. She brings to bear relevant passages from Ellison's "Hidden Name and Complex Fate," and quotes Toni Morrison, in a 1976 interview, saying that at the time of composition she had been reading slave narratives "for sustenance." In her reading, Professor MacKethan remarks, Toni Morrison "would necessarily find the beginnings of the black writer's historical interest in names" (*CEA Critic* 49, nos. 2–4).

or that which is incongruous in conduct." We follow Milkman from his birth in 1931 into the early 1960s, with allusions to contemporary real-life events and figures—like Emmett Till and Orville Faubus—sprinkled through the pages. Most of this time, Milkman is living with his family in the black section of a city on the shore of Lake Michigan: his father, Macon Dead II, a hard-fisted collector of rents; his mother, the former Ruth Foster, daughter of the only black physician in the community; and his older sisters, Magdalene named Lena (so she is almost always referred to), and First Corinthians. Living nearby and a scandal to her brother are Milkman's Aunt Pilate, an elderly woman of bizarre energies who has the distinction of having been born without a navel; her daughter, Reba, and Reba's daughter by an unknown male, Hagar, with whom Milkman has a brief and feverish affair.

The plot gradually focuses on a number of sacks of gold nuggets, thought to be hidden in a cave down in Danville, Pennsylvania, where Milkman's grandfather, the first Macon, had run a farm many years before and where he had been ruthlessly murdered by a gang of rednecks. Milkman, instructed by his greed-driven father, goes off in search of the gold.

For Milkman, the treasure is a promise of freedom, of escape from the unbearable tensions of his family household, and the opportunity to create his own being, at the age of thirty-two, in total disjunction from his pressuring kin. For his closest friend, Guitar Bains (so nicknamed because he had always wanted to play that instrument), the gold represents quite another resource. Guitar is to share in the acquired wealth, and he will use it to fund a secret society he has joined; it is called The Seven Days, and its mission is to kill a white person, any white person, in response to the killing anywhere in the United States of a black person. Milkman himself is uninterested in Guitar's program of revenge; among all the aspects of a generally boring life, he finds "the racial problems that consumed Guitar the most boring of all." But he is willing to divide the treasure, and departs for Danville, Pennsylvania, and points south. He fails to find any gold;

but he finds a great many other things, including himself. As we shall see.

What is most stirring and provocative in *Song of Solomon* comes to us through and out of this complex pattern of characters and incidents—and above all, the whole business, one might say the whole mythology, of names. *Song of Solomon* is a book of names, a novel about naming. The grotesque family name, to begin with, was the gift of a drunken white soldier at the Freedman's Bureau in 1869. After Milkman's grandfather had declared that he came from Macon and that his father was dead, the soldier wrote "Dead, Macon" in the space provided for the former slave's name. This first Macon, who could neither read nor write, chose a name for his daughter by pointing blindly to a word in the Bible. "Like a Christ-killing Pilate," complained the midwife; "you can't get much worse than that for a name." But Pilate, as a young girl, treasured her name so much that she tucked it into her ear, attached to an earring.

Place names too have antic origins. The street the Dead family lives on, known locally as Not Doctor Street, received its name through the stubbornness of the neighborhood residents. Ruth Dead's physician father had lived there, and his reverential black patients sent him innumerable letters addressed to Doctor Street. The annoyed city legislators issued an edict that the avenue "had been and always would be known as Mains Avenue and not Doctor Street." The black population simply blocked out a phrase in the edict, which now read, "would be known as . . . Not Doctor Street"; and so it irrepressibly was. In the world of *Song of Solomon*, even farm animals are granted special names, like the first Macon's plowhorse President Lincoln, and his hog General Lee.

Names are what people think about and talk about in *Song of Solomon*, names and their relation to individual identity. The first Macon's wife is said to have approved the name bestowed on her husband at the bureau. "Mama liked it," her son remembers. "Liked the name. Said it was new and would wipe out the past." Her grandson

Milkman does *not* like his name. "Let me tell you somethin, baby," Guitar offers. "Niggers get their names the way they get anything else—the best way they can." In a later exchange, after listening to Guitar's white-killing plans, Milkman wonders why his friend does not follow the lead of Malcolm X and call himself X, so as "to let people know you don't accept your slave name." "I do accept it," says Guitar. "It's part of who I am. Guitar is *my* name. Bains is the slave master's name. And I'm all of that."

Milkman's steadily deepening consciousness of the tangled sources and the extraordinary suggestiveness of names is given a kind of ultimate expression in the echoing, ritualized litany that passes through his mind when he is flying back north after his Southern venture. He is thinking about all the black men he has known, North and South. "Their names," he says to himself. "Names they got from yearnings, gestures, flaws, events, mistakes, weaknesses. Names that bore witness. Macon Dead, Sing Byrd, Crowell Byrd, Pilate, Reba, Hagar, Magdalene, First Corinthians, Milkman, Guitar, Railroad Tommy, Hospital Tommy, Empire State, Small Boy, Sweet, Circe," and so on through some three dozen more nicknames (including Muddy Waters, Jelly Roll, Fats, and Leadbelly) in one of the great outbursts of the poetry of names in our literary time.

It is also, this litany, the ultimate product of Milkman's entire quest, and his testimonial to it. In Danville, Pennsylvania, a visit to the old cave is unprofitable, though he is now willing to credit his aunt's claim that the ghost of her father once appeared and spoke to her there; communion with the past is becoming a beckoning possibility for him. It is in Danville that, through an incredibly aged black woman called Circe, he learns for the first time the real names of his paternal grandparents: Jake, the ex-slave who was drunkenly renamed Macon Dead; and Sing, a woman of mostly Indian blood (like Frederick Douglass's grandmother, the reader is likely to reflect).

Milkman journeys down to the tiny village of Shalimar, Virginia, and here the story comes to its climax. Outside the general store, children are singing a song about "Jay the only son of Solomon"; except for the first line, it is a series of meaningless musical sounds. Making his rounds in the village, with a persistence he scarcely understands, Milkman comes upon a series of disclosures, some partly invented but others authentic, which put him in touch with the whole of his genealogy over four generations. He comes to know the names of his grandmother Sing's family: Heddy Bird, his great-grandmother; Crowell Byrd, his great-uncle; Susan Byrd, his living second cousin. Most important for him, he finds out where his father's father came from: from Solomon and Ryna, who in some olden time begot twenty-one sons, and the last one Jake.

The children are singing again, and now, the narrator says, "Milkman memorized all of what they sang." For this song of Solomon contains hieroglyphically the story of his clan and the origins of his own identity.

> *Jake the only son of Solomon*
>
> (to Milkman's ear, "Jay" has hardened into "Jake")
>
> Come booba yalle, come booba tambee . . .
> Left that baby in a white man's house
> Come booba yalle, come booba tambee
> Heddy took him to a red man's house . . .

and

> Solomon and Ryna Belali Shalut
> Yaruba Medina Muhammet too,
> Nestor Kalina Saraka cake,
> Twenty-one children, the last one Jake . . .

and

Solomon done fly, Solomon done gone
Solomon cut across the sky, Solomon gone home.

"These children," Milkman tells himself exultingly, "were singing a song about his own people!" The weird-sounding names—Belali, Shalut, Yaruba, and the rest—must be the names, respelled, of other sons of Solomon; and the baby left in a white man's house and taken by Heddy (Bird) to a red man's house was his own grandfather, Jake renamed Macon Dead. There returns to Milkman's memory the song he had been hearing all his life, the one sung by his Aunt Pilate: "O Sugarman done fly away / Sugarman done gone." The name of Solomon changed to Sugarman as his song traveled north, and as an actual family and an actual history traveled into myth.

If, with an effort, we draw back from the hypnotic texture of *Song of Solomon*, we can make out something of its thematic interweaving: that is, the varying attitudes to black identity, the different sources of personal identification, and the methods of acquiring a survivable self that the novel juggles with, embodies, discards, embraces. It is a narrative *précis* of black cultural history. The method of Frederick Douglass, which might be formulated as Adamism with a dash of the fictional, is confusedly followed by Milkman until he abandons it in Shalimar, at the moment he abandons without regret his search for the gold nuggets. The mode of accepting an identity imposed by the white world—the mode enacted for a space in *Invisible Man*—is represented in *Song of Solomon* by Milkman's father; and it is scornfully dismissed by Guitar. "I don't have to tell you," he says to Milkman, "that your father is a very strange Negro. . . . He behaves like a white man, thinks like a white man. . . . After *seeing* his father shot down by [some crackers] how can he keep his knees bent?"

But Guitar's method of self-affirmation, as I read it, is no less resolutely repudiated. It is acknowledged within the novel to be a great and terrible modern reality, for which the evils of historical conduct are primarily responsible; but it ends by transforming Guitar into an incurable fanatic. It has more than a little in common with the proposition of James Baldwin, that "one had to make oneself up as one went along . . . in the not-at-all-metaphorical teeth of the world's determination to destroy you."

Let me return to the basic distinction. Both the Douglass-style intention and the Baldwin-style intention rest on the belief that a black man's identity has to be *created:* created pretty much out of whole cloth and, shrewdly or polemically, as against the enveloping white environment. *Song of Solomon* moves toward an opposite conviction: that black identity has to be *discovered,* that it is lying there awaiting discovery amid the broken connections and the lost relationships of black history and kinship.

The act of discovery, needless to say, is itself in its own way creative. Judging from *Song of Solomon,* it can even be perceived as a literary act. Milkman's discovery involves the decoding of songs and poems, the clarification of verbal messages, the constant revision of old tales, the deciphering of names. It requires a struggle with the shifting essences of black mythology, and especially with the literary arrangements they can give rise to. *Song of Solomon* is unmistakably of the American late 1970s in being a novel that brings to bear upon its major theme, its myth of identity, a distinctive literary awareness, a pervasive sense that story telling, novel making, the careers of poems constitute the milieu where the answers to the big human questions may be looked for.

It is equally of the 1970s in the stance it eventually assumes regarding that theme. As we glance around us today, we observe a quite widely shared black ambition to identify oneself by identifying one's fore-bears. The older myth of invisibility that flourished into the 1960s and produced at least one masterpiece, with its interior motto that "nobody knows my name" and its feeling that a man must somehow be his own begetter, is giving way in the present era to the quest for family and the legendary prowess of far-off ancestors. We may think of Alex Haley's engrossing if imaginative book about his ancestry, *Roots;* and I would draw your attention to the charming memoir, pointedly called

Generations, by the gifted black poet Lucille Clifton. *Song of Solomon* is a larger accomplishment than either of those, and partly because it gives a clearer narrative voice to Ralph Ellison's remark about a descendant taking on certain high qualities of a predecessor.

The legendary Solomon flew off through the air from Shalimar, cut across the sea and flew all the way back to the Africa from which his people had come. "Oh, man!" Milkman exclaims in a shout of triumph to his landlady and bedmate, Sweet. "He didn't need no airplane. He just took off; got fed up. *All the way up!* No more cotton! No more bales! No more orders! . . . He flew, baby . . . flew on home . . . back to Africa." Milkman absorbs the legend, and takes to himself its message of actuality: which is, in a grand metaphor of human freedom, that a man *can* learn to soar, to ride the winds of the world. This is what the discovery of names and family has given him. He has learned his name, and it has made him free.

(1981)

PART THREE

Critics of Literature

I write this on a Tuscan hillside, surrounded by cypresses, villas, and farmhouses, but quite bereft of the books I would need to consult if I were to attempt any close comment on Francis Fergusson's immense contribution to our literary understanding. That contribution is unique in its way; it has profoundly affected the way we perceive the structures—that is, the patterns of momentous development—of dramas and novels; and I should like to offer a general remark or two about it. Under the circumstances, however, I hope I'll be forgiven if I begin with a few personal reminiscences. They are intended primarily as a form of *hommage*.

For some time Francis Fergusson seemed to recede in front of me. I do not mean intellectually: in that regard, he was always quite out of sight. I mean almost literally. His essays—on *Oedipus the King*, on *Hamlet*, on Henry James—had struck me with something of the force of religious revelation, and I was eager to meet him and talk with him, to ask him to elaborate on some of his most stimulating but oddly elusive critical concepts, primarily of course the complex notion of "action." But I arrived at Bennington College in the fall of 1948 to discover that Fergusson, who had taught there for a dozen years, had just taken terminal leave to become a Fellow at the Institute for Advanced Study in Princeton. His shadow loomed with magisterial grandeur at Bennington. His presence was felt in the special orientation of literary studies, in the critical vocabulary on campus, even in the college's library resources (it was because of Fergusson that the little library surprisingly stocked Pico della Mirandola's *Oration on the Dignity of Man*, a text that was crucial for a course I wanted to give). I even came to grow impatient with the reports of his intellectual heroics and his powerful lingering authority and acquired quite a false impression of him as a gray eminence and canny dialectician whose rather dark influence none could dispel.

He was at Princeton University for a few years, organizing and presiding over the remarkably distinguished and successful series of Gauss Seminars in Literary Criticism. But by the time I in turn reached Princeton, in the early 1950s, he had moved on (via Indiana) to Rutgers, whose president created by fiat the position of University Professor chiefly to make possible an appointment for Fergusson. During his last year at Princeton, I happened to talk with Richard Blackmur, who was telling me about some large plans for a school of humanities at Princeton University. What was the purpose of such a school, I asked. Blackmur replied at once: "To keep Francis Fergusson around." The answer made perfect sense; but insofar as that was its excellent intention, the plan did not succeed.

It was thanks in good part to Fergusson that I too eventually moved over to Rutgers, where, in 1954, toiling hard, I at last caught up with him. I must admit I pressed a little in the early days of our friendship (or perhaps I should say my discipleship and his benevolent patronage). We invited him with his wife, Marion, to dinner on a series of summer evenings, and Nancy Lewis, working from dawn, served a variety of sumptuous lobster dishes, which, as it turned out much later, Fergusson detested. He was much too kind to say so, however, and it was not long before I realized that my image of him as a towering authoritarian was ludicrously wrong and that Fergusson was a man of remarkable simplicity of spirit, of warm affections and unquestioning loyalties, as well as extraordinary tenacity and clarity of mind—and in the most casual conversations, one of the greatest teachers I had ever known. (My own experience is that the great teachers I have encountered—Fergusson, F. O. Matthiessen, Mark Van Doren, Newton Arvin, Stringfellow Barr—reveal their capacities even more in conversation than in the classroom.)

In the winter of 1958, I was in Paris for a week, holding discussions with Albert Camus. The latter was directing rehearsals for a revival of his play *Caligula*, and I received his permission to bring Francis Fergusson, who was also in town, along to the theater one afternoon. My wife and I had just come from Munich, where the pre-Lenten *Fasching* was in progress, and we brought and gave Fergusson one of the anticly designed black masks that gentlemen wear to the more exuberant of the *Fasching* gatherings. I can still see Fergusson striding across the Pont Royal, under a gray winter sky, his coattail flapping while he dangled the black mask from his hand with no more self-consciousness than a child and discoursed spiritedly on Henry James's *The Golden Bowl*. At the theater, Camus shook hands warmly and said how glad he was to meet Fergusson: *The Idea of a Theater*, he declared, was the best book on tragedy he had ever read.

Fergusson's reputation in Europe is enormous, perhaps greater than in his own country, where learned academics sometimes look askance at any colleague who tends to have truly fresh and—for students—persuasive ideas. Effortlessly, Fergusson has managed never to be absorbed into the establishment. But once in Venice, for example, I ran into an internationally renowned professor of Italian literature and expert on Dante who was clutching and exulting over Fergusson's book *Dante's Drama of the Mind*. Later that same year, in Rome, I spent an afternoon with Alberto Moravia and Giorgio Bassani, who was at that time director of the Rome School of Drama. I happened to mention Francis Fergusson, and the other two immediately exclaimed that *L'Idea del teatro* was an absolutely exceptional book and for Bassani in his professional work a kind of bible. I am told that it is not unheard of to elicit similar responses in Japan.

There are, needless to say, a great many more memories, all happy to contemplate, in a friendship that has lasted for more that fifteen years. There was the winter evening when my wife and I went to dine at the Fergussons', who had also invited the Jason Epsteins down from New York. (When Epstein was given free reign to begin the epochal Anchor paperback series, the second book he selected for publication was *The Idea of a Theater*.) It was snowing when we arrived, and before dinner was over drifts had completely blocked the Fergussons' driveway. Bunks were found for all of us, and Fergusson had just enough bourbon on hand to keep us satisfied till we had exhausted ourselves in talk, mainly, as I recall, about current literary periodicals and the feasibility of starting a new one. I was struck then, as I always am, by Fergusson's combination of quiet serenity and utter muscularity of intellect. He would no more compromise a literary opinion than he would cut off his own hand. Not that there is ever a question of imposing his views on others; he is much too good a teacher for that. A couple of years ago, he came up to Yale to see the production of Robert Lowell's *Prometheus*, and we asked Robert Brustein and his wife to join us for dinner. Brustein, the exceedingly tough-minded and vigorously forward-looking dean of the Yale Drama School, said that nothing on earth would keep him from the opportunity of meeting Francis Fergusson, who had been his literary idol for years. There was much harmonious and sociable talk about the performance the Fergussons were about to see; but Fergusson's account of the play later, in the *New York Review of Books*, did not conceal behind its courteous and elegant rhetoric the fact that he considered it a dramatic mess, a wild flailing of sometimes brilliant language around (to Fergusson's stern critical sense) an inertness of action.

But perhaps my most enduring recollection of Francis Fergusson is in his garden, tending the flower beds and pointing out the tracks of the foxes and deer that sometimes stray out of the woods at the foot of the slope. It is no bit of fancy to say that this is what Fergusson has always been doing. Unconcerned with the establishment and the academic literary fashions of the moment, almost unaware of them, he has gone on steadily cultivating his garden.

Francis Fergusson's key critical concepts are strikingly prehensile. Carefully applied to any work of literature that has a germ of the dramatic in it, they permit us to *take hold* in the most convincing manner. They work a kind of magic in the classroom; they are indeed teaching instruments, the product of a strenuously active mind that is persistently concerned with the process of learning and of teaching. And yet they do not come to us easily; if they are, so to speak, ideas that grasp, they are curiously difficult to grasp themselves. Nothing more straightforward, theoretically, than Fergusson's proposition that the first stage of a dramatic action is best identified by an infinitive of purpose: "to find the killer of the former king"; "to avenge the murder of one's father." Yet it took me, at least, no few years before I could make critical use of that principle with any assurance.

One reason, I think, is that American criticism and the minds of our best students have been pretty thoroughly romanticized in recent decades, while the intellectual temper of Francis Fergusson (like that of most others of his critical generation) is essentially classical—as, in his case, classicism was modified and thickened by the medieval vision of reality, and as the latter was thereafter modified and to some extent secularized by Shakespeare. Fergusson's critical eye looks and invites us to look at human motives, at the human spirit in purposeful motion, at human personalities thrusting against one another in a significant illuminating clash of cross-purposes; but the romantic eye watches the human spirit examining itself, descending into itself, experiencing itself; and the romantic imagination, whether creative or critical, is most aroused by the spectacle of its own workings. Fergusson, or shall we say the Fergussonian critic, inspecting *The Scarlet Letter*, observes an austere conflict between Dimmesdale's impulse to confess, Chillingworth's will to discover, and Hester Prynne's determination to conceal. For the romantic critic, all this is very nearly beside the point; what he perceives as central is Hawthorne's imagination manipulating characters and incidents in a painful effort to wrest meaning out of the indecipherable and to invest phenomena with symbolic significance.

The analysis of action in a novel like *The Wings of the Dove* permits us to penetrate the thick and initially baffling haze of oblique allusion and get at the source of the novel's momentum—the ailing Milly Theale's anguished desire *to live*, essentially to experience the most fully rewarding relationship with another human being; that purpose runs up against the strategically concealed counter motives of Kate Croy, her Aunt Maude, Lord Mark, and the ineffectual but slowly maturing Merton Densher. We observe the rich play of what Fergusson would call Henry James's "histrionic imagination," leading as it does and all so convincingly at last to the very nearly religious vision entertained by Densher, that moment of "perception" which, according to Fergusson, the purposes and the passions serve to beget in the thoroughly dramatized literary work. Henry James is of course the most avowedly dramatic of novelists; but even with a writer less vigorously histrionic, the analysis of action can be an indispensable approach. With Edith Wharton, for example, as we search the handsomely detailed settings and the meticulous description of women's wear to see just what kind of an action is being started and by what means, we come rather quickly to realize how limited and uncertain is the willpower of most of her male characters, and how easily their dim, gentle aspirations are defeated by smaller-minded but stronger-willed young females. The actions in Edith Wharton's best novels are, I suppose, what Fergusson would identify as "pathetic"; and just as the initiating purpose is usually vague and wistful and the passions muted, so the ensuing perception remains blurred and ambiguous, a general sense of the pathos of the human condition.

Fergusson's application of Dante's theory of the fourfold meaning of poetry deserves a paper in itself; since I do not have at hand his book on Dante and his other pertinent discussions, I can do no more than mention it. Nor indeed do I fully understand it. But perhaps I can refer to a part of Fergusson's theory of dramatic meaning—namely what I take to be his view that the *allegorical* level of any literary work that rises thereto is a certain revelation about the secret drift of human history, or, as the case may be, of the working out of God's purposes and promises within human history. Now, this is not only unromantic; it is downright un-American. History as an object of scientific study may have great appeal to intelligent Americans; but when it comes to literature, the Amerian critical mind is usually immune to such hints as may be bodied forth—the larger, remoter historical, or historico-mythic developments the main action may be representing.

And yet, when we concentrate on this aspect, how much that had gone unnoticed in major American novels (to stay with them) becomes visible. *The Scarlet Letter*, in one perspective, is a dramatic essay on the evolution of the New England temper from Elizabethan days to Hawthorne's time, with subtle apprehensive insinuations about the future. *Billy Budd*, or one version of it, surreptitiously adumbrates a theory about the nature of modern revolution. In *The Wings of the Dove*, the anagogic moment of vision is preceded and made possible by the subtly gathering image of a Europe, an entire human community (the Western world, we feel in retrospect, on the eve of the First World War), fatally succumbing to some implacable corroding force; and Francis Fergusson himself has compared the dark grandeur of the historical vision in *The Golden Bowl* to that of Virgil's *Aeneid*. If Edith Wharton's fiction resolutely and significantly holds back from anything like the anagogic, the small but perfectly understood social and moral history her actions imply shows itself only to greater effect—a movement exactly toward the ambiguous and the morally confused.

And we need only mention *Absalom, Absalom!* to become aware not only how important the historical dimension of a novel can be, but how cautious our assumptions must be about the relationship implied by a writer of genius between the historical on the one and the dramatic and individual on the other. Is Sutpen's finally disastrous career a synecdoche as it were of Southern history? Of American history? Of modern history? Is there a cause and effect relation—is Sutpen the product and victim of Southern history; or is the South the victim of men like Sutpen? No one of these questions can be answered confidently in the affirmative. But they are among the questions Francis Fergusson would have us ask; and no reader who believes that what *Absalom, Absalom!* is really about, first and last, is the struggling process of the creative or myth-making imagination will even come to them.

They are crucial questions because they make our minds stand up and ask about ourselves: where do *we* stand, with our habits and actions and beliefs, on the long, menacing, hope-arousing arc of history? They are sources of identity. Francis Fergusson's critical theories and practices have a kind of severely beautiful purity to them. They are uncontaminated by private idiosyncrasies, and they are not distracted by the clamor of *immediate* history. But they are profoundly, organically implicated in the processes of life—that is, with the allegory that, knowingly or not, we are all caught up in.

(1969)

13

The Surviving Self

*The Bit Between My Teeth. A Literary Chronicle of
1950–1965
Edmund Wilson: A Study of Literary Vocation in Our
Time, by Sherman Paul*

E dmund Wilson turned seventy about six months ago, and
the occasion is being variously observed and celebrated.
Wilson himself has just given us the third of his "literary
chronicles," a gathering of essays published in the last decade and a
half. His publishers have brought out new editions of the two earlier
ones, *Classics and Commercials* (1950) and *The Shores of Light* (1952), so
that Wilson's fascinating chronicle of his own and his country's literary
preoccupations from 1920 to the current year is now available intact.
Sherman Paul, professor of English at the University of Illinois and the
author of admirable books about Emerson, Thoreau, and Louis Sulli-
van, has written a discreet and discerning account of Wilson's career
thus far. Edmund Wilson is certainly, as Mr. Paul says, "our pre-
eminent man of letters." As a literary critic, social reporter, and travel
writer, as poet, playwright, and short story writer, as novelist and
historian—and as a performer, in general, on an astonishingly and
sustained high level—Wilson is "perhaps the last of the great profes-
sionals." It is a good moment, with the help of the new books, to

reappraise this enduring prodigy, to try to identify him and to calculate his impact and influence.

The Bit Between My Teeth (a title that reminds one of the double-edged phrase Wilson used for another collection some years ago, *A Piece of My Mind*) contains three dozen essays, several of very considerable length. The range of interest, knowledge, and critical power is extraordinary, as always; and the achievement, to use a word Wilson mistrusts, is massive. Wilson talks about American subjects from the pre-presidential Theodore Roosevelt to the work of the novelist Dawn Powell and James Baldwin, and English writers from Swinburne to Kingsley Amis. He contributes what is nearly a small book on the Marquis de Sade; and to the original and enormously enthusiastic review of Malraux's *Psychologie de l'Art* he has added a long, slightly apprehensive note on its revised version, *The Voices of Silence,* expressing the belief that Malraux puts too much faith in the world of pure art forms, and that he "must look for salvation from some other source than from the products of modern painting." There are two reverential probings of *Dr. Zhivago,* and a number of remarkable essays on words, clichés, and languages. But the real subject throughout is never precisely the writer or the text in question, but Edmund Wilson's personal encounters with each of them. Each essay thus contains a sort of small "action"; and this, along with Wilson's resolute, wonderfully lucid, and ever-pursuing style, is what gives the essays their unrivaled momentum, the peculiar and direct force with which they communicate and go on communicating.

When the encounters have been literal ones, Wilson can reminisce about the antics of Fitzgerald and Hemingway, about being taken to meet Max Beerbohm in Rapallo, and to call upon Logan Pearsall Smith, the author of *Trivia,* in Philadelphia. Elsewhere, the encounter is with the mind and imagination at work in a book, in letters, novels, poems. Speaking of de Sade, to whose complete writings Wilson had at last got access, he tells us that "I am in the habit of reading at breakfast, but I found that *Les 120 Journées* was the only book that I could not face while eating." Other encounters and re-encounters prove more appetizing—for example, with the fiction of James Branch Cabell, which Wilson helped to resurrect, and the poetry of T. S. Eliot, which Wilson esteems, if anything, the more highly because of his lifelong watchful wariness of Eliot's nonhistorical and (to Wilson) antipathetic if important brand of criticism. Two of the most spirited items in the entire volume report on Wilson's encounters with himself: two imaginary, not to say hallucinatory, interviews (one appropriately called "Every Man His Own Eckerman"), in which Wilson holds forth with gusto on the accomplishments and absurdities of contemporary arts and letters.

Like every book Wilson has written, *The Bit Between My Teeth* is, in short, a part of his continuing effort, in the phrase of Hawthorne, "to keep open an intercourse with the world"—with all phases of the world. He misses no opportunity to indicate his sense of the current condition of man. In a review of some books about bees, insects, and fossils, Wilson pauses to reflect that "The present age is not one of the great ages of the self-dramatization of man," and that while apes are found to be more human than was once believed and insects more rational, man is becoming more bestial and instinctual. And in an extensive memoir of his experiences with foreign languages, Wilson exploits a group of Hungarian grammars—prepared in various languages for various tourists and invaders (English, American, Russian, German)—to show how each grammar displays in its "story exercises" the habitual concerns of the nation in question. The American text contains exercises dealing with a G.I. trying to pick up a girl in a restaurant, the Russian introduces an ironworker meeting or looking for communist comrades in Budapest ("Where are the Chinese? Are there no Chinese workers here?" "Why, yes, they are here," and so on). This almost incredible feat of learning is accompanied by a subterranean chuckle like that of an erudite Sidney Greenstreet, while Wilson demonstrates that the cold war has even permeated the field of linguistics.

Wilson's determination, against increasingly terrible odds, to keep a meaningful intercourse between his highly, sometimes crankily independent self and the world or worlds he has lived through is essentially the theme of Sherman Paul's valuable and very well ordered study. The book is un-Wilsonian in that the author makes little effort to confront and explore Wilson the man, having indicated in his subtitle that he is interested rather in an instance, or *the* instance, of devotion to the literary calling in our time. Nor, despite that, does Mr. Paul have much to say about Wilson's distinctively *literary* criticism after the epochal *Axel's Castle* (1931). Volumes like *The Triple Thinkers* and *The Wound and the Bow* are barely mentioned in passing. Further, and what may be the same thing, while Mr. Paul deals perceptively and persuasively with Wilson's one-time involvement with Marx and Marxism, he skimps on Wilson's subsequent involvement with Freud and his Freudian interpretations of literature and the careers of writers. Wilson's Marxian encounter with history—as Mr. Paul aptly describes *To the Finland Station* (1940)—might have been revealingly balanced by Wilson's encounter, aided by Freud, with the troubled self and the traumatic imagination. But in an act of uncommonly clear-eyed critical piety, Mr. Paul has carefully charted the significant externals of Wilson's life and the key rhythms of his career, from his birth in May 1895 to the publication of his *Apology to the Iroquois* in 1964.

In the twenties, Wilson appears as a young man dedicated to enticing poets and novelists back into the public world, to finding how the new literary techniques eventually defined in *Axel's Castle* might be used "in a public way," and the modern creative imagination be drawn into "the service of social action." In the thirties, he is a person vicariously experiencing and writing about historical social action, reading Michelet and revering Lenin, striving to "redirect the bourgeois mind" toward socialism, while at the same time and in the name of an unswerving individualism he wanted to rescue Communism from the communists. In the forties, he is a brilliant but disaffected literary journalist (this was the time of *Classics and Commercials*). In the fifties, he becomes a world traveler, a sort of cultural anthropologist on what turned out to be a religious enquiry (this was the time of *The Scrolls from the Dead Sea*).

In recent years, Mr. Paul sees Wilson making "the passage home," directing his attention to that American scene and history over which he had yearned and despaired in *Memoirs of Hecate County* (1946). The first culmination of this phase was *Patriotic Gore* (1962), Wilson's large-scale study of the imaginative responses North and South—of statesmen, soldiers, writers, housewives—to the Civil War. This may be Wilson's critical masterpiece. But one has the impression that it is part of a still larger scheme, that Wilson is compiling nothing less than an exceedingly personal history of the American imagination from the early nineteenth century onward—an appraisal of the America that lies within the reach of his own experience, that of his lifetime and the transmitted lifetimes of his parents and grandparents. This, Wilson said at the close of *Red, Black, Blond and Olive* (1956) and after declaring that he would publish no more "records of foreign travel," is, after all, "the life that I ought to know best." To know this America is, for Wilson, to know himself.

But Wilson's American researches and meditations have made him steadily more somber. His political passion is unsubdued, but it is now, Mr. Paul points out, a sort peculiar to our time. As against a fascination with the individual's participation in the great movements of history thirty years ago, Wilson has become profoundly concerned with the sheer "endurance and survival of the individual"; with the survival of "minority societies" like his New York state neighbors the Iroquois, to whom Wilson wrote an open letter of apology; and "with the persistence of varieties of life." And he is, so to speak, robustly gloomy because he believes, like many of the rest of us in our less articulate way, that these things may be fatally threatened by a conglomeration of mindless or idea-less forces—political, technological, financial, and emotional forces.

The theme is not new with Wilson. As early as 1950, in a grim apocalyptic farce called *The Little Blue Light,* Wilson envisaged the entire country taken over by a group devoted to pure blind power, without a shred of ideology; and he symbolized in the climax the obliteration of both political and aesthetic idealism. But Wilson is always inveterately American in his indictment of America. The argument of *The Cold War and the Income Tax* was undermined for many readers by Wilson's revealed and disconcerting ignorance of our tax laws; but it was, really, an icily furious contribution to the special American tradition of protest that goes back to Thoreau and is being continued on university campuses across the nation—a tradition of personal outrage over the way America is behaving itself. The opposite note is rare indeed. The only expression of hope that Wilson has given of late comes in an essay about George Kennan, and it must be the most stringently modulated utterance of its kind. The favorable public response to Kennan's book about Russia, Wilson says, picking his words with care, "has surprised me and seemed to me encouraging as a sign perhaps of a stirring in the direction of a relativistic intelligence."

Wilson's apocalyptic tendency is American, too, in its derivation from his Calvinist background. One of his ancestors married a Mather; his grandfather was a Presbyterian minister; and at the family home and later at The Hill School, Wilson was enveloped in a rather thick hard-line Protestant atmosphere. He was able to resist and survive it; but he has retained a portion of the Calvinist religious temper, as it were in displaced form. Wilson knows this, is intrigued by it, and wants to exorcise it. "It may be," he tells us in the postscript to *Red, Black, Blond and Olive* and in the most striking passage of self-examination he has written, "that an atavistic Protestantism predisposed me toward the Marxist morality"—that is, "to the religious element that Marx and Engels smuggled into their system." Such self-examination, which is itself a Calvinistic habit, led Wilson to reject the Marxist "mythology," and all other mythologies, including that of "Jehovah-Elohim and the persons of the Trinity." These may have been admirable, Wilson thinks, for their time and historic purpose; but they tend inevitably to collide with one another, and they must be discouraged and got rid of. Yet Mr. Paul is undoubtedly right in insisting that Wilson is "of a religious disposition." He is regularly drawn to those great thrusts and energies of (as Wilson would say) the purely human spirit, which have given rise to religious mythology. And his imagination is hospitable to images of religious grandeur—including the dark grandeur of catastrophe, of an American apocalypse.

Wilson, in other words, is a very American scholar. He has acknowledged the deep and long-standing influence of Taine, and he has rehearsed the lessons he learned from Vico. But his more immediate lineage descends from Emerson, who similarly displaced a religious intensity into humanistic forms. For Wilson as for Emerson, that device pertains to the American scholarly role of mediator, of seeking to establish and preserve lines of communication between his countrymen and the shifting realms of ideas and of imagination. Wilson descends as well from William Dean Howells, who combined a socialist faith with a courageous and highly influential appreciation of literary greatness, whether expatriated like Henry James or quintessentially native like Mark Twain. To some extent, Wilson follows after Van Wyck Brooks, in the effort to focus a broadly cultivated mind upon the American literary and social scene of the past century and a half. Like those others but especially like Emerson, Wilson has also been a mediator of a different sort—between what might be called the contending spirits of Enlightenment and of Romanticism. His work, as Daniel Aaron has observed, is animated by two major impulses: an impulse toward order, good form, the gracious life, free inquiry, and a rationalistic hostility to mysticism; and an impulse toward the politically and morally revolutionary, the psychologically and aesthetically scandalous. Wilson himself has always admired those, like Edith Wharton and John Jay Chapman, who have cut loose from their conservative background and yet kept their ties with it. He respects and sometimes longs for the old, but he constantly emerges to take serious account of the new. This is one reason why he has spoken to the condition of each new generation of readers.

If Wilson descends from Emerson and, though less so, from Howells and Brooks, who today can be said to descend from Wilson? Mr. Paul argues correctly that Wilson has never tried to impose an orthodoxy, and that he has no "explicit method or discipline." Having no discipline, he has, not surprisingly, had few disciples. But Mr. Paul also argued, in an uncharacteristically glowering footnote, that Stanley Edgar Hyman's "treatment of Wilson in *The Armed Vision* (1948) accounts for Wilson's almost total neglect in the schools." This, if Mr. Paul will forgive me, is nonsense every which way. Hyman's essay was notably ungenerous and, for its gifted author, myopic; he has removed it from later editions. But his strictures on Wilson's critical procedures, Wilson's not infrequent inaccuracies, and his insensitivity to most of modern American poetry: these raise questions worth considering. But on the one hand, Wilson is not in fact neglected in the schools. *Axel's Castle* remains for most literary schoolmen the classic treatment of "symbolism" and perhaps of any new literary movement; and the schools have yet to get over Wilson's Freudian reading of *The Turn of the Screw*. On the other hand, what, beyond that, can the schools *do* with Wilson's work? It is just its antischolastic largeness of interest that make it inaccessible to the current academic pedantry.

Wilson is not so much an influence—like F. R. Leavis or Northrop Frye—as a standard, an example. He is the representative man of letters, in Emerson's meaning of the adjective. He is not a typical but a supreme instance—of utter integrity of opinion and of indifference to the intellectual fashions of either the metropolitan marketplace or the departments of English; of unflagging intellectual energy; and especially of the magnanimous vision and the conviction that the whole range of human experience and activity is the object of the humanistic intelligence. It is not hard to name writers, here and abroad, who have striven after and in various degrees have achieved these qualities—each, following the example of Wilson, in his own personal manner and voice. One need only mention the names and think about the many-faceted work of humanists like Kenneth Burke, Lionel Trilling, the late Richard Chase and Alfred Kazin in this country, and V. S. Pritchett and Frank Kermode in England. But who has been hanging around in the world of letters these past thirty years and has not felt the impact of Wilson, and felt refreshed and encouraged by his mere presence in that darkening and narrowing world?

Wilson, above all, has survived. Not only has he kept on living to the seventieth birthday being celebrated; he has survived as an ever more forceful and independent self. At the close of *Hecate County*, the narrator flees the demonic confusions of a drinking party and goes home "to rejoin there my old solitary self, the self for which I really lived and which kept up its austere virtue, the self which had survived through these trashy years." There speaks Wilson, and he speaks again in the postscript to an article on Stravinsky: "In youth, we admire the heroes, the affirmers, the 'lords of life.' Later on, when we have had some experience of the difficulty of practicing an art, of surviving to grow old in its practice, when we have seen how many entrants drop out, we must honor any entrant who finishes." Wilson has not yet finished—far from it. But he has survived and grown old in the practice of a noble profession. Pesky, skeptical, apocalyptic, rich with prejudices, Wilson has been the greatest, because the most heroically individual, practitioner of his generation.

(1965)

Theatricals

The Duke of Palermo and Other Plays, with an Open Letter to Mike Nichols

In his new book, Edmund Wilson continues the exploration of the American scene that has been his main, if by no means his only, critical occupation during the past decade or so. *Patriotic Gore* (1962), that extraordinary study of Northern and Southern reactions to the Civil War, was a key moment in this perhaps culminating phase in the career of America's first man of letters; *The Cold War and the Income Tax* and Wilson's letter of apology to the Iroquois Indians were later and minor moments. Wilson's appraisal of the contemporary condition of his own country and its decline from older, more heroic and idealistic days has made him steadily more somber (as I remarked in these columns a few years back); and well it might. The new volume bears further and important witness to these matters—Wilson's intensifying concern with the state of things American, and the pain and displeasure it gives him.

Wilson's persistent interest in theater is also reflected here. The book consists of three plays mostly written quite recently—two of them fulllength, one limited to a single scene—and an open letter to the producer Mike Nichols, recommending titles for a proposed American National Theater devoted to reviving forgotten landmarks of American drama. The letter is an engagingly quixotic act of artistic patriotism, and it offsets a little the onward driving satire of the plays and their work of cultural demolition. But even in the plays, where the prevailing mode is comedy slithering betimes into farce, a kind of zest (if scarcely a note of hopeful good cheer) mingles with the somberness. All told, *The Duke of Palermo*, while not perhaps adding a great deal to Wilson's immense literary stature, solidifies our sense of his glowering but also witty and boundlessly energetic humanism. The latter is one of our great cultural "valuables," and the new volume gives us, happily, a fresh occasion for inspecting it.

The first of the plays is a comedy about a play called *The Duke of Palermo*, so to speak a hoax about a hoax. It is set in a small New England liberal arts college, where the first production is being given of a work that may just possibly be a genuine and recently unearthed Elizabethan tragedy by one Henry Chettle—with the even more remote possibility that Chettle was abetted here and there by none other than William Shakespeare. Wilson's academic community is not a place one would want to visit often, much less live in. But the serious heart of the satire is Wilson's dedicated love of literature—"the palace of literature," as Homer Winslow [*sic*], the popular English professor who claims to have discovered the old play, calls it—and the chilling seizure of that palace by several kinds of modern critics and scholars.

They are represented, for example, by a certain Spooky Simms, the departmental chairman, who declares fat-headedly that Yeats's poem "The Wild Swans at Coole" does not, as he had once thought, invoke the symbolism of the Mass but rather the symbolism of homosexuality—"wild" is, of course, a pun on Oscar Wilde, and "swans" is an obvious reference to *Swann's Way* by the equally left-handed Marcel Proust. A visiting pedant from California, a Professor Creech, reports with tightening lips that he has not taught a class or met with students in thirty-five years. Winslow, on the other hand, because of his talent for infecting football players with an enthusiasm for poetry, is regarded by Creech as a mountebank.

Wilson thus has his say about those disparate elements in the academic world that kept him out of fashion there for a number of years, and in the course of it he spoofs some of the dreary connivings of academic politics. As to the soi-disant Elizabethan blood-drama, Wilson gives us the whole of it in an amiable tour de force which reveals Wilson's command not only of the fantastic intricacy of Elizabethan plot structure but also of the nearly unrecoverable slang of the time ("Were I to play at barleybreak with you," a lass called Lucia tells the clown figure, "I'd soon find myself in Hell with a knave and a cungerhead"). Parody of the grand old modes is much in style these days: one recalls the remarkable intellectual wit of John Barth's line-by-line parody of *Oedipus Rex* in *Giles Goat-boy,* and the wildly antic entanglements of language and action of Thomas Pynchon's "Jacobean tragedy" in *The Crying of Lot 49.* Wilson's Winslow supplies a very suggestive reason: "We needs must live the poets that we cherish. . . .

Nor peer at them from scholarly removes. Each man perhaps must forge the book he loves."

At the play's end, the young hero, Chuck Chambers, is invited to teach Greek at Harvard, after that institution (where Wilson, a while ago, taught for a year) has been taken over by the young rebels, an instructor who writes comic songs has been made president, the doctoral degree outlawed and learned books forbidden, and the trustees are in lunatic asylums or on LSD. All this is good fun, and the seventy-three-year-old Wilson displays his usual skeptical sympathy with the revolutionary impulse. The combination in Wilson of the rational and enlightened with the rambunctious and radical is as admirable as it is rare; his radical side has the more force and point exactly because it does emerge from the traditional side. Still, one does have the startling impression of some impossible merger between George Kennan and Norman Mailer.

Having dismantled the worst of academic scholarship and literary criticism in *The Duke of Palermo,* Wilson turns his attention, in the short piece *Dr. McGrath,* to another unsavory American phenomenon, virulent anticommunism. The title figure is a hard-line Calvinist preacher, an intellectually seedy descendant of Jonathan Edwards and a dispenser of latter-day "terror sermons." His opponent in debate, a liberal humanist named Duquesne, incorporates something of Wilson himself: born into the Calvinist tradition, like Wilson, he has also grown out of it and beyond it, and is now an agnostic who is nonetheless fascinated by the religious question and is learned especially in Jewish religious history and gospel scholarship. In speaking of the age of Jesus, Duquesne audibly echoes Wilson's words in *The Scrolls from the Dead Sea:* "there was someone remarkable there—a religious leader of genius—who inspired the Christian legend." (Wilson's second book on the scrolls, incidentally, will be a revised and expanded version of the earlier one and will be called *The Dead Sea Scrolls: 1947–1969;* it will appear this coming June.)

By means of Duquesne, Wilson draws again the analogy he first suggested in *Red, Black, Blonde and Olive* between the extremes of communist doctrine and of Calvinist doctrine. If this implies an analogy between implacable communism and implacable anticommunism, I should like to record my entire agreement. But then, in the play, religion and politics give way to another of Wilson's old loves, Freudian psychology, and the revelation that Dr. McGrath's religious hatred and political bigotry are rooted in an adolescent experience of incest. He is en route, at the end, to humanization.

The value of Wilson's new comedies, like that of his earlier and rather stronger plays (*The Little Blue Light* and others), lies less in their stage-worthiness than in their play of challenging ideas. It is difficult, for me at least, to judge any play on the basis of the printed text alone; but neither of these plays strikes me as very arresting theater, and both indeed show something of that curious tonelessness and slight stiffness of characterization that afflict much of Wilson's imaginative, as against his critical and historical, writing. There is an old-fashioned air to them, too: Dr. McGrath, for all his allusions to Vietnam and other topics of current agitation, really puts me in mind of some ministerial red-baiter of the early thirties—say, Father Coughlin. But Wilson's ideas remain provocative and altogether pertinent, whatever their dramatic form; and Wilson stands as a powerful reminder that the American theater need not be immune to the workings of sheer thought.

The same can be said of the third play, *Osbert's Career; or, the Poet's Progress,* which Wilson calls "a comic strip," and which I found least easy to imagine on the stage. (No doubt I shall be informed at once that it was produced with great success last year in a small upstate theater.) It was begun in the middle twenties, continued at the start of the thirties, and completed in 1968; and Wilson feels that he had made some fairly accurate predictions in the older portions. He undoubtedly did: about the increasing colorlessness and lack of privacy in American life, about cultural sterility as reflected in architectural style, about fascism of both the European and the American varieties, and about the relation of literature to revolution. These are issues of liveliest importance; but the farcical allegory in which they are embedded is a bit hard to bear down on.

The letter to Mike Nichols is quite of a piece with the sense of America satirically projected in the plays, and with the more general and passionate concern for historical American culture that lies behind it. That concern also motivated Wilson's long letter published last summer in the *New York Review* (where the letter to Nichols likewise appeared), attacking an institution called the Center for Editions of American Authors, a branch of the Modern Language Association assigned to prepare textually perfect new editions of a broad range of major and minor American writings. Wilson complained that too many volumes were devoted to second-rate writers, and that the editors were pedants of untrustworthy literary judgment. But the fact is that Wilson simply has a different idea about historical culture than the scholars he is indicting. The scholars, he feels, are like Professor Creech in *The Duke of Palermo,* out of touch with the living reality of the older literature, peering at it "from scholarly removes," and bent not on keeping or bringing it alive but on entombing it. For Wilson, the classical American writers compose a past that we, the living, must be nourished by or starve.*

It is out of this conviction that Wilson has proposed to Mike Nichols the creation of a American National Theater. It is a capital idea, but one assumes gloomily that it would never work. For example, *Uncle Tom's Cabin,* especially if the dramatization by Augustus Thomas is as good as Wilson says it is, would be indispensable in such a theater. It ought to be produced as apocalyptically powerful in its own right (the

---

*Wilson's was a major voice in the discussions that led to the formation of what became The Library of America. This splendid enterprise, under the general supervision of Richard Poirier, has now produced scores of volumes of American writers from the beginnings through the mid-twentieth century; each volume is superbly but discreetly edited, and designed for comfortable reading. It is certainly the publishing achievement of the epoch, as regards the sustaining of American culture.

novel has only recently been accorded its great critical due), and to correct the absurd error in the current use of the phrase "Uncle Tom"—a usage which, since Uncle Tom in fact rebels and is beaten to death, is as wrong as referring to The Monster as Frankenstein. But the mind lurches at the thought of the tumultous and maybe violent demonstrations that would attend the raising of the curtain, and that would continue, deafeningly, no matter what the play was actually trying to say.

Still, playing the game with Wilson for another moment (since one so wistfully endorses his proposal), we can agree that the repertory might begin with Anna Cora Mowatt's *Fashion; or Life in New York* of 1845, if only to indicate some of the early conventions of American drama—the farmer as natural man contrasted with the effete Europeanized easterners, and so on. From later in the century, something by David Belasco (Wilson suggests *The Girl of the Golden West*, though I believe Belasco was not the sole author of the play) and especially by Clyde Fitch should be included. Fitch's best plays are well constructed, meticulously adorned, and not unduly superifical portrayals of the new, money-based social breed in New York before the First World War. They could stand, as still alive and kicking, alongside the early novels of Edith Wharton—with whom Fitch collaborated in 1906 on an impressive if commercially unsuccessful play version of *The House of Mirth*.

Wilson's happiest selection—apart perhaps from William Vaughn Moody's *The Great Divide*, also of 1906—is Langdon Mitchell's *The New York Idea*, which opened in New York in that same puzzlingly fruitful year of 1906, with Mrs. Fiske and George Arliss in the cast. Mitchell was the son of S. Weir Mitchell, the eminent Philadelphia physician litterateur, and a Newport neighbor and admirer of Edith Wharton. His play, I venture, derived from what is probably Mrs. Wharton's best short story and her most exemplary little comedy of manners, "The Other Two" (published in 1904); and it gives engrossing dramatic life to the Wharton brand of social comedy—the awkward, subtly revealing, and amusing mishaps that befall the social intercourse of divorced persons, and the deeply troubled and contradictory feelings that may stir below the well-bred, divorce-denying surface. I indulge myself with these literary relationships only to suggest how Wilson's theater would bring back into existence not merely a number of salvageable plays, but a long, thick, vital chunk of American literary history. And somewhere in the midst of it would be the indomitable figure of Edmund Wilson, musing, commenting, linking together, conjuring up.

(1969)

A Critic of History

The Portable Edmund Wilson. *Edited, with an Introduction and Notes, by Lewis M. Dabney*
The Forties. From Notebooks and Diaries of the Period. *Edited, with an Introduction, by Leon Edel*

A decade after his death, Edmund Wilson seems assured of a conspicuous place in the canon of twentieth-century American writing, though its exact location is still to be settled. Even his literary identity is in dispute. *The Portable Edmund Wilson,* edited by Lewis M. Dabney, who teaches at the University of Wyoming, is an almost overrich intellectual feast that displays Wilson at work in a great variety of genres. And yet it contains none of his fiction except a barely mobile story, "The Man Who Shot Snapping Turtles"; no example of his drama or poetry except his unsparing parody of "The Hamlet of A. MacLeish" ("The Omelet of A. MacLeish"); nothing about the income tax or Canada or the Dead Sea scrolls. Wilson sometimes spoke of himself as a journalist, citing as his heroes and predecessors the likes of De Quincey, Poe, and Shaw, but this was mainly a way of establishing his distance from whatever school of literary criticism happened to be in the ascendancy. We can call him a man of letters who was primarily a literary critic, with a special bias toward history and biography. Or, perhaps more simply, a critic of history.

To suggest the extraordinary reach of the man, one need only list the most powerful and comprehensive essays in *The Portable Edmund Wilson,* those on Marx and Engels, Dickens, the Supreme Court's Oliver Wendell Holmes, and the Philoctetes myth. Those far-ranging endeavors are linked by the most obsessive and compelling motif in Wilson's repertory and his most fertile contribution to critical understanding: the inestimable literary value of trauma and neurosis. This Freudian theme was given its major expression, of course, in *The Wound and the Bow* of 1941. Examining the *Philoctetes* of Sophocles— the drama of the hideously wounded great Greek archer—Wilson came upon "the conception of superior strength as inseparable from disability"; in André Gide's play *Philoctète* he discerned a larger implication, that "genius and disease, like strength and mutilation, may be inextricably bound up together." But that principle had already been central to Wilson's appraisal of *Das Kapital* in *To the Finland Station,* in which he argued that Karl Marx's savage, history-changing world vision ("Here all is cruel discomfort, rape, repression, mutilation and massacre") sprang from his outrage over the unspeakable poverty of the Marx family's London life and his bad conscience about inflicting those wretched conditions on his family.

Oliver Wendell Holmes's cast of mind, and especially his chilly juridical belief that in historical fact might does make right, Wilson traces persuasively to Holmes's military adventures, his injuries and narrow escapes from death during the Civil War battles of Ball's Bluff and Antietam. Indeed, Wilson's honor roll is composed mostly of the wounded. It was Edna St. Vincent Millay's creative struggle with her nearly psychotic terrors and with her desperate loneliness that in part explains Wilson's high opinion of her poetry; and his profoundly ambivalent lifelong involvement with Abraham Lincoln began with

William Herndon's portrait of Lincoln as "a great lawyer who was deeply neurotic" and who, while fighting spells of nightmare depression, managed to steer his country through "the crisis of society." Discovering this Lincoln in the year after his father's death in 1923, Wilson was able belatedly to understand Edmund Wilson Senior, a brilliant lawyer who was subject to misery of spirit and hypochondria and who enormously admired Lincoln as a fellow sufferer and warrior. And we may take the hint and inscribe Wilson Junior too somewhere on the list.

In the world of letters, then, Wilson was anything but that merely "impressionistic critic" he was often said to be. He was not much given to critical theorizing ("impressionistic" is a term used by theorists about nontheorists), but he had a pronounced and recognizable way with literary texts. His focus, as Mr. Dabney observes in his introduction to *The Portable,* the most cogent overview of Wilson's career yet written, "is biographical. He sees society through the individual, takes style as a mirror of personality, and has the old nineteenth century interest in authors as persons." This was why he was at odds with the New Critics, who concentrated on the text, not on the writer, and was in fact scorned by some of them. "Imagine," I recall an accomplished New Critic saying to me about Wilson in the early 1950s, "imagine devoting your whole life to literature and missing the entire point of it." But his special concerns led Wilson to critical insights that were quite half a century ahead of his time.

In a review of Van Wyck Brooks's *The Pilgrimage of Henry James* in 1925, Wilson rejected Brooks's moralistic good-versus-evil interpretation of James's later work—an interpretation that would prevail for decades to come—and proposed instead a series of subtly staged conflicts between different sets of ideals and aspirations. In an article in 1928, he deplored the lack of critical attention to the first-rate writers of the American past and contended that an intelligent study of them would "show how Hawthorne, Melville and Poe, besides becoming excessively eccentric persons, anticipated, in the middle of the last century, the temperament of our own day and invented a method for rendering it." (A couple of years ago, with very considerable labor, I devised a seminar for college teachers on this exact notion, sure that it was my original idea—"premature modernity" was my phrase for it—and preened myself on the ground-breaking nature of the enterprise.)

Toward the close of *Axel's Castle*, his 1931 study of the Symbolist movement, Wilson, quoting Paul Valéry, foresaw a possibility that literature might become an art "based on language as a creator of illusions, and not on language as a means of transmitting realities," and that it would survive chiefly as a game. He was optimistically doubtful about this eventuality. But fifty years later a heralded school of critics is maintaining that all literature since the dawn of time has been a linguistic game having no serious connection with reality.

As the twenties gave way to the Depression of the thirties, Wilson made coast-to-coast excursions into contemporary reality; but the examples of his sociological reports in this collection—on Henry Ford, on the miners of West Virginia—don't hold up very well. I'd have preferred an essay or two on the Victorians or the Lincoln chapter from *Patriotic Gore*, Wilson's ambitious study of Civil War writers. But Mr. Dabney may have been justified in including these pieces from the *New Republic* as preparation for *To the Finland Station* of 1940, that masterwork about the intellectual origins of the Russian revolution. Here, as V. S. Pritchett once put it, Wilson performed as "a critic in whom history is broken up into minds."

The decade of the forties was a crest time for Wilson: *To the Finland Station* was followed by *The Wound and the Bow*, with its studies of Dickens, Kipling, and Hemingway; *The Shock of Recognition*, an invaluable anthology of American writers talking about other American writers; *Memoirs of Hecate County*, his collection of short stories; *Europe Without a Baedeker*, sketches of postwar England, Italy, and Greece; and the collection of literary essays, *Classics and Commercials*. All this work went forward despite, or because of, a number of personal crises, one of which led to a divorce from Mary McCarthy and marriage to

Elena Thornton, a cultivated and charming European-born magazine editor.

Descriptions of those private experiences are lucidly interpolated by Leon Edel into *The Forties,* his selection of Wilson's notebooks and diaries of that decade—and the interpolations may be the best part of the book. I don't otherwise see the purpose of the compilation. A long section consists of Wilson's notebook entries in Italy just after World War II, which show him at his least interesting. Years before he had lectured F. Scott Fitzgerald on the superiority of European to American civilization, but now he had retreated into a wordy and superficial parochialism. We are made forcibly privy to Wilson's sexual doings with Elena, session by session, all of which I found vaguely offensive and embarrassing. (I could not but be arrested, however, by a sequence at Lenox, Massachusetts, in 1947 in which a nice if mildly inaccurate little picture of Edith Wharton's former home, The Mount, is followed by a rhapsody about "Kissing E.'s feet, with their insteps so high on the inside and their dense network of fine blue veins.") One turns back with relief from such stuff to the magisterial essays of the same period, like the one about the impact, both crushing and galvanizing, on Charles Dickens of his father's three-month imprisonment for debt, and even to the robustly wrongheaded discourse on detective fiction, "Who Cares Who Killed Roger Ackroyd?" and the accompanying pieces in *Classics and Commercials.*

Most of *Patriotic Gore,* published in 1962, appeared originally during the fifties in *The New Yorker,* with which Wilson was long affiliated. Lewis Dabney, like many others, regards *Patriotic Gore* as Wilson's supreme achievement and provides a generous sampling from it in *The Portable:* on Holmes, Harriet Beecher Stowe, General Grant and his memoirs, Mary Chesnut and her diary, a trio of Southern generals. These are stirring historic-literary re-creations, and the book does have a certain somber and durable magnificence. But for me it is damaged by Wilson's strenuous demythicizing of the war itself—his rejection as irrelevant of such matters as the fate of the Union and of the institution of slavery—which he seems not fully to have understood was itself an attempt to demythicize a vast segment of American culture.

Within that culture, meanwhile, Wilson continued to play a vigorously shaping role until his death in 1972. Mr. Dabney tells us that the obituaries referred to Wilson as "the last man of letters." The phrase isn't clear; Wilson, though a sizable man of letters, was not the final member of the species or the most complete representative in this century. He was curiously inept, for example, with modern American poetry (as against Russian and ancient Greek); he overrated Edna Millay, was deaf to Hart Crane, and dismissed Robert Frost as an extremely dull writer of "very poor verse." His own most attractive verse was comic, with a cultural sting. He included the following in a Christmas booklet he sent to his friends in 1952:

Said Mario Praz to Mario Pei:
"Come ti piace the Great White Way?"
Said Mario Pei to Mario Praz:
"It's polyglots."

Wilson's grumpy withdrawal from the contemporary American scene in his later years was never altogether convincing. "When, for example, I look through *Life* magazine," he remarked on reaching sixty in 1956, "I feel that I do not belong to the country depicted there, that I do not even live in that country." Wilson's inability to apprehend the religious impulse seems another drawback; though in this regard, his atheism could be expressed with such valor and briskness that the most devout might be beguiled. "The word *God* is now archaic," he wrote in another article of 1956, "and it ought to be dropped by those who do not need it for moral support." Wallace Stevens never said it better.

Wilson's formidable intelligence, meanwhile, grappled unceasingly with literature and with history and with the minds and personalities that made them. The reader is drawn into the agon of a characteristic Wilson essay and stretched and toughened by it as by few other critical writings of the epoch. It is exhilarating to read *The Portable Edmund Wilson*, and it is humbling.

(1983)

14

L ike Edmund Wilson, Malcolm Cowley may be considered first of all a literary chronicler. But Cowley, over almost half a century, has created a unique role for himself as chronicler *from within*: that is, of the contemporary American world of letters and the major stages it has passed through during his lifetime. The value and cogency of his successive chronicles—from the classic *Exile's Return* in 1934 to this arresting new memoir of the 1930s*— derive in part from Cowley's personal experience of the human drama, the anguish and the comedy, out of which literature arises. But they derive no less from hs singularly acute sense of what constitutes a literary generation. Speaking of the writers of the 1920s in *Exile's Return*, Cowley remarked that "they were a generation, and perhaps the first real one in the history of American literature," something that led one caustically skeptical reviewer, Lewis Gannett, to snort with disdain. Cowley would no doubt repudiate the second part of his

---

The Dream of the Golden Mountains (1980).

contention; he has since discovered, as he said in the stimulating lead chapter of *And I Worked at the Writer's Trade* a couple of years ago, that a series of distinguishable literary generations can be charted in this country starting at least as far back as the mid-nineteenth century. But the analytic principle is a sound one.

It is also most appropriately American. American literature has customarily moved forward not by schools and manifestos, in the Gallic manner, but by generations—not by programs and assemblies but by a sort of half-accidental simultaneity, at once nourishing and challenging. The irony is, though, that the 1930s generation explored in *The Dream of the Golden Mountains* is the one literary age in our annals that did attempt to launch itself by programs and multiply signed statements, that held congresses, founded leagues, and formed international alliances. The aim of course was to enlist the sympathies and energies of American writers in the desperate conditions of the native working class, to summon them as witnesses to the collapse of the capitalist system and the eventual triumph—in what used to be called "the long view"—of the worldwide communist cause.

The conditions were indeed appalling, and the governmental actions—the routing of the threadbare bonus army by machine-gun squadrons and cavalry; the granting of $90 million not to the stricken city of Chicago, as its mayor requested, but to Chicago's leading bank—were so callous and outrageous that one can still grind one's teeth at Cowley's calm narrative of events. Yet as generations go, this one was relatively short-lived. Cowley's account begins just after the Wall Street crash in late 1929, when he joined the staff of the *New Republic*; and it ends in the first year or so of Roosevelt's second administration.

Cowley gained firsthand knowledge of the rapidly deteriorating state of the American outlands, the palpable threat of class war and a homegrown fascism, in visits to the Harlan County (Kentucky) mining district and elsewhere, in the company of potent literary spokesmen like Dreiser and Dos Passos. He absorbed a good deal more from his perch at the *New Republic* in Chelsea Square, New York. This was the *New Republic* of Bruce Bliven as managing editor; George Soul, the soft-spoken, scholarly economist; Stark Young, the drama critic; and Edmund Wilson, book reviewer and wandering recorder of the American jitters. The magazine's circulation could never be reckoned as more than about five thousand; but in the 1930s, it became the most important message center—for political and economic inquiry, for theorists and fanatics, for troubled Americans and lively, fast-talking foreigners—in the nation. At the same time, Cowley, in intervals between collecting information and writing articles, was assailed on several sides by communist apocalyptics. And so, both horrified by what he had seen and read about and exhilarated by the visions he had been made privy to, Cowley allied himself in the spring of 1931 with the Communist party.

If he never formally joined the party, it was probably (Cowley now surmises) because the Communist program had such an observably debilitating effect on the writers who actually espoused it. Cowley, already engaged in an ardent and long-enduring love affair with the English language, could not help noticing that the party leaders wrote atrociously. Beyond that, the kind of work they exhorted Americans to produce, in particular "the proletarian novel," was to be almost programmatically crude, formless, uncontaminated by bourgeois niceties of art. (In a telling analogy, Cowley compares this kind of thing to the didactic crudities of early Christian art.) What Cowley does not quite say is that in most instances it was also irrelevant: you can't have a proletarian novel if you don't have a proletariat to begin with.

The whole enterprise, in fact, went against the American literary grain, and this as much as anything helps account for the generation's brevity of tenure. Cowley and others like him (among whom I include my teenage self) were caught up in the dream of a genuinely better and more humane world far off in the golden mountains. It was an honorable and inspiriting dream—Cowley felt "full of humility, the desire to serve, and immense hopes for the future"—and nothing that befell it has made it vulnerable to derision; but this was not the way for writers to set about realizing it. It is not only that American writers, or the best of them, have never worked well in harness together, and have been congenitally uneasy with causes. It is also that the Communist program for writers blinded them, for a period, to their real subject matter, what was really going on in the lives and minds of Americans, as well as to the source of Roosevelt's enormous popular appeal.

Cowley is persuasive in explaining what at the time seemed to many of us baffling and vexatious: the failure of intellectuals by and large to appreciate the vigorous improvisations and artful zigzagging of Roosevelt and the first New Deal, and their dismissal of Roosevelt as the temporary prop of an incurably sagging capitalism. But Roosevelt was in touch with his country and the needs of his countrymen; the writers and intellectuals *engagés* on the whole were not; and when the latter grew grudgingly or dishearteningly aware of it, the enterprise sputtered and subsided.

At one point, Cowley apologizes for a quite detailed digression into economic matters "in what started out as a literary memoir." The details are necessary to understand the barometric pressure of the age; but *The Dream of the Golden Mountains* is not lacking in the kind of personal and literary anecdote that Cowley handles so gracefully. There is a sad, retrospective glimpse of Hart Crane, off to Mexico to write "The Broken Tower," one of the great lyrics in the American canon, to enter into an intense affair with Cowley's former wife Peggy Baird, and to commit suicide. Dreiser is observed at a gathering in his studio, with "his scrubbed lobster-pink cheeks and his chins in retreating terraces," declaiming that "The time is ripe for American intellectuals to render some service to the American worker." Cowley describes a visit with Scott and Zelda Fitzgerald in 1933 at their home outside Baltimore: Scott trying to pick a quarrel and then flashing "his bad-boyish smile"; Zelda's face emaciated and twitching, her skin weather-beaten. There are pleasant encounters in Tennessee with Allen and

Caroline Gordon Tate ("We'd like you to meet our Yankee friend," the Tates would say cautiously, introducing Cowley to their neighbors). Kenneth Burke appears briefly, displaying his genius and his innocence in lecturing a largely Communist audience about the need to apply middle-class values to the revolutionary effort. Burke is such good company that one wants to see more of him.

But another theme emerges, somewhat unexpectedly, to serve as a recurring counterpoint to the mixture of political and literary history. Let me call it the pastoral theme. Cowley confesses in the preface that in 1930 he was "still a country boy" ("the plowboy of the western world," the poet John Peale Bishop called him). Cowley empathizes at a glance with the plight of the embattled Iowa farmers; and the one thing he liked about the New Deal was its conservationist policy—he found himself "mildly attracted to Roosevelt because he had planted trees and wanted to save the countryside."

The entire narrative is punctuated by a series of withdrawals into the rural. Cowley always writes an uncommonly agreeable prose, easy, limpid, slightly out of the corner of the mouth; but his prose rises toward the fabulous and the poetic when he goes back to the country. In Riverton, Connecticut, where he is finishing *Exile's Return*, Cowley walks ten miles through the snow every afternoon, finding and mumbling aloud the words he will employ next day; in the evening he stands at the bar of the little inn talking to two old men about the effect of the spring thaw upon the ice-scape—one of the men regularly recalling the spring of of 1875 when the ice, "going out," had carried away the bridge, the other repeating, like the burden of a song, "I been here fifteen years and I ain't seen the ice go out but twice." And here is Cowley commuting back from New York to the Connecticut shore it the summer of 1935:

> Even the train ride to Niantic was magical, at dusk on a
> Thursday evening. I found a seat by the window, where I
> could look out at the shore. Between the ugly towns were flat

salt marshes, pale green even in midsummer when most of the countryside was turning brown. Little islands of darker green rose out of the marshes, they were round clumps of oak trees growing on rocky soil, each island floating on its marsh against a background of gray-green twilight.

Karl Marx, it has been famously said, was not a country boy. In these periodic immersions in pastoral New England, Cowley seems to have found a way of being that touched his deepest chord, one to which the essentially urban Marxist vision never reached; and this may finally be why—along with those other and important literary considerations—he never could accept the Communist creed. He did not abandon his social sympathies, but he stopped living there. Malcolm Cowley and his gifted wife Muriel came home for keeps at last, in the spring of 1936, when they bought seven acres and an empty barn in the little town of Sherman in western Connecticut. "There," Cowley says, "I could fish and hunt in season, grow a big garden, and still spend three days a week at the *New Republic* office." The poignant fading of the dream of the golden mountains was being somewhat mitigated by the reality of the green Connecticut hills and woodlands.

(1980)

Bibliographical Afterword

In the same year (1980) that Cowley published *The Dream of the Golden Mountains*, he also produced *The View from 80*, reflections on the experiences of aging and of seeking a pattern in the long life. These were followed in 1985 by *The Flower and the Leaf: A Contemporary Record of American Writing Since 1941*, edited by Donald W. Faulkner. *The Selected Correspondence of Kenneth Burke and Malcolm Cowley, 1915–1981*, letters between the two lifelong friends beginning in their teens (they first met in western Pennsylvania when Cowley was three and Burke four), very ably edited by Paul Jay, appeared in 1988. In 1990, Viking, for whom Cowley served as literary advisor for more than forty years, published *The Portable Malcolm Cowley*, a signal text in the Portable series Cowley himself had begotten in the 1940s with Portables of Hemingway, Faulkner, and Hawthorne.

The Portable Malcolm Cowley, which runs to nearly six hundred pages, includes autobiographical excerpts from *Exile's Return*, *The Dream of the Golden Mountains* and *The View from 80*; essays on eighteen American writers, most of them Cowley's contemporaries and in several cases acquaintances or even friends, with other essays on naturalism, the revolt against gentility, mythic elements in American literature; a selection of poems from *Blue Juniata* (first published in 1929); "a brief selection of correspondence (1917–1961)," letters to Burke, Robert Penn Warren, F. O. Matthiessen, Faulkner, Hemingway, John Cheever, and others; and a section "On Writers and Writing," containing such titles as "The Writer's Working Day," "A Defense of Storytelling," "On Criticism: The Many-Windowed Houses."

The volume is edited with an introduction and notes by Donald W. Faulkner, and it is a model of editorial intelligence, judgment, and intimacy with its subject. The subject is at once Malcolm Cowley the person, his voluminous writings, his literary career, and his characteristic performances; and the intimacy is manifest in a compilation that is, so to say, Malcolm Cowley in action—an expansive literary memoir of our most accomplished literary memoirist.

The editor's introduction concludes with a paragraph that rings bravely at the start of the 1990s. It is a paragraph cowritten by Donald Faulkner and Cowley and handsomely sets the tone for the book that follows:

> In distinction to what eulogizers have said about Cowley, among them, that he served to establish an American canon, Cowley's effort was to set standards which, he hoped, would

make both writers and critics acknowledge a sense of literary tradition, the openness of that tradition to new views, and finally, means to give new writers a sense of the possibility that exists in extending that tradition. Cowley said of forthcoming generations of American writers, "They will be as different from those of the 'Lost Generation' as Hemingway and Faulkner were different from every American author who preceded them, though without ceasing to be in the American tradition. The tradition grows and changes, but persists. Eventually it will include everything honest and new and written with patient rigor, like a good line of verse, so that it becomes unchangeable."

Malcolm Cowley died in 1990.

(1991)

15

In several different ways, V. S. Pritchett, as a writer, draws our attention to the phenomenon of age. "It has often been said," he observes in an essay on E. M. Forster in *The Tale Bearers,* "that the British venerate old age." One hears the note of skepticism in that remark, but Pritchett suggests that the British cult, such as it is, may be a Victorian legacy, since "the Victorians solemnly sought to get over youth as quickly as possible and assume elderly airs"; and he draws a contrast with France, where, he says, "old age is often publicly derided." In this country, one is tempted to add, we tend to be uncomfortable with old age, and prefer to isolate it for scientific and sociological inspection; we seem divided, as a nation, between child-worshipers and gerontologists. I think the British are in the right of it. Almost the only thing I *don't* have against Ronald Reagan, as a presidential candidate, is his age; the evidence is not encouraging, but it is just possible that his easygoing mediocrity may have gained a measure of wisdom about practical affairs in the course of his nearly three score years and ten.

In his own case, though, Pritchett has acknowledged an odd psychological pressure as the years advance. He began *Midnight Oil,* the second of his two superb autobiographical volumes, with these words: "This is the year of my seventieth birthday, a fact that bewilders me. . . . I understand now the look of affront I often saw in my father's face after this age and that I see in the faces of my contemporaries. We are affronted because, whatever we may feel, time has turned us into curiosities in some secondhand shop." That was written in 1970, and Sir Victor—he was knighted a couple of years ago for his literary accomplishments—is now in the year of his eightieth birthday. He may be something of a miracle, but he is hardly a curiosity. It would be impertinent to say that he is still going strong. He is, quite simply, flourishing—as always.

It has been quite an "always." Over the decades, Pritchett has produced five novels, including the classic *Mr. Beluncle* at mid-career, and half a dozen collections of short stories—a form in which, according to the expert opinion of Elizabeth Bowen, he is "the most important English practitioner." He has few peers as a travel writer, and largely because he shares the quality that, in talking about *The American Scene,* he attributes to Henry James: in whatever place he finds himself, Pritchett is always on the lookout for the story in it. *The Spanish Temper* challenges the best work of its kind in English, and Pritchett also has written about the cities of Dublin, London, and New York. (The book on Manhattan bears the title *New York Proclaimed;* what New York does, Pritchett has said, is to proclaim itself, and he is so right.) Then he has given us two fairly recent biographies of Balzac and Turgenev and, counting *The Tale Bearers,* some eight volumes of essays in literary criticism. Pritchett writes faster than I can read. Even as I made my way through *The Tale Bearers,* I noticed that Pritchett was appearing almost weekly, with new, long, literary essays of the same unfailingly high order, in *The New Yorker* and the *New York Review of Books.*

Interestingly enough, Pritchett has never, so far as I know, written poetry for publication, and he avoids writing about poetry or the lives of poets. One reason may be that in his time, our time, the discussion of poetry has fallen chiefly into the hands of academic critics—a breed for which, I have to say wincingly, Pritchett reserves his rare expressions of scorn. Speaking of Max Beerbohm in *The Tale Bearers*, he confesses in an aside to a fear of "what would happen to Max if he were put through the American academic machine. There seems to be a convention that this machine must begin by stunning its victim with the obvious." As to the new American critics, the structuralists, Pritchett has been heard to say that they are really engineers rather than readers of literature. Warming to this theme in *The Myth Makers*, published last year, in a review of Victor Brombert's study of Flaubert—a book for which Pritchett otherwise voiced considerable admiration—he deplored "the present academic habit," therein exemplified, "of turning literary criticism into technology." The duty of the critic, he went on, "is to literature, not to its surrogates"—meaning, by the latter, modes of philosophy, psychology, and science. "Literary criticism," he concluded, "does not add to its status by opening an intellectual hardware store."

As a critic, V. S. Pritchett seems to inhabit not a hardware store but some sort of open-air pavilion, with the myriad books protected by a roof and the sounds of the human world flowing in freely and bracingly. He can, of course, be an astute close analyst of prose style when he wants to be. In the course of a piece on Saul Bellow, whom he engagingly credits with having "the most effusive intelligence of living American novelists," Pritchett quotes a passage from *Humboldt's Gift*:

> A wonderful talker, a hectic non-stop monologuist and improvisator, a champion detractor: to be loused up by Humboldt was really a kind of privilege. It was like being the subject of a two-nosed portrait by Picasso, or an eviscerated chicken by Soutine.

"One recognizes the voice at once," Pritchett comments; "it has the dash, the dandyism, the easy control of side-slipping metaphor and culture-freaking which gives pace to Saul Bellow's comedies." And in that critical comment, in turn, one recognizes Pritchett's own comic spirit; one sees and hears the broadening smile, the little chuckles, the sudden burst of laughter that so frequently accompany his literary or personal pronouncements. As imaginative writer, as critic, as autobiographer, Pritchett is a lover of the comic. How he relishes the recorded moment when Oscar Wilde asked a lady whether Max Beerbohm ever took off his face and revealed his mask!

The Tale Bearers is a companion volume to *The Myth Makers*. The latter collection dealt entirely with non-English-language prose writers, Pritchett showing himself at home and at ease with an astounding range of individual writers, bodies of work, national cultures, and literary ages: from Pushkin to Pasternak and Solzhenitsyn in Russia; from George Sand to Jean Genet in France; Kafka and Strindberg; and an assortment of Latin American writers, among them Borges and Gabriel García Márquez. In *The Tale Bearers,* the subjects are mainly British and American—an exception being Lady Murasaki's medieval Japanese *Tale of Genji,* which, however, Pritchett treats by comparing the English renderings of that extraordinary novel by Arthur Waley (half a century ago) and by the American scholar Edward G. Seidensticker (1976).

More often than not, the occasion for discourse is a new biography: of Rider Haggard—Pritchett did not read Haggard during his lost childhood and was nearly sixty before he took his "first plunge into the choking verbiage of *King Solomon's Mines* and *She*"; of Kipling, Conrad, T. E. Lawrence, Forster; and, in a section called "Characters," of Jonathan Swift, Richard Burton, Frederick Rolfe. Pritchett is never better than when he is considering a writer's life and his writings in offbeat association with each other. At other times Pritchett examines new fiction by Graham Greene, Saul Bellow, Ruth Prawer Jhabvala, and others; and there are some texts revisited, like Henry Green's first novel, *Blindness,* reissued in 1977, and Edmund Wilson's *To the Finland Station.*

Pritchett's gift for the luminous, often witty summary remark serves him handsomely as he covers these large stretches of literary ground. To the examples already offered, let me add his perception that in *To the Finland Station* Edmund Wilson performed as a critic "in whom history is broken up into minds." Wilson, he continues, is an artist "in the sense that he is a man possessed. Give him the subject and it fuses with his whole person as if something like Mesmer's famous magnetic fluid had flowed into him." Pritchett's well-modulated prose is a constant pleasure; it is never self-admiring and never out of keeping with its subject. In *Midnight Oil* Pritchett quotes some heady, youthful stuff he wrote on a mountain in Tennessee, where he was responding to the unaccustomed scenery and listening to the local vernacular. "What," he asks with amused dismay, "can be the origin and meaning of those bizarre lyrical outbursts, those classy metaphors and finicking adjectives. . . . I had come out in a rash." There is no evidence of rash, of the faintest rise in temperature, in the unforced style of *The Tale Bearers.*

I would be the last to harness Pritchett with anything like a "theory" of literature, theories being what he is most wary of when it comes to literary talk. But he does have developed views about the varieties of literary personality, about the sources of personality and the ways it can get articulated in language and narrative theme. And he has long indicated a homegrown distinction—it strikes me as Pritchettesque rather than Freudian, though Freud contributed to it—between writers of a prepuberty and those of a postpuberty imagination (as he once put it, between Whitman and Shakespeare). The former species is at least as fascinating to him as its opposite. About Kipling, for whom Pritchett has always declared a profound and somewhat unfashionable respect, he says—mark the words—that:

> His lasting attraction as a writer is his gift of conveying the magical. It springs from his childhood in Bombay and Lahore,

and he never lost it entirely. . . . Kipling worshipped children, and easily and seriously abandoned himself to their private minds. . . . He saw childhood as the sacred age out of which it was painful and shocking to grow.

And more harshly, about Swift: "Swift is an instance of the infantilism of genius; he was a self-regarding child-egotist all his life." For this connoisseur of the ages of man, needless to say, mature writers like Conrad and Graham Greene likewise disclose their odd obsessions and winning peculiarities.

It is possible to cavil at Pritchett, though one does so with an apologetic smile. He is perhaps too generous with his superlatives. In reviewing novels, he quotes at too great length for my taste (this was a minor flaw in his book on Turgenev). He skids momentarily in identifying Henry James as a Bostonian, indeed as "a Boston snob"; the author of *The Bostonians* could not have been anything but what he was, a New Yorker born and bred. In trying to cope with the weird mix of Catholicism and the American deep south in Flannery O'Connor, Pritchett is uncharacteristically turgid. But he occupies today a nearly solitary position as a literary critic in the great tradition—standing between literature and human society to greet the books as they come, passing the word back and forth.

(1980)

Bibliographical Afterword

A decade has passed since the above was written, and Sir Victor has now celebrated his ninetieth birthday. In the intervening years, he has published a book on Chekhov, edited the *Oxford Book of Short Stories,* and seen to the publication of his *Complete Collected Stories* and the most recent collection of his literary essays, *Lasting Impressions.* The latter two appeared almost simultaneously in his ninetieth year.

The short stories, eighty-two in all, were saluted by Paul Theroux (with whom Prichett collaborated on a tiny enterprise in 1982) as "his greatest triumph"; he added, "There's nothing like Pritchett's short stories in the language." Frank Kermode called Sir Victor "a great story writer," and went on (in a New York *Times* review) to offer an astute description of the recurring rhythm of a Pritchett story: "Commonplace people going through their domestic routines . . . until one realises that they suffer the passions of the great." Eudora Welty, than whom no one knows better, said of Pritchett that he is "one of the great pleasure-givers in our language."

Lasting Impressions offers us twenty-seven essays and articles written between 1961 and 1987 and appearing in *The New Yorker,* the *New York Review of Books,* the *London Review of Books,* the *New Statesman,* and elsewhere. The pieces themselves are mostly abbreviated, but the range is fabulous: Sholom Aleichem, Simone de Beauvoir, Browning, Alexander von Humboldt (the great German scientist, 1769–1859, who founded the science of meteorology, traveled ten thousand miles across Russia, and was said to be the most famous man in Europe after Napoleon—who, Pritchett says, hated and suspected him), Le Roy Ladurie (a contemporary French historian of medieval France and author of a book about the intimate and daily life of the people of the mountain village of Montaillou, at the time when the Inquisition was invading it to crush the local Cathar heresy), Malraux, Walker Percy (and his image of the hero as a sick clown amid the "sex-mad, science-mad, pleasure-mad contemporary life"), Salman Rushdie ("a great novelist . . . a master of perpetual story-telling," whose 1980 novel *Midnight's Children* is "really about the mystery of being born"— Pritchett admires it greatly but wishes Rushdie wouldn't push his symbols so hard), Bernard Shaw, John Updike (*Rabbit Is Rich*—Updike "is both poet and historian," and his first three Rabbit novels "are a monumental portrayal of provincial and domestic manners"), P. G. Wodehouse ("The never-never-land is irresistible. . . . All nationals seem to have another self, preoccupied with sustaining illusions. Isn't this what comedy is about?"). What comedy is about—to take that last question out of its parentheses—is what V. S. Pritchett's lifelong career has been all about.

(1991)

R ichard Ellmann was born in Highland Park, Illinois, of Rumanian and Russian Jewish immigrant parents, in March 1918. He went east for his undergraduate and graduate education at Yale, and taught for a year at Harvard; but his literary career began in the summer of 1945, when, on an extended leave from his duties with the OSS in London, he made his first visit to Ireland and, in Dublin, came to know the widow of William Butler Yeats.

Dick had been drafted into the Navy in 1943, and managed to get himself stationed at a headquarters near Paris, where he spent time writing citations for less literate higher-ups. He was recruited into the OSS by Norman Holmes Pearson, his former Yale professor, and served in England for the rest of the war. At Yale, he had been at work on a dissertation about Yeats and varieties of magic. In Yeats's homeland, being introduced to the poet's widow, young Ellmann opined: "Really, I think, Yeats was more a magician than a poet." Mrs. Yeats was enchanted, and eventually turned over fifty thousand pages of unpublished Yeats manuscripts to her visitor: autobiographical notes, drafts of poems, letters, and diaries. Out of all this, in 1947, there came *Yeats: The Man and the Mask.* There are those who think it may be Ellmann's best book, if only because it gives somewhat freer play to purely literary and critical considerations than do the later volumes.

Dick joined the English department at Northwestern University in 1951, and remained there until 1968. In his university life—as his classmate and longtime friend Charles Feidelson has put it—he was a member of a recognizable postwar academic species: a teacher with a touch of the poet. Dick Ellmann wrote literary biography and bio-graphically informed criticism; but he wrote in good part for the sheer pleasure of writing, for the joy of elegant and pungent and telling expression. Writing about literary matters for Dick was an action in language—and an action, it can be said, of singular grace.

The life of James Joyce, which appeared in 1959, began as a much more limited endeavor than the monumental eight-hundred-page vol-ume it finally became. Once again, Dick endeared himself to helpful individuals—Joyce's relatives and friends and his literary executor, Harriet Shaw Weaver, among them—and was given access to hordes of materials. Dick's ingratiating manner was anything but a pose. He really was interested in other people, in what they were like and might say to him. (He can be recalled remarking that he had just run into so-and-so, and then giving an enthralled account of what that person had talked about.) It is this same imaginative interest in people that is so palpable in the engaging figures of his biographical narratives.

James Joyce is incontestably one of the great literary biographies of our time: an extraordinarily rich interweaving of the story of James Joyce, of his ancestry and family and associates, of the city and society of Dublin and the country of Ireland, of the several developments of modern and modernist literature. The Joycean writings are born, grow, and live amid these other stories as characters of finally classic stature. Ellmann rarely analyzes a text *apart* from biographical fact. But Joyce's imagination and language are made present to us, literarily and as biographically suggestive, from the outset. Each of the thirty-seven chapters is headed by a quotation from *Finnegans Wake:* from atop the opening account of the Joyce ancestry ("Wharnow are alle her childer, say? In kingdome gone or power to come or gloria be to them farther?") to the closing chapter on Joyce's last years in Zurich and his death ("Quiet takes back her folded fields. Tranquille thanks. Adew.") And in the final monologue of Anna Livia Plurabelle in the same text, Ellmann characteristically finds a recapitulation of the endings of all Joyce's previous books, finds a question addressed by Joyce to Nora Barnacle thirty-four years earlier, finds a memory passed on to him by an American woman friend of having been carried by her father through a fair in Kentucky, detects the North and South Walls of Dublin Bay, and behind the book's closing word, the article *the,* he lets us hear Joyce saying that it was the least forceful word he could hit upon, "not even a word . . . scarcely a sound between the teeth, a breath, a nothing."

Richard Ellmann's human and literary love affair with Ireland continued through an edition of Joyce's letters and assorted essays into a biography of Oscar Wilde, published in 1987. If he felt an intensifying kinship with the literary Irish, it was to an extent because he felt himself, like them, to be an outsider: and even more like them, an observant and a participant outsider, beginning, as well might be supposed, in his undergraduate years at Yale in the late 1930s. Charles Feidelson remembers Dick Ellmann on a spring evening in his junior year, announcing his intention of going out into the Branford College courtyard to watch the activities of "tap-day": the ritual tapping of juniors for the then socially and racially exclusive senior societies. "You can't possibly expect to be tapped!" Feidelson exclaimed. Of course not, Dick answered; but he wanted to mingle, to see what it was all about, to be there on the scene.

Writers like Yeats, Joyce, and Wilde also appealed to Dick Ellmann because of their theatricality, their grand showiness, and because of the abundant humanity that kept their histrionics in balance. He loved their irrepressible humor and joke making. Dick was himself an uncommonly sweet-natured specimen of humanity, with a mix of gentleness and strength. Thinking back, we evoke a quizzical twisted smile and a fondness for joking. It was Dick who first told some of us the anecdote about the fellow who said that if he were Rothschild, he would be richer than Rothschild . . . because he'd do a little teaching on the side.

The Irish aspect was also represented by Mary Donahue, whom Dick met when she was teaching at Wellesley; they were married in 1949. Mary had an enlivening Irish background, and in endless conversations with her, Dick worked out his understanding of the great Irish phenomenon. His dependence, like his attachment, was enormous. When Mary suffered a ruptured aneurism in her brain in 1969, collapsing in the kitchen of their New Haven home—Dick Ellmann now being professor of English at Yale—he said to one of her surgical attendants that if Mary should die, his intellectual life would come to an end.

Oscar Wilde is not less magisterial than *James Joyce*. Here are the teeming social and cultural milieux that Wilde lived in and passed through: Oxford, London, Dublin, the United States from coast to coast, Paris, Rome. Here is Wilde's internal duality as represented externally by Walter Pater and John Ruskin. Here needless to say are plentiful examples of Oscar Wilde's wit; but here as well is the accompanying wit of Richard Ellmann. Quoting from two different descriptions, one by Wilde and one by Henry James, of a recently displayed painting that showed Love, as a beautiful young boy, confronting the gray-draped form of Death, Ellmann observes: "When they come to the beautiful boy, Wilde is all atremble, James all aslant."

In this biographical story, Wilde becomes perforce a tragic figure; and the story itself is deftly shaped as a tragedy, with the familiar qualities of the overweening, the stubborn fatal choice, the ensuing disaster, the blindness leading through pain to understanding. If *Oscar Wilde* is not, even so, quite the accomplishment that *James Joyce* is taken to be, it is only because Wilde was not of Joyce's artistic magnitude by any final reckoning. Ellman thinks otherwise. The book's closing sentence is this: "Now, beyond the reach of scandal, his best writings validated by time, he comes before us still, a towering figure, laughing and weeping, with parables and paradoxes, so generous, so amusing and so right." William Butler Yeats points us toward a judgment on the biography. Wilde, Yeats wrote a friend, was "an unfinished sketch of a great man." Richard Ellmann has finished the sketch.

His own last phrases apply to Ellmann himself: so generous, so amusing, so right; and, we may add, so staunch. About a year before *Oscar Wilde* appeared, Dick Ellmann was stricken with what is known as Lou Gehrig's disease: a creeping paralysis from which he died in May 1987. He had been Goldsmith Professor of English at New College, Oxford, since 1970. Not long before the end, there took place at Oxford the election of the university's new chancellor. Dick was virtually immobile and bereft of speech. But he decked himself out in his academic regalia—he was an M.A. Oxon—and had himself carried down to the Senate House to vote. American as he was, he was bound to have his say on the British field of action.

(1989)

17

T oward the end of this richly furnished memoir,* Irving Howe lingers with sad exasperation over the demise of the new left in the late 1960s, and the way it had repeated the disastrous errors of earlier radical movements: "posturings of rectitude, fantasies of violence, a complete incapacity to attend the pulse of American experience." It is by reference to that last phenomenon—the observable rhythms of actual life, especially in this country—that Howe has come more and more to test an idea, an attitude, a political loyalty, a critical position, even to some extent a literary text. And as he rehearses his "intellectual autobiography" from about 1933 onward, he constantly brings to bear on it, ruefully or trenchantly, his successive discoveries of the realities of human history, as against the caterogies of ideology, whether political or aesthetic.

This is the best kind of pragmatism, and it makes for a winning narrative. Howe does full justice, for example, to his youthful involve-

A Margin of Hope: An Intellectual Biography.

ment in radical politics, especially as a member of the Trotskyist group. The Trotskyist "sect" (Howe's word) gave him and his teenage associates "the sense that we had gained not merely a purpose but a coherent perspective upon everything happening in the world," so that never before or since has he lived "at so high, so intense a pitch, been so absorbed in ideas beyond the smallness of self." The chief ideological position provided by the Trotskyists, needless to say, was implacable hostility to the Stalinist "betrayal of the socialist revolution" and to Stalinism as a force on the American scene. Yet Howe recognizes without rancor the marginal nature of Trotskyism as a would-be movement in America: "once the Trotskyists ventured on a politics of their own, trying in the America of Franklin Delano Roosevelt to resurrect the tired bones of Leninism, they shrank to a historical oddity." More than most backward glances at this political period by sometime radicals, Howe's is perfectly willing to acknowledge the historical fact of the Rooseveltian achievement and to appreciate it: "The major cause of socialist decline could be put in one word: Roosevelt. That canny politician, half savior and half confidence man, ruined us." That is exactly right, every wry word of it, as is Howe's additional notation that Roosevelt triumphed despite having failed to pull us out of the Depression until we were rescued by the war.

In 1942 Howe helped organize a new political gathering, not quite a party, calling itself the Independent Socialist League, with a political style, Howe recalls, quite different from that of the Trotskyists—less dogmatic, "softer in tone and texture," with a good deal of earnest talk about "the proletariat." This enterprise, as that last foreign-born phrase might hint, was practically formulated not to get very far; and in any case about this time Howe was drafted and sent to Anchorage, Alaska, where he spent two years sorting records and reading any volume that came across his bunk (a biography of Stalin, Gibbon's *Decline and Fall*, the essays of Matthew Arnold), and catching an occasional glimpse of a courtly, white-haired sergeant named Dashiell Hammett.

When he came back to New York and the postwar world, Howe discovered that history had continued to outwit the theorists: the war had not brought down the enemies, capitalism was flourishing in the Western countries, and Stalinist Russia was stable and expanding. Taking a long look at it all, and with a shy burgeoning admiration for America's political system, Howe and his friends began to agree "that for us the prime value was democracy, and that without it we could not even imagine a desirable socialism." They took to calling themselves Social Democrats. It was a long journey, this trip to democracy. But it has an allegorical fitness to it, beginning, as it should have, with the great garment workers' strike of 1933, and its radicalizing impact on Howe's family and Bronx neighborhood, moving persistently if erratically toward reality and the real historical imperatives, and arriving where it should have arrived.

It was as a Social Democrat that Howe, in 1953, founded the magazine *Dissent,* an intellectually sturdy periodical that would more than justify its existence a decade or so later. But by 1953 Irving Howe had also become a literary commentator of increasing weight and ability. Soon after the war, he had fallen among those writers and theorists whom Howe himself has designated as "the New York intellectuals," and about whom he published a long, searching essay more than a decade ago. The center of energy for this gentry was of course *Partisan Review,* to the faintly dubious enshrinement of which William Barrett, a former editor, has recently contributed his memorial, *The Truants.* Revisiting that scene in memory, Howe finds again that it was as disunited as it was lively. "Of visible community there were few signs that I could see," he writes, meditating on the entity presided over by Philip Rahv. "This was a gang of intellectual freebooters," and he quotes with pleasure the allusion of Harold Rosenberg to "the herd of independent minds."

Howe credits *Partisan Review* and the New York intellectuals of the 1950s with establishing for American readers the enormous fact of

European literary modernism. This may be true in a general way, though Harry Levin, up north at Harvard, had been leading the charge for a decade or so (his critical biography of James Joyce came out in 1941, at which time Levin was also teaching a seminar on Proust, Joyce, and Mann). And Howe, who was never really a card-carrying member of the metropolitan literary party, himself did as much as anyone to propagate modernism, with his anthology *The Idea of the Modern* and, among others, his volume of essays, *The Decline of the New*.

A common cultural flaw among those addicts of modernism, Howe acknowledges, was an ignorance of, and an indifference to, the native literary tradition. Howe takes this as a less serious defect than I do; in retrospect there is something curiously limited and walleyed about the European enthusiasms of *Partisan Review* at just the moment (the 1950s) when American literature for the first time was being fully explored, codified, appraised, and celebrated by such critics and scholars (following the example of F. O. Matthiessen) as Alfred Kazin, Daniel Aaron, Richard Chase, Marius Bewley, Charles Feidelson, and Leslie Fiedler. But again Howe errs toward modesty: he had from the outset of his critical career been addressing himself to American writers—books on Anderson and Faulkner (1951, 1952) and then essays on Henry James, Dreiser, E. A. Robinson, Edith Wharton, and his own contemporaries.

The simultaneous appeal of modernism, with its characteristically conservative political temper and its revulsion from everything that might otherwise be called "modern," and radical politics, with its asserted faith in the future historical victory: this has long been a familiar and yet a mysterious phenomenon. No one has represented that twin commitment more eloquently than Irving Howe; and in *A Margin of Hope* he goes back over the paradoxes and tensions involved—to conclude with another look at the momentous event that caused the hidden anxieties, as Howe puts it, to break out into the open. This was the award—by a jury that included Eliot, Tate, Auden, and Robert Lowell—of the Bollingen prize to Ezra Pound for his *Pisan*

Cantos of 1948. A great deal of ink has been spilled over this episode (and at one point, when Allen Tate challenged William Barrett to a duel, it seemed that some blood might be spilled as well); but in my view it has never been handled better than here by Irving Howe. My judgment is no doubt colored by our shared opinion of Pound, whose work and voice make us grimace.

But on the issues of the Bollingen case, Howe is worth listening to:

> Two separate questions were entangled here: one, the public propriety of honoring a profascist and anti-Semitic writer even if he had written the best poetry of 1948, and the other, far more complicated, whether or how fascist or anti-Semitic matter can be lodged in poetry taken to be great.

As to the first, Howe proposes that the jury might more wisely have held that Pound probably did write the best poetry that year, but that when aesthetic standards and human values clash, the latter must be taken as primary; and so no award would be given for 1948. The second and more troublesome question led Howe to reconsider the principle of "aesthetic autonomy." He ascribes to the New Critics in this era a position that would not in fact be explicitly espoused until the still newer critical breed of the New Haven persuasion twenty-five years later—and rejects it. This is the view that

> a poem was not to be grasped in its essential being through references to the world of familiar experience, for the poem is not an "imitation" of that world, the poem inhabits a realm of its own. The offending lines in the *Cantos* thus would not contain a statement in the sense that an essay contains statements; those in the poem must be seen as self-contained matter.

The "statements" referred to included such lines as "Pétain defended Verdun while Blum/Was defending a bidet"; and Howe finds it impossible to accept any theory that divorces those lines from an external historical reality. In all sincerity, and in the words of an English military friend, I couldn't possibly begin not to disagree with him less. Pound's Pisan poem, on occasions like this, is so morally revolting as to be aesthetically rotten.

For five years, beginning in 1949, Howe lived in Princeton, where his wife had a job teaching Latin. He would later decide that he had been repelled by the "chilled graces and Anglophile snobbery" of the university and the town, but he adds his own colorful testimony about the local literati to that, recently, of Russell Fraser in his fascinating but vexatious biography of R. P. Blackmur, and Eileen Simpson's vivid and moving recollections of the Princeton clan of gifted, self-dismantling poets, her husband John Berryman and Delmore Schwartz among them. (As a matter of fact, the shrewdest and the most intimately knowledgeable account of literary and intellectual life in Princeton during this epoch is an unpublished—but eminently publishable—two-hundred-page report written by Robert Fitzgerald for the Rockefeller Foundation.*)

As it happened, it was in Princeton and at this time that I first met Irving Howe, and here I should confess that it has been an eerie experience for me to read this memoir. I can name a number of other people of a certain age who will have the same dislocating reaction: one's own life seems to unfold before one in these pages, stage by remembered stage, slightly blurred here, a bit misplaced there, with some of the names changed. In my case, the parallels with Howe's life

*The report was published by the Northeastern University Press, in late 1984, as *Enlarging the Change: The Princeton Seminars in Literary Criticism, 1949–1951.* In his preface Fitzgerald said that he had not thought about the report for years—"until I was reminded of the post-war Princeton circle by a scholar and critic who had come on that scene just after I left it and now looked back on it with attachment. I dug my carbon out to show it to him. The next thing I knew he had mentioned it in print as 'eminently publishable,' and the Northeastern University Press had asked to see it."

story carry forward through college and war years, a remotely comparable political alertness, apprenticeship in the postwar literary periodicals (I was a *Hudson Review* boy, being too bookish and American for *Partisan;* Rahv always called me "professor"), a lengthy spell and a Gauss seminar at Princeton, *und so weiter*. The parallels are symbolized for me by our common affection—a politicoliterary affection, as it were—for the writings and the personal presence of Ignazio Silone.

This being so, I permit myself some divergences of opinion about the cultural history we have both lived through. As to the crucial part of that history that we did *not* share, the American Jewish experience, I can only say that for this outsider Howe moves through the perplexities and the passions with great intellectual dignity. But Howe strikes me throughout as a bit tone-deaf regarding the religious pulsations of the age, Christian or otherwise. He observes with bafflement the religious striving of a Newton Arvin ("I probably missed its finer shadings," he says, which suggests he missed much more than that); and there is no cognizance, amid the cultural welter Howe is so handsomely evoking, of the theological performance of a Jacques Maritain or the cunning, perverse Catholicism of a Flannery O'Connor.

Howe in turn may want to diagnose me as tone-deaf on the political side; for I do differ from him in a long-standing inability, historically nurtured, to fear and detest communism (any mode of it) as much as I have feared and detested fascism and the Nazis. And wisps of the old, harsh, discarded dialectics seem still to cling to Howe when he writes, speaking of the anti–Vietnam War movement: "We were stuck, those of us who opposed American involvement in Vietnam yet did not favor a communist victory." This leaves an awful lot of us stranded atop the excluded middle.

But Howe is staunch on the McCarthy period, and shows none of the signs one notices with dismay elsewhere of rearranging his mind about the evil; he has the right to recall with pride having written and acted on the conviction that McCarthyism was as threatening nationally as Stalinism was on the international stage. But probably Howe's finest hour was in the late 1960s, during his bruising encounters—in fact and in the pages of *Dissent*—with the new left, the SDS, and other factions of the moment. Booed more than once in public for his desperate rationalism, his attachment to democratic procedures, and expressed historical awareness, Howe kept his head while platoons of intellectuals and political savants were all around him losing theirs. The best he got for his pains was an amiable admonishment from a political theorist at Amherst: "The trouble with your Social Democratic politics is that it's so boring." The comment, Howe says, has haunted him ever since. "Between my political beliefs and the dark reaches of our century there is obviously a gap." Maybe so; but it may also be the gap that saves. It has protected him from the instant fanaticisms of our era; and it has brought him time and again to insist that public rhetoric, however worthy the cause, show a respect for what he calls "the actualities of our lives."

But *A Margin of Hope* is far more than a mulling over of political and literary attitudes and experiences. It is a work of literary distinction, beautifully composed—its artful pacing would repay close study—and set forth in prose rhythms of an exceptionally high order. One of the happiest things to watch over the decades, in the world of American letters, has been Irving Howe's development as a prose stylist, to the point where, to my ear, his is the most resonant voice we have on anything that touches our cultural situation, our civilized discontents.

In this autobiography, the style quickens and illumines the whole long act of memory, as some of the passages quoted may perhaps indicate. It can equally provide superbly worded snapshots of individual figures. Here is Robert Fitzgerald, a fellow book reviewer at *Time*, keeping his cool at the weekly conference "by assuming an air of unbroken gravity, as if he were a monk bound hostage to a gang of heretics." Here is R. P. Blackmur in Princeton: "Small, neatly turned out, a shade dandyish, speaking in a weighty, murmurous monotone."

About Hannah Arendt, Howe says that "she bristled with intellectual charm"; think that over. He conjurs up for us with dark enjoyment the persona of Louis Kampf, an M.I.T. professor and member of the new left who somehow got himself elected president of the Modern Language Association. After listing some of the critical stances taken by Kampf at a forum in Philadelphia—Jonathan Swift, Marcel Proust, and the whole body of Greek tragedy were to be dismissed as counter-revolutionary—Howe goes on: "Yet I know Louie, he isn't really a commissar, he wouldn't hurt a fly, he has simply been driven out of his wits by the *Zeitgeist*." And there are graver portraits, like that of the Columbia historian Richard Hofstadter, a New York neighbor who gave off "a mild glow of charm and sanity" such that "there was profit even in his silence." Howe attributes to Hofstadter, as he does to Lionel Trilling, the supreme quality of "liberalism of spirit."

Howe ends with an unavoidably jaundiced look at the present:

> This is a moment—the early eighties—of peculiar sordidness. It's as if the spirit of the old robber barons has been triumphantly resurrected, as if the most calloused notions of Social Darwinism were back with us, as if the celebrations of greed we associate with the nineteenth century were reenacted a century later.

The utterance is not despondent, but vigorous, coldly wrathful, that of a learned and experienced man about to gird up. Hence the hope.

(1982)

PART FOUR

A View from the Source

homas Hardy is a particular case in point in any consideration of Robert Penn Warren's literary descendancy. Talking to an interviewer in 1974, Warren suggested that the appeal of Hardy's poetry (along with that of Yeats) for the southern Fugitive writers was its deployment of "the folk element within the larger reaches of the imagination." "Hardy's use of folk materials . . . touched some of these people very deeply," Warren said—"these people," of course, being John Crowe Ransom and the others who enlivened the Vanderbilt University scene in the 1920s.

This was in thoughtful retrospect, and in view of half a century of creative experience. What happened initially was much more simple. On a July weekend in 1925, soon after Warren's graduation from Vanderbilt, John Ransom drove up from Nashville to Guthrie, Kentucky, a matter of fifty-odd miles, for a visit at the Warren home. He was accompanied by three of Warren's college friends, and, as Warren explained to his other chief faculty advisor, the group of them ate meals, played poker, went swimming in the river, and then stretched out on blankets under the trees and read poetry.

Ransom led the way in a reading of Hardy's poems; he was "mad for Hardy," Warren would recall, and would later edit Hardy's *Selected Poems*. On this occasion, Ransom memorably read aloud the poem "Wessex Heights," and its slow evocation of highland places where the lone self can seek its own truth seems to have fired young Warren's imagination:

> There are some heights in Wessex, shaped as if by a kindly
>   hand
> For thinking, dreaming, dying on, and at crises when I stand,
> Say, on Ingpen Beacon westward, or on Wylls-Neck
>   westwardly,
> I seem where I was before my birth, and after death may be.

"I was never the same," Warren has remarked. "I thought, this is the real thing, and I still think it is."

It was when he returned to Hardy's poetry on his own, apparently, that Warren began to discern and to cherish the mixture in it of the folk and the traditional. In Warren's fledgling poetic practice, such a mixture is observable as early as "Pondy Woods" in 1928, in which the circling buzzards harangue the doomed fleeing black man in tones alternately of T. S. Eliot and of a Kentucky redneck. The mix continues and thickens through "The Ballad of Billie Potts" in the 1940s down to "Folly on Royal Street" in the 1970s. This latter-named memoir of Baton Rouge and New Orleans days begins with an echo of Milton's lordly "Samson Agonistes" and moves on or descends to the saltily idiomatic:

> Drunk, drunk, drunk amid the blaze of noon,
> Irrevocably drunk, total eclipse or,
> At least, almost, and in New Orleans once . . .
>   Sunday and the street
> Blank as my bank account

With two checks bounced—we—
C. and M. and I, every
Man-jack skunk-drunk
came.

Another and darker attraction of Hardy for the Vanderbilt writers,
Warren remarked, was his notion of fate. "A fatalism was deeply
ingrained in the southern mind. Things could not be changed. A sense
of entrapment . . . Hardy touched this nerve." Elsewhere, in a more
formal context (an essay on Hemingway), Warren spoke of literary folk
who perceived the individual as confronting a hostile and meaningless
universe, and presented as succinctly representative Thomas Hardy in
his little poem "Hap," with its dire image of "purblind doomsters." In
the face of such a universe, Warren observed, Hardy had something to
sustain him: "a strong sense of community"—but a *secret* community,
existing apart from social institutions and often at odds with them.

Warren recognized in Hardy, and all the more with the passing
years, what he treasured in his own experience, a private community
that in his account of it nourished and restored and transformed him.
It comes into view seriatim in his poetry: his father, Robert Franklin
Warren, and his mother, Anna Ruth Penn ("side by side, Ruth and
Robert," in the graceful phrasing of a poem in 1957); his grandfather
Gabriel Penn (to whom Warren addressed half a dozen poems, the best
perhaps being the one called "Court Martial"); his boyhood friend
Kent Greenfield (whose bird lore and foreshortened baseball career are
revisited in "American Portrait: Old Style"); his wife, Eleanor Clark
("Birth of Love" is her special enshrinement, but she figures in many
another poem); their children, Rosanna and Gabriel (the volume
Promises of 1957, the turning point in Warren's poetic career, was
inspired by their arrival in the world); other friends described in poems
or named in dedications.

So Thomas Hardy the poet, as purveying these themes and enacting
these strategies, was taken by Warren at a young age into his personal

canon, his assembly of earlier writers whose work and vision were of particular and enabling value for him. With this I come, if a bit laggardly, to a statement of my subject: which is, exactly, the makeup, the *making* up, of Warren's own literary canon—and, not less, that making process as a model of literary canon making.

There has been a burst of talk and a fury of debate within the American academy and between its members in recent years about the whole phenomenon of canon formation, with discordant ukases about canon dismantling and re-formation. Like so much else in the academic world these days, the matter has become strenuously politicized; conservatives and liberals alike are quick to push their programs. Throughout the discussions and polemics and voluble revisionings, the most disconcerting assumption, for anything like an onlooker, is that it is the discussants themselves, the professorial critics and theorists, who determine the list of canonical writings—the ones most to be revered and taught and written about—in our present day. The academic canons are real enough: they exist and have an air of authority about them, and it would be a brave student or untenured faculty member who would disregard them in any given case. But they have very little to do with *literary* reality: that is, with the life of literature. For in fact it is and always has been much rather the *practitioners,* the poets and novelists and essayists, who beget the really important literary canons, those with weight and meaning, in any generation. And the manner of it is perfectly exemplified by Henry James in his lecture on Balzac in 1905, aptly called "The Lesson of Balzac." "Let me . . . frankly say," James told his audience, "that I speak of [Balzac], and can only speak, as a man of his own craft, an emulous fellow-worker, who has learned more from him of the lessons of the engaging mystery of fiction than from any other."

There you have it: the fellow worker, the person of the same craft, in an acknowledgment of lessons learned and applied. Poets, even more than prose writers, can be seen displaying this tactic over the ages: it is one of the great recurring acts of literary history, from the sixteenth-century French poets who called themselves the Pléiade and who rejected the medieval poetic tradition and urged instead the study and emulation of Homer, Pindar, Horace, and Petrarch, down to T. S. Eliot discarding Milton in favor of John Donne and the metaphysicals out of his personal creative urgencies, and soon after that Hart Crane and Wallace Stevens canonizing Whitman and Emerson to comparable purpose. And it may be ventured that critics have, traditionally, best pursued their calling—in this business of canon making, that is—when they have inquired into the whys, the wherefores, and the consequences of the canonical choices of their literary betters, the poets and novelists contemporary to them.

The figure and posture exemplified by Henry James, anyhow, are the ones we recognize when Robert Penn Warren writes about the precursors, English and American, who have meant the most to him. Eudora Welty caught the matter in a phrase when, at a meeting to celebrate Warren in New York in 1990, she spoke of Warren's superlative essay on Coleridge's "The Rime of the Ancient Mariner" (1946), and said that Warren's mobile analysis of the poem gives us "one poet's vision of another's." It was indeed via just such fellow-envisioning that Coleridge was taken into Warren's canonical entourage. For Warren, Coleridge counterpointed Hardy when it came to an assessment of the human situation. In a fine article of a few years back, Monroe K. Spears suggested, with a bit of serious punning, that Warren should be identified not as an American Hardy but as a "Hardy American": partly because Warren reflected a sense of "personal responsibility for older American literature," and partly because Warren (this was how the pun worked) was hardier, staunchier, in his general views than his Dorset predecessor. Setting texts from the two poets alongside each other, Spears found that Warren is "much less bleak and grim than Hardy. . . . He believes in the existence of joy and love because he has experienced them." The rendered experience of joy was what, among other things, Warren discovered in Coleridge.

He discovered it in that pivotal moment in "The Ancient Mariner" when the mariner, alone on his stricken ship, the Albatross around his neck, the dead crew lying near him on the deck, watches the flashing water snakes and is suddenly overwhelmed by their beauty:

> O happy living things! no tongue
> Their beauty might declare:
> A spring of love gushed from my heart,
> And I blessed them unaware. . . .
>
> The self-same moment I could pray;
> And from my neck so free
> The Albatross fell off, and sank
> Like lead into the sea.

As Warren puts it in the 1946 essay, the poet-mariner recognizes and proclaims the One Life that runs through all living things: "the chain of love which binds human society and the universe," and the vision of which (these are Coleridge's words) summons forth "the deep power of joy." Warren came close to an express formulation of the Coleridgian theme, and its living import for him, in the toughly abstract closing lines of his 1973 poem "I Am Dreaming of a White Christmas." Here the poet, puzzling over and trying to understand his dream-vision of a childhood Christmas in Kentucky, and of a family life once treasured and now lost and gone, declares at the end:

> This
> Is the process whereby pain of the past in its pastness
> May be converted into the future tense
>
> Of joy.

Coleridge's canonical status for Warren also derived, to an extent, from his precursor's technique of glossing in "The Ancient Mariner." In the margin of the passage quoted from, it can be recalled, one sees

Coleridge's comment: "By the light of the moon he beholdeth God's creatures of the great calm. . . . He blesseth them in his heart. The spell begins to break." That mode of dialoguing between poet and text was a feature of Warren's poetry from earliest days, and was never manuevered more effectively than in "The Ballad of Billie Potts" in 1943 (at a moment when Warren may well have been beginning to work on the Coleridge essay*). In this work, the gloss appears as discursive commentary in the author's voice, interpreting and expanding upon the action described in the narrative, which itself has the air of an anonymous folk ballad. The discursive and the narrational relate to one another as the high style and the vernacular. Thus, when little Billie decides to run off from Kentucky to the far west and make his fortune and prove his manhood, we have, first, the story telling:

> Little Billie had something in his clobber-head
> By way of brains, and he reckoned he knew
> How to skin a cat or add two and two.
> So long before the sky got red
> Over the land between the river,
> He hobbled his horse back in the swamp
> And squatted on his gams in the morning dew and damp
> And scratched his stomach and grinned to think
> How his Pap would be proud and his Mammy glad
> To know what a thriving boy they had
> In the section between the rivers

And then the gloss, set off by parentheses:

> (Think of yourself riding away from the dawn,
> Think of yourself and the unnamed ones who had gone

*The essay was mostly written, in fact, in the spring of 1945, when Warren was the Poet in Residence at the Library of Congress—and meditating, one may conjecture, on the status of poetry in America and its relation to its English forebears.

Before, riding, who rode away from *good-bye, good-bye,*
And toward *hello*, toward Time's unwinking eye;
And like the cicadas had left, at cross-roads or square,
The old shell of self, thin, ghostly, translucent, light as air;
At dawn riding into the curtain of unwhispering green . . .

Think of yourself at dawn: Which are you? What?)

A somewhat similar interplay of story and voice takes place in Warren's novel of 1950, *World Enough and Time*; and it reached a sort of fulfillment in the verse-drama *Brother to Dragons* (1953, revised 1978), where the author not only meditates at length upon the terrible doings (chiefly the murder of black slave boy in 1800s Kentucky), but engages in ghostly conversation with the play's major figure, Thomas Jefferson.

This is not a survey of the whole of Warren's self-begotten literary ancestry (much less is it an inventory of his vast reading). Such a survey would be worth making; and in this case, of a writer who is a far-ranging literary critic and historian as well as a poet and novelist, it would amount to a decent-sized book. Among the other English figures to whom Warren was variously beholden, mention would have to be made of Wordsworth ("Wordsworth knew what he was up to," Warren once opined with sage approval), A. E. Housman ("Housman-esque nostalgia" was a favorite subject for imitation at Vanderbilt, he remembered), and Joseph Conrad. Warren devoted one of his most potent essays to Conrad's *Nostromo*; he had a deep natural affinity, at once imaginative and intellectual, with the author of that novel and of *Lord Jim* and *Under Western Eyes*. Further in Warren's English background, we make out Edmund Spenser, whose *Faerie Queene* supplied the cunningly appropriate epigraph for *World Enough and Time*; the plays of Shakespeare—Warren first read them in a well-thumbed multivolume set belonging to his mother, and which he kept by him all his life; and the nondramatic writings of the Elizabethans, which Warren taught in his classes at Louisiana State University and later.

The Bible is everywhere in Warren, in epigraphs, titles, themes, language. Warren read it at a young age, from start to finish at the rate of three chapters a day, to earn a gold piece (five or ten dollars—later, he wasn't sure which) offered by his father. The paternal influence no doubt contributed to the continuing importance of the Bible for the mature Warren; but that same mature personality also shared, learned from, and constantly rearticulated the Old Testament's brooding sense of human history struggling to reveal its inmost meaning and purpose.

In the hypothetical survey we have broached, an entire chapter could be given to Dante and the *Divina Commèdia*. Warren has adverted more than once to the years when he was wholly immersed in Dante: roughly from 1939 to 1946, when *All the King's Men* was going through its metamorphosis from play to novel; and the novel's epigraph is taken from *Purgatorio* iii: *"mentre chè la speranza ha fior del verde."* It is spoken by the spirit of Manfredi, the Ghibelline warrior who was killed at Benevento in 1266 and whose body was denied burial in sacred ground by Pope Clement IV. It expresses Manfredi's belief that, for the repentant sinner, there is always hope—"a green blossoming of hope"—of ultimate salvation. Warren added the line as an afterthought to suggest something about Willie Stark: that he too was a human mixture and redeemable, that (in Warren's comment) he underwent a "deathbed reversal of feeling . . . like Manfredi." This is the implication of Willie's dying words to Jack Burden: "It might have been different. . . . You got to believe that."

In other words, there was at work for Warren at this time a structure of moral outlook sufficiently like that of Dante for him to call upon the *Divina Commèdia* as a guide to the understanding of his protagonist. The Dantean moral vision is even more strongly present in *At Heaven's Gate*, the novel that preceded *All the King's Men* (in 1943). Warren has been willing to say that the Seventh Circle of the *Inferno* "provided, with some liberties of interpretation and extension, the basic scheme and metaphor for the whole novel." The Seventh Circle presents sinners who have been guilty of violence against nature; and in Warren's retrospective notation, "All of the main characters [in the novel] are violators of nature." Warren has declared in particular that the financier Bogan Murdock and the homosexual Slim Sarrett "are straight out of the Circle." They are modern Tennessee versions of Dante's usurers and sodomites. One records with tolerant regret, in the 1990s, that Warren in the 1940s followed Dante's view that homosexual activity was a violation of the natural; but one notices as well that, like Dante, Warren looks upon the power-and-money-grasping Murdock far more harshly than he does Sarrett.* Meanwhile, the epigraph for *Rumor Verified*, the 1980 volume of poems, is taken from the closing lines of the *Inferno*, where Dante, following Virgil up out of the underworld, sees far ahead "*delle belle cose*": "some of the fair things that Heaven bears; and thence we came forth to see again the stars" (translation by John D. Sinclair). The passage could have been drawn upon in many another connection, for it hints at the characteristic Warren intuition about the *possible* emergence from terrible pain and even horror into the presence of beauty and a hard-won future joy.

The role of Dante in Warren's last novel, *A Place to Come To*, is more problematical. The protagonist of that story, Jed Tewksbury, earns a Ph.D. at the University of Chicago with a dissertation entitled *Dante and the Metaphysics of Death* (the writing of it coincided with the dying of his young wife), and he later becomes a widely esteemed professor of Comparative Literature and a Dante specialist. But it is central to the narrative theme that Jed is an almost completely disengaged individual: disengaged from life, from love, from self, from history, from literature, and not least from the poetry of Dante Alighieri. It was an oblique form of canonizing when, seeking a person of towering

---

*The most memorable representative of sodomy as a sin against nature in the *Inferno* is Brunetto Latini, Dante's revered teacher; and for most readers, no figure in the *Commèdia* seems more humanly sympathetic. Slim Sarrett in *At Heaven's Gate* is an indefensible manipulator of the selves of others. But he is given some of the wisest saying in the novel, and it is in any case his manipulativeness rather than his homosexuality that the novel condemns.

literary achievement from whom it would appear most inexplicable and reprehensible for an intelligent scholar to be disengaged, Warren chose Dante.

Robert Penn Warren, in the words of Monroe K. Spears, made evident a sense—this was especially true in his later years—of "personal responsibility for older American literature." In this regard, Spears adduces Warren's growing attention to Melville's and Whittier's poetry and the novels of Dreiser. To this abbreviated list we should immediately add the name of Nathaniel Hawthorne. Warren's major statement about Hawthorne was in an essay of 1973, and it is, one might say, at once intensely responsible and intensely personal. Nowhere else does Warren give us so clearly the impression of one practitioner looking at, musing upon, and learning from another. In the opening sentence, Warren describes the cluster of tensions that Hawthorne lived and wrote among; as one listens to it, one would do well to "think Warren":

> He lived in the right ratio—right for the fueling of his genius—between an attachment to his region and a detached assessment of it; between attraction to the world and contempt for its gifts . . .; between a faith in life and a corrosive skepticism . . .; between aesthetic passion and moral concern; between a fascinated attentiveness to the realistic texture, forms and characteristics of nature and human nature, and a compulsive flight from the welter of life towards abstract ideals.

As Warren moves from one Hawthorne story to another, he is also moving from one aspect of his own work to another. He stresses the filial theme in Hawthorne's "The Gentle Boy" and "My Kinsman, Major Molineux," and there comes to mind the recurring drama of father-and-son in Warren's writing, in "The Ballad of Billie Potts," in the verse play *Brother to Dragons*, in *All the King's Men* and *World*

Enough and Time, and in the many poems Warren wrote about his own father. Warren observes that Hawthorne regularly turned to tales of violence and passion, "but the violence and passion had to be in the past, for, as he put it, poetry "is a plant that thrives best in spots where blood has been spilt long ago." And we think again of *Brother to Dragons,* with its gruesome murder of a black slave boy by two nephews of Thomas Jefferson in 1811 Kentucky; of *World Enough and Time,* and its tale of killing and pursuit in the Kentucky of a decade or so later; of *Wilderness* and *Band of Angels,* set partly back in the Civil War years. Warren examines a recurring phenomenon in Hawthorne, "the obsessed man": Ethan Brand, Goodman Brown, Rappaccini, Chillingworth; and we remember Jeremiah Beaumont in *World Enough and Time* (a novel, in Warren's formula, "about the pathology of romanticism"), the bedeviled farmer Gillum in the harrowing poem "School Lesson," and perhaps the suicidal dentist in "The Day Dr. Knox Did It."*

All these themes and ingredients, Warren says near the end of his essay, were revelations of what he names "the obsessive concern of Hawthorne's work"; and this was "the struggle to achieve self-knowledge." Warren sees everything Hawthorne ever wrote as an effort at self-discovery and self-understanding, mixed in with the effort toward self-masking and self-evasion; and this is precisely why Hawthorne holds so high a place in Warren's canon. The same principle may be applied to Robert Penn Warren, which means that the essay on Hawthorne too is an effort at self-discovery, with a portion, as may be, of self-concealment. For this is the way literary canons are in the reality of things pressed into existence.

There was a measure of surprise, almost of scandal, in academic circles when, in 1971, Warren brought out a selection of the poetry of John

*John Burt first led this writer to see the Hawthorne-Warren motif of the obsessed man, in his distinguished Ph.D. dissertation at Yale in 1983, "American Romance and the Bounds of Sense."

Greenleaf Whittier with a sixty-page introduction. The latter is in its way a more striking example of canon making than the essay on the solidly established Hawthorne ("solidly" at least until recently, when Hawthorne has become a favorite target of the new literary radicals). Warren is again dealing with matters of abiding interest in his own personal and literary life. For one thing, Whittier in his early career represents the danger of succumbing to the style of the fashionable poets of his time: what Warren called "the inane gabble" of N. P. Willis, Lydia Sigourney, and Longfellow at his worst. Only by "getting rid of the 'poetical' notion of poetry," Warren writes, was Whittier "able, eventually, to ground his poetry in experience," which is where Warren came to think it should be grounded.

Warren took to himself the poetry of Herman Melville in much the same way. In an early essay on Melville, a review of a small selection of his poetry by F. O. Matthiessen, Warren said: "It must be admitted that Melville did not learn his craft. But the point is that the craft he did not learn was not the same craft which some of his more highly advertised contemporaries did learn with such glibness of tongue and complacency of spirit." In a much later essay, Warren described Melville's ultimate achievement in language, which again invites us to "think Warren": "He was aiming at a style rich and yet shot through with prosaisms, sometimes casual and open and sometimes dense and intellectually freighted." Warren was underscoring in both Melville and Whittier what he had accomplished in his own poetic development: an escape from any kind of bondage to the fashionable contemporary (in Warren's case, the dangerous influence of T. S. Eliot, hardly an inane gabbler by Warren's or anyone else's reckoning), a grounding of the poetry in personal experience (the whole history of Warren's evolution is implicit in that phrase), the admitting of "prosaisms" and the vernacular into the poetic vocabulary.

The figure of Whittier the abolitionist held a strong appeal for Warren, above all because Whittier was "a man of peace and a man of reason" drawn by historical pressures into the world of violent discord.

More than any of his canonized precursors, or at least more overtly, Whittier was the socially responsive artist: that nineteenth-century persona that Ralph Ellison (in his comments at the celebrational New York meeting mentioned earlier) found Warren inheriting and re-embodying. Warren of Kentucky honored Whittier of Massachusetts because, while Whittier "never compromised on the question of slavery, . . . he steadily insisted"—in opposition to the Garrisonian abolitionists—"on viewing it in human and institutional terms."

It was when Whittier brought his developing poetic skill to bear on his political convictions, as we have heard Warren saying, that he arrived at literary success: as in "Letter to a Missionary" in 1854, where the godly Kansas preacher, cunningly ventriloquized by Whittier, reports with satisfaction on his recent doings:

> I tarried overnight [at Westport, Kansas], to aid in forming
> A Vigilance Committee, to send back,
> In shirts of tar, and feather-doublets quilted
> With forty stripes save one, all Yankee comers. . . .

And there was "Ichabod" four years earlier, a delicately devastating operation on Daniel Webster for abandoning his previously unequivocal antislavery position. But for all its historicopolitical content, "Ichabod," in Warren's view, is on its deepest level about the betrayal of children by the father. It thus suggests the real "experience" that Whittier grounded his best poetry in, and so belongs to those poems where Whittier deployed his most compelling themes: the poems of family, of parents and children, of siblings lost, childhood remembered, and age foreseen.

Whittier's masterwork in the genre, of course, was *Snow-Bound: A Winter Idyll*, the 759-line poem published in 1866. It is a full-scale evocative reminiscence, tender, sad, and lively, of the family circle almost fifty years before: the Whittier family with two guests gathered comfortably inside the substantial old farmhouse in Haverhill, Massachusetts, while a fierce December snowstorm rages outside. We are introduced, as the rhymed couplets glide forward, to the poet's father and then his mother, to a brother, two sisters (both dead by the time of the poem, the death of the younger, Elizabeth, being the occasion for the memoir), an uncle, the master of the district school (much admired by Whittier), and the eccentric, adventurous Harriet Livermore (last heard of, Whittier tells us in a note, wandering in Syria with a tribe of Arabs who treated her as a holy madwoman).

In his commentary Warren once again gives us one poet's vision of another's. Warren's time-saturated mind was particularly intrigued by the manner in which each individual in the company "brings into the poem a specific dramatization of the problem of Time." Interlaced with this is the theme of bereavement: as of 1866, every member of the original Whittier family is dead, except Greenleaf and his brother, Matthew. The final perspective is that of the present temporal moment: the immediate post–Civil War world, with its fearsome dangers and great possibilities. Warren sees Whittier—in lines that rang in Warren's imagination—offering the act of memory of a sustenance in the trials of the moment:

> I hear again the voice that bids
> The dreamer leave his dream midway
> For larger hopes and graver fears;
> Life greatens in these later years,
> The century's aloe flowers today!
> Yet haply, in some lull of life,
> Some truce of God, which breaks its strife,
> The wordling's eyes shall gather dew,
>   Dreaming in throngful city ways
> Of winter joys his boyhood knew. . . .

Snow-Bound is the unmistakable precursor for Robert Penn Warren's strange, powerful poem of boyhood memory already mentioned, "I

Am Dreaming of a White Christmas," written in the early 1970s when Warren was in the thick of his affair with Whittier. Here, in an act of emulation, the elderly poet looks back across the decades to a family gathering on a winter day: in this case on Christmas morning, perhaps in 1915, in the little living room of the old home in Guthrie, Kentucky; and before the work is ended, the dreamer, following Whittier, has left his childhood scene for the urban world. We are made aware—we can scarcely be said to be introduced to them—of the father and the mother, the poet as child, the younger sister, the baby brother. The Warren poem asks to be understood as playing *against* its predecessor, beginning with a title borrowed from Irving Berlin, which casts a curious jazzy light over the proceedings: an interpolation of the musically vernacular, to declare the poem's contemporariness, as it were its post-Freudian and, if you will, its postmodernist nature.

Warren's "White Christmas" is hallucinatory, a drama of vision. "The Natural History of a Vision" is the subtitle, and we come upon the ingredients one by one, stage by stage, as the poet dreams his dream. It begins:

> *No, not that door—never! But*
> Entering, saw. Through
> air brown as an old daguerreotype fading . . .
>
> Through brown air, dust-dry, saw.

What the poet saw was an old bed, now stripped of coverings, the mattress littered with yellowing newspapers; then, the old Morris chair, bought by the parents after their marriage, for the father to sit in; then the father himself.

> The big head. Propped
> Erect on the chair's leather pillow, bald skin

>   . . . I have not
> Yet looked at the eyes. Not
> Yet.
>
>   The eyes
> Are not there. But
> Not there they stare at what
>
> Is not there.

The mother comes into view:

>   Now staring
> She sits in the accustomed rocker, but with
> No motion . . .
>
> On the brown-lacquered face
> There are now no
> Lips to kiss with.

A hearth is there, but no fire in it. Suddenly the Christmas tree appears, the boughs long since denuded of green; below it, the poet espies three packages. And then nearby, three chairs, which the poet had not noticed before:

>   The little red chair,
> For the baby. The next biggest chair
> For my little sister, the little red rocker. Then,
> The biggest, my own, me, the elder.
>
> The chairs are all empty.

Warren, as we see, is manipulating the motifs of the precursor poem, but by a different, even a unique, method. The dream-vision mode permits him to do simultaneously what Whittier could do only by phases: to bring the long-ago family scene back into sight *and* to present the mother and the father as long since dead, mummified, eyeless; to resurrect the Christmas setting and to describe it as faded and withered, a thing of the far past. Having accomplished this, the poet moves on—to quote Warren on the final section of the Whittier poem—from "the old agrarian way of life" to a new urban order: literally, in section 9, to New York City.

> Where I was
> Am not. Now am
> Where the blunt crowd thrusts, nudges, jerks, jostles,
> And the eye is inimical. Then,
> Of a sudden know:

> Times Square, the season
> Late summer and the hour sunset, with fumes
> In throat and smog-glitter at sky height.

After inspecting the urban dreamscape for a number of lines, the speaker, as though in a final gesture toward *Snow-Bound,* is displaced again, into the Nez Perce Pass between Montana and Idaho, where snow is beginning to fall. The poem ends in an echoing version of the closing sequence in *Snow-Bound,* with the action of memory undoing the pain of loss. We quote for a second time:

> This
> Is the process whereby pain of the past in its pastness
> May be converted into the future tense

> Of Joy.

But at this point we should pause to acknowledge a certain fact. The academic warriors busy demolishing old literary canons and erecting new ones would pay little heed to Warren's re-canonizing of the likes of Hawthorne and Whittier. The main intention of these folk, in fact, is to question the validity of *all* those nineteenth-century oldsters: elitist white male WASPs at best, working to perpetuate outworn class interests, and as dead, the lot of them, as the father and the mother in Warren's "White Christmas" poem. The concomitant intention has been to replace those people with writers hitherto regarded as socially or literarily marginal: women writers, black writers, American Indian writers, political writers, folk-culture voices, and similar varieties. Some of the most beneficial work done by academic critics of late has unarguably been to make such figures accessible, to get them into print and into prominence. So it must be reported that Robert Penn Warren, functioning as always in his fellow-practitioner capacity, was focusing on many of these outsiders, celebrating them, and drawing them into his personal canon twenty and thirty years ago.

Warren's essays on Hawthorne and Whittier and the more substantial of the essays on Melville were written for an anthology, co-edited by Cleanth Brooks and me, called *American Literature: The Makers and the Making*. The anthology appeared in two volumes in 1973. For the first volume, along with his other contributions, Warren offered informed and astute discussions of political writers—Garrison, Frederick Douglass, and others; southern humorists and tall-story tellers; "Folk Songs of the White People" and "Folk Songs of the Black People"— Warren's concern with folk material, as was suggested pages back, is genuine, learned, and long-standing; and American Indian poetry and oratory. In the second volume Warren was responsible for two long sections on black literature, running from Charles Waddell Chesnutt and W. E. B. Du Bois through Jean Toomer, Zora Neale Hurston, and Richard Wright; discussions of post–Civil War songs ("The Cowboy's Lament," "Casey Jones," "John Henry," "Paul Bunyan"); and a consideration of composers of the blues (among them Jelly Roll Morton, Ma Rainey, and Bessie Smith).

A word should be said about Warren's concern with political writing: it is a significant adjunct to one central aspect of his literary career.

A striking if confusing feature of the new canonists has been their emphatic political bent; just now, it seems to be going beyond the emphatic to the fanatical, in a politicizing of the cosmos and the entirety of the human being. In a replay of one extreme tendency of the 1960s (when, for example, classical texts with others were dismissed from the curriculum because of their political failings), text after text, from Shakespeare to Hemingway, has been brought to the unforgiving bar of ideological acceptability. But what is so puzzling is the almost total lack of connection with, interest in, or comment upon the *actual* political and social world in which these historicizers live. Political correctness and political indifference seem to go hand in hand. These theorists appear to be as divorced from the world outside their ruminations as did their theoretical opposites, the deconstructionists. Warren, by distinctive contrast, was always taking his part in the history of his time, speaking out publicly on the issues alive in the American social and political world to which he belonged, accepting and enacting his role as a socially responsible literary artist.

There was the contribution to *I'll Take My Stand* (1930), where he seemed to assume a fated fixity in the racial structure of southern society; the book-length essay *Segregation* (1956), where he brought the matter down into the actual and the experienced; and *Who Speaks for the Negro?* in the 1960s, a dedicated searching out and interviewing of black leaders across the land—Malcolm X, Roy Wilkins, Martin Luther King, Mrs. Claire Harvey (of Jackson, Mississippi, founder of Women Power Unlimited), Ruth Turner (full-time worker for CORE and at the center of the black community movement in Cleveland), Stokeley Carmichael, Dr. Kenneth Clark, James L. Farmer, James Baldwin, Ralph Ellison, and many another. The superb little book *The Legacy of the Civil War* (1961) looks at the heritage of that war as it operates within the ongoing culture of the two combative elements— what Warren decidedly did *not* honor or canonize: for the South, "the Great Alibi," the military defeat as an excuse-all explanation for every shortcoming or inaction; for the North, "the Treasury of Virtue," an assurance of moral superiority, ratified by victory, that carries the region through every public misdemeanor. It is in this ample context that Warren's anthology profiles of Calhoun, the abolitionists, and most of all perhaps Abraham Lincoln gain peculiar force.

As to Warren's creative lesson from black literary expression, we can notice as one small instance that the title of his novel *Band of Angels* was taken from the spiritual "Swing Low, Sweet Chariot." Warren had the warmest admiration for black spirituals and the blues, and said of the former, specifying "Swing Low," that they were highly and consciously organized literary compositions, with strong dramatic and poetic qualities. Black voices can be heard increasingly in Warren's later poetry, lending verve to the rhetorical mix. And a paradigm of Warren's development in this connection is the 1975 poem "Old Nigger on One-Mule Cart Encountered Late at Night When Returning From Party in the Back Country."

The encounter named in that headline title occurred in the 1930s, when Warren was teaching at Louisiana State University. The speaker, driving home after a party enjoyably lavish with liquor and sex, almost collides with a cartload of junk driven by a black man; he excoriates the other, scraping by him, as "fool nigger, ass-hole wrong side of the road, naturally." The event is at least semifictional. The word "nigger" was forbidden in Robert Warren Senior's household; this does not mean it was never used (Warren's brother Tom had recourse to it), but it is doubtful that Warren himself often employed it. The ugly phrases serve within the text exactly to measure the *distance* the poet has traveled from the moment of their utterance to the present moment, forty years later in snowbound Vermont, when of a sudden he recalls the old incident. (There has been more than one sadly tone-deaf reading of this poem, whereby it is taken as stereotypically racist: a model of missing the point.) It is a human and a moral distance, a cultural and social and literary and linguistic distance.

The seventy-year-old poet imagines the black man, later in that evening, making his way peaceably to his shanty home, pausing outside, "face calm as prayer," then entering and lying down to sleep. The speaker addresses him directly, recognizing him now as brother and as father; as mentor; almost as saintly, canonizable. We may perhaps think of the black farmer as a gentle singer or hummer of a blues song, the descendant of a black slave who once sang spirituals. He is the one to whom the poet is ready to refer his literary offerings, his whole literary career, the career that brought him from the scurrilous epithets quoted—and from the spurious little imitation of T. S. Eliot which the poet recollects having scribbled boozily that same evening—to the language and the attitudes of the evolving poem:

> And so I say:
> Brother, Rebuker, my Philosopher past all
> Casuistry, will you be with me when
> I arrive and leave my own cart of junk
> Untended from the storm of starlight and
> The howl like wind of the world's monstrous blessedness.

When he comes to Indian expression, Warren does not withhold his feelings about the unspeakable American history that lay behind it. "Avarice, arrogance, and brutality collaborated over and over again, with the inevitability of natural law, to repeat the old pattern": that is, of broken promises and cruel injustice. "The continuing theme of the eloquence of the Indian orator," Warren says, as he introduces transcribed speeches by Chief Joseph, Chief Logan, Chief Black Hawk, and others, "was the ongoing ordeal of his people." Warren's last long poem, *Chief Joseph of the Nez Perce* (1983), shows him performing his customary role—canonizing via emulation—to an unexampled degree: to the point of adopting his precursor's very voice. He has Chief Joseph retell the story contained in the anthology oration, the chief's heroic attempt to lead his people (in 1887) from Idaho through Montana to freedom across the Canadian border, malignantly pursued by American forces. In an analogous literary way, the Ghost Dances

Warren included in the anthology as "Indian Poetry" became the inspiring source for a visionary moment in the 1979 edition of *Brother to Dragons*. "Over the whole earth they are coming," runs one of the Ghost Dances, "The buffalo are coming, the buffalo are coming." And at the climactic moment of reconciliation and redemption in *Brother to Dragons,* the voice of Meredith Lewis breaks into a hypnotic choral chant:

> Dance back the buffalo, the Shining Land!
> Our grander Ghost Dance dance now, and shake the feather.
> Dance back the whole wide gleaming West anew!

The focus in this discussion is on literary predecessors from the nineteenth century and previous ages; but a word is in order here on those writers closer in time to Warren who also meant a great deal to him. First of all, most obviously, there are the fellow southerners; but Warren's relationship to them was of so special a kind that it would properly call for treatment within a different framing. Warren has written some of the most appreciative essays we have on the fictional art of Katherine Anne Porter and Eudora Welty (with both of whom, as well, he enjoyed a nourishing friendship); and his recognition of William Faulkner—explicitly in commentary, and by implication in his own fiction—was of the same early vintage as that of Malcolm Cowley. But these figures were not precursors for Warren; they were siblings, members of the same regional family. Even Faulkner, only seven years older than Warren after all, was really an elder brother, if also something of a challenge and a standard. Warren came by the lot of them naturally; he did not choose them for canonical intentions.

The exception among the southerners ought to be Mark Twain; but one of the puzzles in this phase of the Warren story is the relative faintness of the Mark Twain presence. "He's a great inventor of language," Warren remarked in a published discussion with Ralph Ellison. "He made a language." It is the only reference to Mark Twain in the entire volume of interviews; and commentators on Warren, following suit, rarely mention Twain at all. Warren did write the long introduction to Twain in *American Literature;* it is Warren at close to his best, especially when he attends to the "deep and mysterious" split in the man and the writer, and when he listens to the narrative voice in *Huckleberry Finn*—"a miraculous solution," Warren maintains, to the problems of narrative strategy Twain was confronting: so miraculous, indeed, that Warren is willing to say that "Lincoln freed the slave, and Mark Twain freed the writer." But that essay dates from 1972, and not from the much earlier canon making epoch.* It may always be argued that the very absence of Mark Twain's name in Warren's literary animadversions over the years suggests a precursorship so powerful that it could not be faced up to. But this too is a topic for consideration elsewhere.

The case of T. S. Eliot, meanwhile, has elements in common with the Faulkner instance, though it is if anything more complex. Warren has spoken on several occasions of the extraordinary impact *The Waste Land* had upon him and many other undergraduates at Vanderbilt, when it came out in the fall of his sophomore year, 1922. Allen Tate apparently brought *The Waste Land* to campus attention; and Warren expressed his gratitude by decorating the walls of the little dormitory room he shared with Tate (and two others) with painted scenes from Eliot's poem. *The Waste Land,* Warren would recall, was memorized and quoted from by many a Vanderbilt student, himself no doubt among them; and it bore heavily on Warren's poetry at least through the mid-1930s. "Letter from a Coward to a Hero," an admirable poem of 1935, is a striking illustration.

*The Twain essay was published in the *Southern Review* in the summer of 1972, before being fitted into the ongoing literary history in *American Literature.* Beinecke Library at Yale also contains a packet of six sheets, handwritten by Warren, with the title "Mark Twain and the Myth of Modernity." It is essentially a bundle of quotations relating to the modern split between the genuine self and the industrialized or technologized self, and served presumably as background to the analysis of *A Connecticut Yankee* in the *American Literature* essay.

> What did the day bring?
> The sharp fragment,
> The Shard,
> The promise half-meant . . .

So the poem begins, in a seductively Eliotic echo of brooding question and answer (as in "Gerontion": "What will the spider do, / Suspend its operations, will the weevil / Delay?"). And later, even more Eliotically:

> At the blind hour of unaimed grief,
> Of addition and subtraction,
> Of compromise,
> Of the smoky lecher, the thief . . .

(Recall "Preludes": "The morning comes to consciousness / Of faint stale smells of beer"; or "Rhapsody on a Windy Night": "The memory throws up high and dry / A crowd of twisted things . . .")

But Eliot, though twenty years older than Warren (old enough to be a young father), was also in his way, like Faulkner, an elderly contemporary (Warren knew him slightly, in fact, and introduced him at a reading in 1961); a towering example for the generation Warren belonged to. Eliot chose Warren, rather than vice versa; and beyond that, Warren's imaginative challenge was not so much to absorb Eliot as to work away from him toward (as it turned out) his own idiomatic mix and stretched-out lines. As late as 1985 Warren reread the whole of Eliot, and admitted to an interviewer that "*The Waste Land* still works. Even with all the nonsense and dissemblance about it, it still works." But though he acknowledged freely in another discussion, in 1982, that he still thought Eliot was "a very great poet," he added, "somehow I like Hardy more; he was somehow a writer I felt closer to." Let it be confessed, however, that the Eliot aspect of Robert Penn Warren is not to be easily disposed of; it awaits further deliberation.

The most telling chapter in the story of Warren's canon making—to return to the nineteenth century where most of the action takes place—was his tortuous relation with Ralph Waldo Emerson: "this rather absurd innocent man," as he once called him. "Emerson cancels evil out of the human algebra," Warren told an interviewer in 1974, and added that "Hawthorne brings it back." Picturing Emerson and Hawthorne meeting on a wood path in Concord, Warren said, "I'm strictly for Hawthorne." He went on: "I really have something that's almost a pathological flinch from Emersonianism, from Thoreauism, from those oversimplifications . . . of the grinding problems of life and personality."

For Warren in a certain mood, Emerson simply denied the world of fact and action. This is the tenor of Warren's witty, troubled, obscurely yearning poem of 1966, "Homage to Emerson on Night Flight to New York." As, in the poem, Warren sits in his seat while the plane hurtles eastward, a volume of Emerson on his lap, he feels, in lines that have become a favorite passage for quotation, that:

> My heart
> is as abstract as an empty
> Coca Cola bottle. It whistles with speed.
> It whines in the ammoniac blast caused by
> The passage of stars, for
> At 38,000 feet Emerson
>
> Is dead right.

In the succession of seven short sections that follow, the poet, striving desperately to "remember something specific" and so to escape the dissolving lure of Emersonian abstraction, recalls a wart he once had on his right forefinger; recalls an old black man who advised him: "*You quit that jack-off and that thing go away*"; a drunken cripple he saw slipping and falling outside the Old Absinthe House in New Orleans one Saturday night; the smell of burned gasoline coming off the Sound; a newspaper being driven by the wind across the runway; someone in the city—his wife?—waiting to recreate the human bond, with lips that may be about to smile.

Warren's mistrust of Emerson is well known, as is the unfairness in his appraisals of Emerson. But the mistrust is manifestly a mistrust of his own imaginative and intellectual tendencies: Warren, in trying to cope with Emerson, is engaged no less in an act of self-discovery than he is in his discussions of Hawthorne. For, as we have said, he himself shared that tension that he attributed to Hawthorne: between "a fascinated attentiveness" to the forms of nature and human nature, and "a compulsive flight from that welter of life towards abstract ideas." Warren did not always hold back from flight; some of his friendliest critics have wished he would desist from ending a lively, earthy poem or prose sequence with some portentous abstraction about Time or History. He was alert to the danger, however—to the tempting and threatening beauty of the transworldly; and he drew Emerson into his poetry as an earnest of it.

Emerson's presence is most palpable in poems of high-climbing or of actual flight (where, he tells us, Emerson is dead right). In the uncommonly stirring "Evening Hawk," the bird is observed with wonder and a kind of terror:

> Look! Look! he is climbing the last light
> Who knows neither Time nor Error, and under
> Whose eyes, unforgiving, the world, unforgiven, swings
> Into shadow.

He is splendid, a more majestic Emerson; Emerson without the smiling courtesies; but he is beyond the human, beyond time and human anxiety. "If there were no wind," the poem concludes, "we might, we think, hear the earth grind on its axis"; and *we* hear Warren contending that Emerson and his like oversimplify "the grinding problems of life and personality." Or take the poem "Mortal Limit" of 1985: it provides a nearly perfect image of the grand adventurous, treacherous impulse toward the transcendent, the greatness and the threat of Emerson—and the lifesaving response to it. The speaker sees "the hawk ride up-draft in the sunset over Wyoming," and asks:

> Beyond what range will gold eyes see
> New ranges ride to mark a last scrawl of light?

Or, the poet says:

> Or, having tasted that atmosphere's thinness, does it
> Hang motionless in dying vision before
> It knows it will accept the moral limit,
> And swing into the great circular downwardness that will
> restore
>
> The breath of earth?

Emerson is, hereby, forever fixed in Warren's literary constellation, but with a built-in warning sign. And this may be the most recognizable of all the forms of canonization.

In his prose comments on Emerson, as against those ambiguous poetic testimonials, Warren allows himself to say, if a bit grudgingly, that Emerson with his associates expressed "the seminal idea of the power of mind," and that this idea was "projected into the only native American school of philosophy, the pragmatism of William James." (It is an odd formulation: that was not precisely the idea that gave rise to pragmatism, but never mind.)

And here we run into a final peculiarity, about which a word of explanation is in order. It is a question of the status of Emerson, and the relation of Emerson to William James. Of all the canonical revisions of American literature in the past decade—that is, by those rare and invaluable critics who retain a belief in literature rather than ideology and the politics of power—the most provocative has been the one that has elevated Emerson to an Olympian place above it all. This has been done with considerable panache, and representing a certain tide of opinion, by Richard Poirier in *The Renewal of Literature: Emersonian Reflections* (1987) and by Harold Bloom in sundry places. As an "experiential critic and essayist," Emerson, Bloom informs us characteristically, is "the mind of our climate, the principle source of the American difference in poetry, criticism and pragmatic post-philosophy" (handsomely chosen words). Poirier, comparably, finds Emerson, his mind and his intellectual disposition, at the head and start of what is best in the truly authentic American literary tradition.

Poirier, with Bloom, is engaged in putting forward an American literary tradition, or canonical sequence, *counter* to the one that (they believe, not incorrectly) has dominated criticism and taste for most of this century and that coincides with literary modernism. That older sequence led from Hawthorne through Henry James to T. S. Eliot and perhaps Faulkner, and that (with many other attributes) does reverence to human sinfulness, to time and history, and to a God external to man. To replace it, a new continuity is discovered and promoted: from Emerson to *William* James to Robert Frost to Wallace Stevens: a procession of free and flexible spirits, uninhibited by history, essentially Adamic in an impulse to begin anew, knowing no God outside the individual consciousness, and each refreshed but uncoerced by his forerunner.

As to Robert Penn Warren, both Poirier and Bloom locate him at the tail end of the old discredited tradition, down among the southern epigones of modernism, though Bloom does so with visible regret— he cannot suppress his enjoyment of Warren's poetry and has indeed been its champion, even if he has to look away from Warren's moral stances and time-addiction.

Now, Richard Poirier is one of the most cultivated and mind-arousing critics we have; and no one is more audacious, enlivening, and genuinely original than Harold Bloom. Poirier's book is brilliant and subtle, enormously well-informed about the history of literary reputations (of persons and movements); a deep and steady intelligence pervades it. Poirier says at one point: "There is no coherent history of American literature, nor, in my view, should there even be an attempt at one. The kind of coherencies we should start looking for ought to have less to do with chronology or periods than with habits of reading (including fashions in classroom pedagogy) and with the way poets 'read' one another in the poetry they write." The first sentence is debatable; histories of American literature, aiming at coherence, may be attempted even in the worst (e.g., the present) of circumstances; but this entire essay might be considered as an extended illustration and verification of the long final clause.

Even so, Poirier, like Bloom, does perform as a critic, albeit a superb one. The perilousness of the enterprise grows apparent when we consider, in context, the case of Robert Penn Warren. It was Warren who was given to saying that history is never tidy, and that no history is less tidy than the literary branch. And Warren, who descends so decidedly from Hawthorne, is also a descendant of William James (much more than Henry James, incidentally), and an advocate of Robert Frost.

This is what Warren had to say about William James in his anthology essay:

> William James, with his roots (in a peculiar way) in Emerson, in his father's religious attitude toward life, in his own scientific training, and in his taste for art, was trying to work out a philosophy that might carry the old values of moral will, social responsibility, democratic conviction, and religious faith into a period that, with scientific positivism on the one hand and cynical opportunism on the other, seemed to deny all such values. Though he was a man of cultivation and taste, he was

not afraid of the "character of vulgar reality," and sought to renew philosophy by making contact with that reality.

One should, for the last time, "think Warren," and as hard as may be, in perusing those lines. For Warren too had "his roots (in a peculiar way) in Emerson"—it was in part his peculiar Emersonianism that drew him to William James; Warren too, in both fiction and poetry, sought to carry forward the old values of moral will and social responsibility; and no writer was less afraid than Warren of making contact with the most vulgar reality in order to reanimate his poetry.

The words, in short, pronounce an intellectually muscular act of self-appraisal; they are the words of the writer in our epoch who, all things considered, best turned the philosophy and rhetoric of William James to his own masterfully original imaginative ends. One could cite Warren's own citation (in the introduction to the Modern Library edition of the novel) of the figure of William James standing behind Willie Stark and the dramatic pattern of *All the King's Men;* or the solicitation of risk in the novel *Wilderness;* or the 1975 lectures on *Democracy and Poetry;* or the accumulating evidence of a sort of obsession with the question of religion in Warren's poetry. But perhaps the poem "Dragon Country" of 1956 may be allowed to speak in this Jamesian regard for many other texts and passages.

"Dragon Country" is a story-telling poem in twelve stanzas, each with four long, uncoiling, dragonlike lines and alternating rhymes. It is set in the Kentucky farmland and Warren's own Todd County during his lifetime; the speaker reminisces about the visitations of a mythical beast wreaking death and destruction throughout the countryside. In this quintessential Warren text, folk materials mingle with religious and philosophical speculation; the high style mixes with the vernacular; vulgar reality is allied to cultivation.

> I was only a boy when Jack Simms reported the first
>   depredation,
> What something had done to his hog pen. They called him a
>   God-damn liar.

> They said it must be a bear, after some had viewed the
> location,
> With fence rails, like matchwood, splintered, and earth a
> bloody mire.

The beast is never seen, but the wreckage continues. Land values fall, fields go untended, and "no longer do lovers in moonlight go."

> We were promised troops, the Guard, but the Governor's skin
> got thin
> When up in New York the papers called him Saint George of
> Kentucky.
> Yes, even the Louisville reporters who came to Todd County
> would grin.
> Reporters, though rarely, still come. No one talks. They think
> it unlucky.

> If a man disappears—well, the fact is something to hide.
> The family says, gone to Akron, or up to Ford, in Detroit.
> When we found Jebb Johnson's boot, with the leg, what was
> left, inside,
> His mother said, no, it's not him. So we took it out to
> destroy it.

Church attendance is on the increase, the narrator observes; the Catholics have sent in a mission. But "that's off the point," he says. It's no more than an expression of fear and need; all the fools do in church is to pray that the Beast will depart. What the human heart demands, the speaker insists, is "language for reality": language articulating the deeper truth of the human condition.

The reverberant final stanza of "Dragon Country" summons up that language, and it is a nearly exact mythicopoetic version of a postulate of William James, in the conclusion of his 1899 essay "What Makes a

Life Significant?" The essay was written after James had spent an exasperating week at the popular educational resort in Chautauqua, New York: a place of healthiness and model schools and a perfect absence of shadows; all in all, in James's words, a place of "atrocious harmlessness." On the return train journey, James asked himself what had been so lacking in the experience, and arrived at this answer: "it was the element that gives to the wicked outer world all its moral style, expressiveness and picturesqueness—the element of precipitousness, so to call it, of strength and strenuousness, intensity and danger."

The final lines of Warren's poem comment on those local fools who "pray only that the Beast depart," and doing so they affirm the Jamesian image of the significant life. In the Warren language and accent, they speak for the necessity of the precipitous in life, of intensity and danger; to this they add the Warrenesque hint about the mysterious possibility of joy:

> But if the Beast were withdrawn now, life might dwindle
>   again
> To the ennui, the pleasure, and the night sweat, known in the
>   time before
> Necessity of truth had trodden the land, and our hearts, to
>   pain,
> And left, in darkness, the fearful glimmer of joy, like a spoor.

(1992)

NOTES ON ORIGINS
AND OTHER AGENDA

Note: All Afterwords and other updatings were written for this volume.

1. "On Translating Virgil." Originally published as "On Translating the *Aeneid:* Yif That I Can," *Yearbook of Comparative and General Literature* no. 10 (1961), pp. 7–15, ed. Horst Frenz. Copyright 1961 by Comparative Literature Committee, Indiana University, Bloomington, Indiana. Reprinted with permission.

2. "Shakespeare's *Pericles.*" This was written in 1962 as the introduction to *Pericles* in the Dell Laurel edition of Shakespeare, edited by Francis Fergusson. The edition came to a stop before it reached *Pericles,* but Fergusson spoke most kindly about the piece. "Reprint it when you bring out a collection of essays," he urged me.

3. "Camus's *Caligula.*" Originally published as "Caligula, or the Realm of the Impossible," *Yale French Studies* 25 (Spring 1960). Reprinted with permission.

4. "Elio Vittorini." The first section originally appeared in *Italian Quarterly* 14, no. 15 (Fall 1960). Reprinted with permission.

Reconsidering Vittorini's career in 1989, I came to realize how many facets I had been unaware of in 1960, and so, after a good deal of reading and collating, I added the second and third sections.

5. "Fugitives from England." Originally published as "Travel and the Modernist Temper," *Yale Review* (Spring 1981). Copyright 1981 by Yale University. Reprinted with permission.

6. "The Facts in the Case of Mr. Poe." Originally published as the introduction to George E. Woodberry, *Edgar Allan Poe* (first published in 1885), in the series *American Men and Women of Letters*, under the general editorship of Daniel Aaron (New York: Chelsea House, 1980). Reprinted with permission.

7. "Henry Nash Smith, *Democracy and the Novel*." Originally published in the *New Republic*, December 23, 1978. Reprinted with permission.

8. "Melville's *Pierre*." This lecture, entitled "The Premature Modernity of Melville's *Pierre*," was delivered as part of a series at the University of Kentucky in the spring of 1981. It was conceived at the time as part of a book-length study to be called *The Premature Modernity of American Literature*, and which would deal as well with Hawthorne, Poe, Emily Dickinson, and others. In the summer of 1978, I conducted a seminar for college teachers, sponsored by the National Endowment for the Humanities, on the general subject (and made thereby, incidentally, some of the most valued associates I have ever come to know). The enterprise proceeded as far as a publisher's contract, but in the early 1980s it was given up: not for lack of interest or belief in the theme but because my attention was pulled elsewhere. I retain the distant hope that some day I may return to Hawthorne's *The Blithedale Romance* re-examined in this context.

9. "The Letters of Edith Wharton." Originally published as the introduction to *The Letters of Edith Wharton,* ed. R. W. B. Lewis and Nancy Lewis (Scribner's, 1988). Reprinted with the permission of Charles Scribner's Sons, an imprint of Macmillan Publishing Company. Copyright 1988 by R. W. B. Lewis, Nancy Lewis, and William R. Tyler. All rights reserved.

10. "E. A. Robinson." Originally published in *American Literature: The Makers and the Making,* vol. 2, ed. Cleanth Brooks, R. W. B. Lewis, and Robert Penn Warren (New York: St. Martin's, 1973), pp. 1829–1837. Copyright 1973. Reprinted with the permission of St. Martin's Press, Incorporated. The editors divided up the general and particular introductions, and E. A. Robinson happened to fall to me. The final essay in this volume, "Robert Penn Warren's Canon of Precursors," contains a word on that anthology.

11. "Ritual Naming: Ralph Ellison and Toni Morrison." This was originally given as a talk in Montreal at the Conference of the Canadian Association for American Studies, in October 1981. The theme of the conference was "Myth in America," and I was asked to comment on *The American Adam* and its emphasis on mythic aspects of nineteenth-century culture.

The reference to "the occasion, about a year back, to re-evoke the atmosphere of the campus" at Bennington (second paragraph) might be elaborated. For a "Ralph Ellison Festival" held at Brown University in September 1979, I offered a highly informal talk, which was ceremonial in nature as befitted the occasion as well as the author, who had himself said, in "The World and the Jug," that "True novels, even when most pessimistic and bitter, arise out of an impulse to celebrate human life and therefore are ritualistic and ceremonial at their core."

I rehearsed some of the figures on the Bennington scene in the late 1940s, and said that the common link among us all . . . was a deep concern with the mythic and ritualistic elements in literature from the ancients onwards. One of our Bibles was Lord Raglan's *The Hero,* with its spelling out of the archetypal from classical times; Joseph Campbell's *The Hero with a Thousand Faces;* Robert Graves's *The White Goddess;* and we attended to "The Cambridge School," headed by Gilbert Murray and Jane Harrison, who were writing about the ritual origins of ancient tragedy.

So, for example, we at once recognized the short story "The Lottery" by Shirley Jackson for what it was: a tribal scapegoat ritual set in contemporary New England. We applauded the element of ritual in the poetry of Theodore Roethke, who had been teaching at Bennington until recently. Howard Nemerov gave a course called "The Myth of the Quest," and Stanley Hyman gave lectures on the premise that myth is nothing other than the narrative working out of rite. . . . Our local hero was Kenneth Burke, and I suppose our Bible of Bibles was Burke's *The Philosophy of Literary Form.* Closely associated with it was Francis Fergusson's *The Idea of a Theater,* which explored myth and ritual in classic, Shakespearian, and modern drama. . . .

As to Ellison's *Invisible Man,* I was glad to recall my judgment (in the *Hudson Review*) when it first appeared: "The novel has that life beyond life which is the nature of art. It is not easy to name a work of fiction since *Light in August* which gives us so much and holds itself so well." Among other things, I also located Ellison and *Invisible Man* in an American literary tradition that runs from southwestern humor to Mark Twain and to William Faulkner before reaching Ellison. The chief characteristic of this tradition, I said, was "the explosive element, that all-hell-breaks-loose element—as in the quilting party in the Luvingood story of George Washington Harris, or that enormously comic tale by Faulkner called 'Was,' in which everything and everybody are chasing everything and everybody else, foxes and slaves and dogs and husbands and women. In *Invisible Man,* all hell breaks loose with a sort of ritual periodicity."

12. "Glimpses of Francis Fergusson." Originally published in *The Rarer Action: Essays in Honor of Francis Fergusson,* ed. Alan Cheuse and Richard Koeffler. Copyright 1970 by Rutgers, the State University. Reprinted with permission. This was written (during a period of leave) at the Villa Boccaccio outside Florence, near Settignano, hence the opening reference to a Tuscan hillside, cypresses, and so on.

13. "Edmund Wilson." "The Surviving Self" originally appeared in the *New York Times Book Review,* December 12, 1965. "Theatricals" originally appeared in the *New York Times Book Review,* March 2, 1969. "A Critic of History" originally appeared in the *New York Times Book Review,* May 22, 1983. Copyright 1965/1969/1983 by the New York Times Company. Reprinted with permission.

14. "Malcolm Cowley." Originally published in the *New Republic,* March 15, 1980. Reprinted with permission.

15. "V. S. Pritchett." Originally published in the *New Republic,* July 19, 1980. Reprinted with permission.

16. "Richard Ellmann." This talk was delivered as a "Tribute" before the American Academy and Institute of Arts and Letters in April 1989.

17. "Irving Howe." Originally published in the *New Republic,* November 1, 1982. Reprinted with permission.

18. "Robert Penn Warren's Canon of Precursors." This is an expanded version of a talk originally given at Vanderbilt University in November

1990, to mark the occasion of the university's Humanities Center being named in honor of Robert Penn Warren.

I would like to record my special thanks to the following:

to Penelope Laurans Fitzgerald, for supplying me with some key information about the career of Robert Fitzgerald;

to John Hollander, who came up with the answers to three fairly abstruse literary questions during a ten-minute transatlantic call between Florence and Woodbridge, Connecticut;

to Harvey Fergusson, for an important date regarding his father, Francis Fergusson;

to Ann Twombly, for her exceptionally careful and perspicuous reading of the copy, and her many acute queries and suggestions about word choice.

INDEX

Douglas, Gawin, 4, 9–10, 11, 12
Douglas, (George) Norman, 76, 81
Douglass, Frederick, 179–183, 185, 187, 190, 192, 193, 277
Doyle, Arthur Conan, 111; *A Study in Scarlet*, 96
Dreiser, Theodore, 228, 230, 251, 269; *Sister Carrie*, 154
Drew, Elizabeth, 30*n*
Dryden, John, 5–6, 8, 10
Du Bois, W. E. B., 277

Edel, Leon, 224
Edwards, Jonathan, xvi
Eliot, T. S., 8, 29–30, 42, 71, 79, 155, 207, 251, 260, 263, 271, 280, 282–284, 287
Ellison, Ralph, xix, 119, 178–179, 183–186, 187, 192, 194, 272, 278, 281, 295, 296–297
Ellmann, Richard, xx, 243–247
Emerson, Ralph Waldo, 140, 145, 147, 162, 185, 205, 211, 212, 263, 284–286, 287, 288
Engels, Friedrich, 210, 221
Epstein, Jason, 200
Euripides, 20

Farmer, James L., 278
Faulkner, Donald W., 232, 233–234
Faulkner, William, xiv, 44, 57, 69, 71, 93, 105, 113, 120, 233, 234, 251, 281, 282, 283, 287, 296–297; *Absalom, Absalom!*, 124, 203–204
Feidelson, Charles, 244, 245, 251
Fergusson, Francis, xiv, xx, 12, 197–204, 296
Fiedler, Leslie, 251
Finley, John Huston, Jr., x

Fisher, M. F. K., 83
Fitch, Clyde, 219
Fitts, Dudley, 20
Fitzgerald, F. Scott, 206, 224, 230
Fitzgerald, Penelope Laurans, 22–23, 24
Fitzgerald, Robert, xii*n*, 18–27, 253, 255
Fitzgerald, Zelda, 230
Flanner, Janet, 78
Flaubert, Gustave, 237
Forster, E. M., 75, 235, 238
Fraser, Russell, 253
Freud, Sigmund, 208, 239
Frost, Robert, 163, 225, 287, 288
Frye, Northrop, 212
Fullerton, William Morton, 131, 137, 138–145, 147, 148
Fussell, Paul, xv, 75–83

Gadda, Carlo Emilio, xv, 72–73
García Márquez, Gabriel, 238
Garibaldi, Giuseppe, 63
Garrison, William Lloyd, 182, 277
Gates, Henry Louis, Jr., 180
Genet, Jean, 238
Gibbon, Edward, 81, 249
Gide, André, 126, 221
Ginzberg, Natalia, 71
Goethe, Johann Wolfgang von, 133, 147, 149
Gower, John, 39–40
Grant, Robert, 134
Grant, Ulysses S., 224
Graves, Robert Ranke, 178, 296
Green, Henry, 238–239
Greene, Graham, xiv, xv, 76, 81, 238, 240